The Trail will be your guide in every chapter as you explore the regions, their communities, and the histories and stories of the people who live there.

Viewpoints

Everyone has a viewpoint about topics they care about. You do, too. This feature presents information in every chapter about a subject that is significant to people living in a region or to those affected by an event.

Voices of Canada

People tell their stories here through letters, diaries, historical records, or newspaper articles. Each one communicates personal accounts that relate to text topics. Together, these stories show our diversity and different experiences as Canadians.

words matter!

This feature provides a definition for a word that is highlighted in the text. Often the word has an unusual meaning, or even multiple meanings, which must be used in the correct context in order to make sense.

Thinking Skills

SKILL POWER

This feature occurs in every chapter. Working through the steps to follow in **Practise the Skill**, either alone or in a small group, helps you use the Skill Power effectively.

Thinking *It Through*

These questions appear with each main topic and focus your attention on major subjects. They ask you to think about the key ideas presented.

Skill Smart

Each time you see this feature, it asks you to do a short, skill-based task, such as find the relative location of a province's capital city. Doing these sharpen your skills.

Voices of
Canada

People, Places, and Possibilities

Donna M. Goodman

J. Craig Harding

Thomas A. Smith

PEARSON

Education
Canada

Toronto

Brand names and logos that appear in photographs provide students with a sense of real-world application and are in no way intended to endorse specific products.

ISBN 13: 978-0-13-198718-0
ISBN 10: 0-13-198718-6

Grade 5 Project Team
Publisher: Susan Cox
Product Manager: Patti Henderson
Managing Editor: Gaynor Fitzpatrick
Coordinating Editor: Rosalyn Steiner
Development Editors: Glen Herbert, Cara James, Mary Kirley, Melanie Myers, Kelly Stern
Production Editors: Allana Barron, Karen Kligman, Anita Levin
Production Coordinators: Helen Luxton, Sharlene Ross
Cover Design: Zena Denchik
Design and Composition: Word & Image Design Studio Inc.
Maps: Crowle Art Group
Illustrators: Brian Hughes, Paul McCusker, Stephen MacEachern , Allan Moon,
          Dusan Petriçic, Rose Zgodzinski
Index: Noeline H. Bridge
Research: Catherine Rondina, Wendy Scavuzzo
Photo Researchers and Permissions: Natalie Barrington, Sandy Cooke, Karen Hunter, Amanda McCormick, Jeanne McKane

Pearson Education Canada gratefully acknowledges Alberta Education's support in the resource-development process and the support of the many teachers/educators who have provided advice and feedback for Alberta Education over the course of the development of *Voices of Canada: People, Places, and Possibilities*.

Printed and bound in the U.S.A.
3 4 5 QC 11 10 09 08 07

ACKNOWLEDGMENTS

Contributing Authors

Lynn Bryan
Andrea Cartwright
Alisa Dewald
Carolyn Hunter

Fiona Kramer
Bev Milobar-den Ouden
Robert Morrow
Edie Reichardt

Program Advisers and Reviewers

Pearson Education Canada thanks its Program Advisers and Reviewers, who helped shape *Voices of Canada: People, Places, and Possibilities* through discussions and reviews of prototype materials and manuscript.

Program Advisers

Melina Akins
Dana Antaya-Moore
Jim Barritt
Louise Breland
Leith Campbell
Maureen Duguay

Ken Ealey
Avis Fitton
Kay Haslett
Dr. Alan Sears
Cliff Whitford

Subject Specialist Reviewers

Bob Beal
Louise Breland
Darcy Dobell
Ken Ealey
Victor Fines
Angela Hall
Carrol Jaques
Robert Leavitt

Dr. France Levasseur-Ouimet
Mark McCallum
Gwen McKnight
Sophie Mitchell
Robert Morrow
Sheila Staats/GoodMinds
Maurice Switzer
Cliff Whitford

Assessment and Evaluation

Anne Mulgrew, Edmonton Public Schools
Jim Scott, Edmonton Public Schools
Colin Woelfle, Edmonton Public Schools

Grade 5 Field-Test Teachers

Pearson Education would like to thank the reviewers and the teachers and students who field-tested *Voices of Canada: People, Places, and Possibilities* prior to publication. Their feedback and constructive recommendations have been most valuable in helping to develop quality social studies resources.

Elaine Clarke, Holy Spirit School, Calgary Catholic SD

Sarah Clarke, Holy Spirit Academy, Christ the Redeemer Catholic Schools

Karen Doepker, Senator Buchanan Elementary, Lethbridge SD #51

Valerie Dowell, St. Timothy Catholic School, Edmonton Catholic SD

Robyn Drews, Centennial School, Edmonton Public SD

Mary Dytyniak, St. Martha Elementary School, Edmonton Catholic SD

Elizabeth Godfrey, St. Patrick, Calgary Catholic SD

Marnie Harrison, R. T. Alderman, Calgary Board of Education

Anna Maria Hrubizna, St. Augustine Elementary Catholic School, Edmonton Catholic SD

Cheryl Johnson, Muir Lake Community School, Parkland SD #70

Dr. William Gordon Kidd, Fultonvale Elementary School, Elk Island SD

Lauri Los, Wildwood Elementary School, Calgary Board of Education

Hyong Ly, Grant MacEwan School, Calgary Board of Education

Lisa McHerron, St. Justin Elementary School, Edmonton Catholic SD

Angie McKenna, St. Justin Elementary School, Edmonton Catholic SD

Janet Mossfeldt, Capitol Hill Elementary School, Calgary Board of Education

Nancy Murphy, Ascension of Our Lord School, Calgary Catholic SD

Bev Milobar-den Ouden, Colchester School, Elk Island SD

Lyle Parr, Father Leonard Van Tighem, Holy Spirit Catholic SD

Wanda Pedersen, George P. Nicholson, Edmonton Public SD

Adam Quraishi, Calgary Islamic School, Private

Diane Rollie, Robert Rundle Elementary School, St. Albert Protestant SD

A. Roppo-Bustillo, St. Timothy Catholic School, Edmonton Catholic SD

Kenda Rudkowsky, Woodbridge Farms Elementary School, Elk Island SD

Kim Schermann Our Lady of Fatima School, Calgary Catholic SD

Michelle Sherlow, Wildwood Elementary, Calgary Board of Education

Kevin Shilling, Grandview Elementary School, Red Deer Public SD

Loretta Stabler, Millarville Community School, Foothills SD #38

Diane Thomas, Manachaban Middle School, Rocky View SD

Lynn Thurston, Wheatland Elementary School, Golden Hills SD

Jenny Watson, Mattie McCullough Elementary, Red Deer Public SD

Marian Zazelenchuk, Ranchlands Community School, Calgary Board of Education

Grade 5 Teacher Reviewers

Pearson Education would like to thank the teachers who reviewed *Voices of Canada: People, Places, and Possibilities* prior to publication. Their feedback and constructive recommendations have been most valuable in helping to develop quality social studies resources.

Kari Archer, Win Ferguson Community School, Elk Island SD

Charlene Assenheimer, Fort Assiniboine School, Pembina Hills RD #7

Karen Bourassa, Mike Mountain Horse School, Lethbridge SD #51

Ken Hakstol, St. Joseph School, Holy Spirit SD

Joanne Heenan, Sherwood School, Calgary Board of Education

Charlene Karpick, Chief Old Sun School, Siksika Board of Education

Janet Wilkinson, Westhaven Elementary School, Grande Yellowhead RD #35

CONTENTS

Getting Started
Travelling the Trail

In 1992, Canada turned 125 years old. To celebrate, the Trans Canada Trail was started as a recreational trail. It was to connect over 800 communities across Canada and span over 18 000 km! Eventually, it would be the longest trail of its kind in the world.

While the Trail is still being built, there are already many completed areas. People hike, bike, horseback ride, cross-country ski, and snowmobile along the constructed trails. Special pavilions show the names of people who helped build their piece of the Trail. In parts of Alberta and the Northwest Territories, people can canoe along a waterway section. Some people have even crossed Canada by biking along the Trail.

Part of celebrating Canada is celebrating the land and the people who live throughout this vast country. The Trail will give Canadians the chance to participate by donating money or land, or by volunteering. Each part of the Trail is unique, reflecting the unique regions of Canada.

A logo is a special sign that gives key information. What does this logo for the Trans Canada Trail tell you? Which languages are on the Trans Canada Trail logo? Why?

Trans Canada Trail

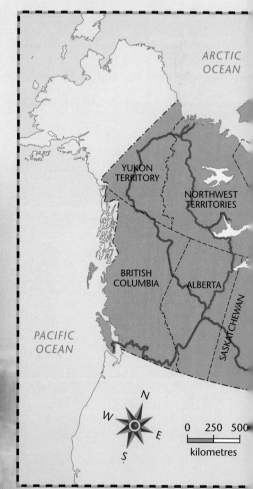

Canada's Stories

It's time to begin your quest across our amazing country. As you read this book, you will explore the different regions of this place we call Canada. Your quest will also help you discover more about the land you call home.

Investigate the landscapes and their diversity. Listen to the stories of the people from our past and those living here now. All of these people make up our country.

Former Member of Parliament Herb Gray, Maniwaki Elder William Commanda, and Québec Lieutenant-Governor Lise Thibeault mix the water of the Arctic, Atlantic, and Pacific oceans in a ceremony in Ottawa in September 2000. Volunteers travelling the Trans Canada Trail carried the water. Why was it important to combine the water from three oceans?

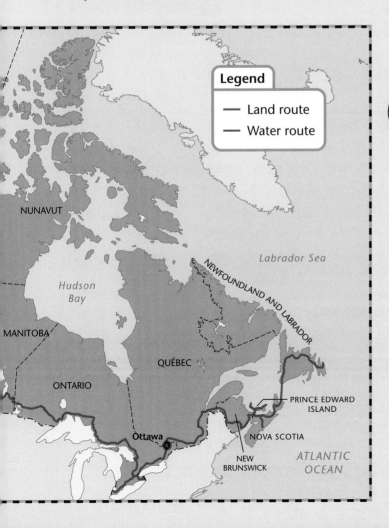

Legend

— Land route
— Water route

NUNAVUT

Labrador Sea

Hudson Bay

NEWFOUNDLAND AND LABRADOR

MANITOBA

QUÉBEC

ONTARIO

PRINCE EDWARD ISLAND

Ottawa

NOVA SCOTIA

NEW BRUNSWICK

ATLANTIC OCEAN

? Inquiring Minds

Here are some questions to guide your inquiry throughout this book:

- How would you explain what it is like to be a Canadian when we live in such a diverse country?
- In what ways do our stories, histories, languages, and ways of seeing ourselves bring Canadians together?
- Is being a Canadian the same for everyone?

During your journey, you will gather clues to answer these questions.

How Can I Learn About Canada's Identity?

By following the Trans Canada Trail, people can learn a great deal about Canada's physical geography. The Trail connects every province and territory and is a part of the particular landscape in each region. It tells a story about the land. You also have a particular story—one that is personal to only you.

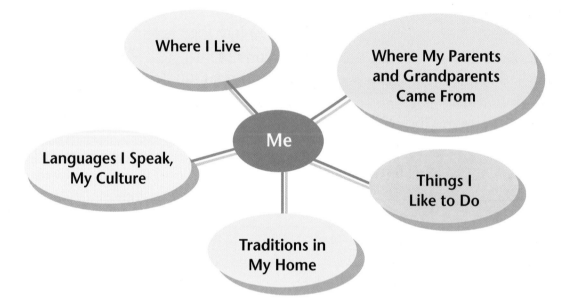

Think about your **identity**. How would you describe yourself? Perhaps you are a soccer player, speak more than one language, or live in a rural area. Describe how a country can have an identity. Name three things that make Canadian identity unique.

Voices of Canada

Our Identity

We have an identity arising out of the rights and citizenship duties we share with others and the sense of public good and ethics that involve us all. It is important to give to people who come to us wanting new lives, wanting to become Canadian, the deepest possible access to the culture of which they are becoming a part.

The Rt. Hon. Adrienne Clarkson, Governor-General of Canada, 1999–2005

What Supports Identity?

In this book, you will find several features that help promote Canada's—and Canadians'—identity. Let's take a look.

The Trans Canada Trail: See an example on page 77. The Trans Canada Trail will guide you through the varied landscapes and stories of the six regions in Canada. Descriptions of the Trail will help you begin to explore the unique geography of each one.

Voices of Canada: See an example on page 31. Read the selections on that page. These are personal accounts of newcomers' reactions to places in Canada. Other Voices of Canada features throughout this book provide parts of legends, songs, letters, diaries, news items, and historical records. Together, they all contribute to our identity as Canadians.

Viewpoints: See an example on pages 120–121. The Viewpoints feature will show you different points of view that Canadians hold about important topics. All of these help make us who we are as Canadians.

Making a Difference: See an example on page 58. This feature describes people whose actions or contributions help change their community and make it better.

Canada Collection: See an example on page 289. The Canada Collection gives you an opportunity to collect pieces of your work about personal accounts of identity and citizenship. How would you react in a certain situation? What would you do to change something for the better?

How Can I Begin an Inquiry?

words **matter!**

An **inquiry** is an investigation to find answers to questions. In this book, the inquiry process will help you learn more about Canada.

Asking questions is the first step in an **inquiry**. Think of things you want to know about Canada's stories, people, and places. Work with a partner or a small group to brainstorm some questions. Use the following question words to help you get started.

What?

Who? When?

Where?

WHY?

How? If?

Who were the first people to live in my community?

How are the characteristics of the land, water, and weather different in the Canadian Shield from the Arctic region?

Why does a railway run through my community?

In order to answer the questions you have thought of, you need a plan. You might try using a chart like the one below. It is called a KWHL chart. See if you can figure out why!

What I Think I Know	What I Want to Know	How I Will Find Out	What I Learned
• Canada has water on three of its borders. • Canada has many different people.	• What is it like to live in other places in Canada?	• Books, magazines, newspapers • Letters, diaries • Television • Photos • Maps • Paintings • Elders • Museums • The Internet • Songs, poems	

Fill in the first three columns of a chart like this one before beginning your research. You might think of more questions or new sources as you look for answers. Fill in the last column while you are doing your research and after you are finished. Can you think of another way to organize your plan? Find out more about the inquiry process on the following pages.

Where did First Nations people first live in my region?

What factors have made my city so big?

What Does Inquiring Critically Mean?

Look at the diagram on these pages. It shows you how you can plan an inquiry. It also shows you how to think critically about the questions you are asking.

Read the questions that accompany "Reflecting" at each stage. These questions should help you become a critical thinker.

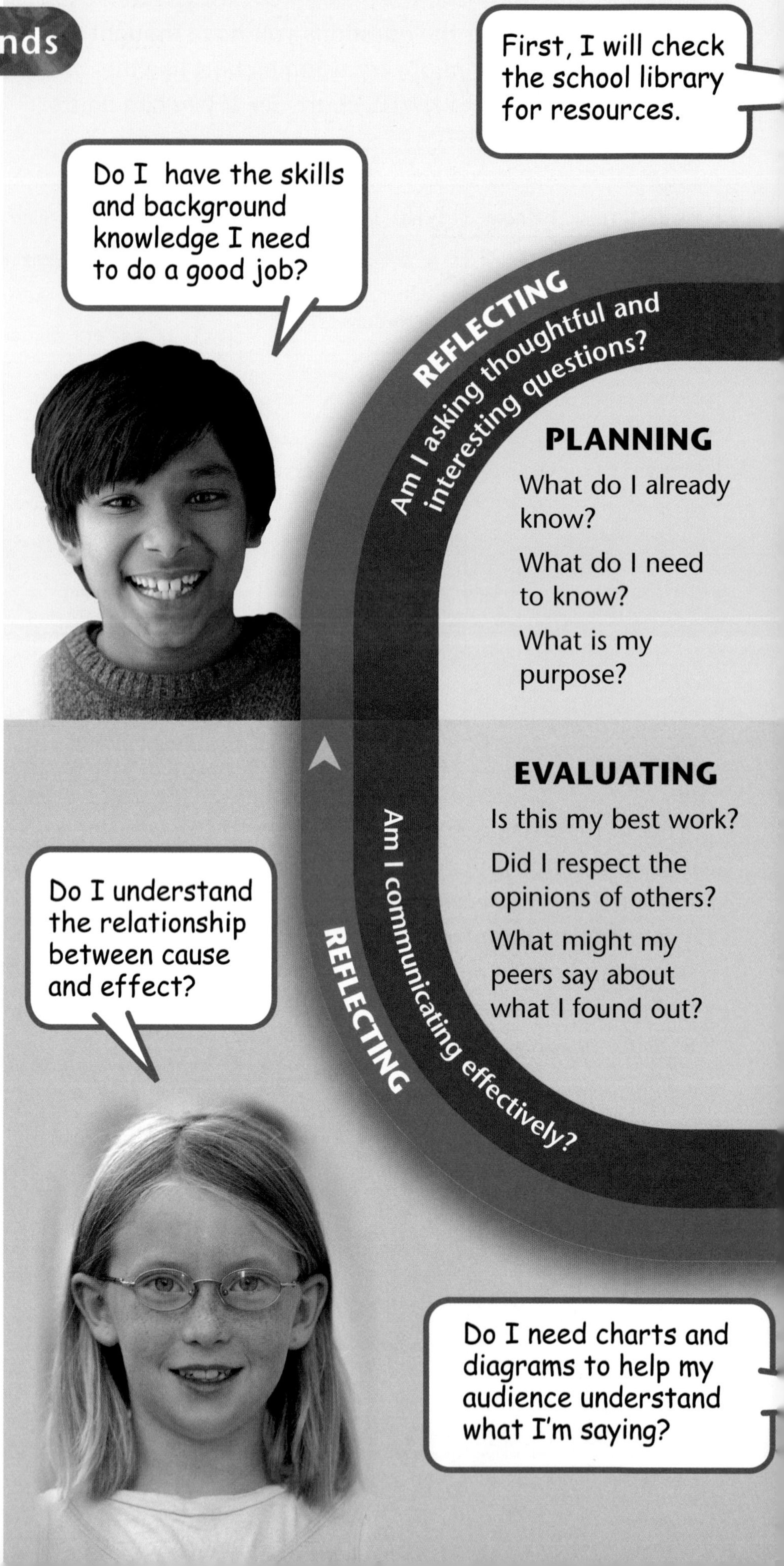

First, I will check the school library for resources.

Do I have the skills and background knowledge I need to do a good job?

REFLECTING

Am I asking thoughtful and interesting questions?

PLANNING

What do I already know?

What do I need to know?

What is my purpose?

EVALUATING

Is this my best work?

Did I respect the opinions of others?

What might my peers say about what I found out?

Am I communicating effectively?

REFLECTING

Do I understand the relationship between cause and effect?

Do I need charts and diagrams to help my audience understand what I'm saying?

My research folder will be a great place to keep my notes and photos. I'll check with my teacher for an update on how I'm doing.

REFLECTING ➤

Am I gathering relevant information?

Am I recognizing multiple perspectives?

REFLECTING

RETRIEVING

How will I decide if my information is relevant and complete?

Can I check my information using more than one source?

PROCESSING

How have I supported my ideas?

Have I thoughtfully sequenced my presentation?

Will my audience understand?

Critical Thinking in Inquiry

CREATING

How will I choose the best format?

Are my conclusions fair?

What materials will enhance my presentation?

Am I reaching well-reasoned conclusions?

REFLECTING

SHARING

Am I considering others?

Will my presentation be interesting to my audience?

Am I being fair-minded in my judgments?

◀ **REFLECTING**

Have I found facts or opinions? What other conclusions might there be?

9

What Is a Good Inquiry?

A good inquiry lets you use many of your skills:
reading, writing, talking, listening, and observing. Start with
something you are curious about. Ask yourself questions such as these:

- What am I interested in learning about Canada?
- What part of Canada in particular do I find exciting?

When you have decided on your questions, consider where you will
find information. Sources may include

- books, magazines, newspapers
- Internet Web sites, films
- photos, paintings
- interviews with family members and friends, people in your
  community

What other sources can you think of?

As you gather information, other questions may occur to you.
These may interest you as much or even more than the first questions.
Do you want to go down a different path or stay with the questions
you asked first? It's fine to rethink your investigation. This is all part of
the process of doing an inquiry.

Look back at the model on pages 8–9 to help you focus on the stages of
an inquiry. After you have collected your information, it is time to
choose a layout for presenting your work. There are many different
formats—a poster, a newspaper article, a short skit, a radio interview.
Choose one that will enhance your inquiry.

Practise the Skill

Look at the map of the Trans Canada Trail on pages 2–3.

1. Find the part of the Trail that runs through Alberta.
2. Think of two questions that interest you about the Trail in your
   province.
3. Take jot notes as you find information.

Build Your Skills!

Make a Tracking Chart

With a partner, discuss why it is important to record where you find information for an inquiry. Make your own chart. Record all the sources you use throughout the year. Use the one shown below as a model.

Date	Source	Location
Sept. 15	Book: <u>Canada Day</u>, by Jack Innes, p. 15	school library
Sept. 17	Internet: "All About Canada"	www.allaboutcanada.ca

Look What You Know Already!

Review the inquiry questions for the year:

- How would you explain what it is like to be a Canadian when we live in such a diverse country?
- In what ways do our stories, histories, languages, and ways of seeing ourselves bring Canadians together?
- Is being a Canadian the same for everyone?

In a small group, make a three-column chart similar to the one below.

Being Canadian	Diverse Cultures	Identity Factors
• •	• •	• •

Under each heading, briefly jot down what each group member knows or thinks.

Create a Canada Collection

This year, you may want to keep a binder or portfolio that tells about Canada's story: its people, places, and land.

- Collect stories, maps, pictures, poems, cartoons, and photos of your work. You will be asked for something specific at the end of every chapter.

Living with the Land

Imagine you had the chance to travel high in space! If you looked down, planet Earth might appear as it does in this photograph. Can you see Canada? It is so vast that it can be seen from space. Even thousands of kilometres away, some geographic features of our country are visible— Hudson Bay, the Rocky Mountains, and the Great Lakes. Find them on this photograph. Throughout this unit, you will learn more about the land, our relationship to it, and how it affects our quality of life.

This unit helps you explore these questions.

■ What are the main regions, landforms, and bodies of water in Canada?

■ Why do natural resources help establish communities?

■ How have the land and the stories and histories of the people in each region shaped who we are as Canadians?

13

Exploring Canada

Have you ever travelled to another part of Canada? How did you get there? Can you imagine travelling there in a wheelchair? Rick Hansen travelled through all ten of Canada's provinces this way! Hansen was a wheelchair athlete who wheeled his way around the world. His goal was to raise money to help people with spinal cord injuries, like himself.

In August 1986, Hansen began his journey across Canada, starting on the rocky shore of Cape Spear in Newfoundland. For weeks and weeks, he travelled west. He wheeled through the valleys of the Atlantic provinces. In Québec and Northern Ontario, he saw the bright colours of the trees as fall began. Soon he was on the Prairies, under a big sky. There were many kilometres still to go.

Crowds would wait for Hansen by the roadside and cheer him on when he passed by. In Alberta, Chief Clifford Big Plume of the Tsuu T'ina First Nation gave Hansen an eagle feather, a symbol of strength and courage. He would need strength, since he still had to go through the Rocky Mountains!

On May 22, 1987, Hansen reached Vancouver. It had taken him nine months to wheel across Canada.

More About. . .

A Big Country

Canada is the second-largest country in the world. Only the country of Russia is bigger.

Canada: Our Stories Continue

When Rick Hansen took his journey across Canada, he explored many different **regions**. He saw coastlines, plains, lakes, forests, and mountains. He met many different Canadians. In this chapter, you will begin to explore six major regions in Canada. You will also learn about the people who live in these regions, and what affects how they live.

Rick wheeled 13 861 km in Canada. It was the longest distance he wheeled in any country on his world tour!

? Inquiring Minds

Here are some questions to keep in mind as you explore this chapter.

- What background information would Rick Hansen have to know in order to make his journey across Canada?
- Where would he look for information?

Let's Explore Canada's

To study Canada, we can divide it into six major parts, or regions. This map shows the six regions we will study. Each region has unique physical features, climate, and natural resources. Look at the map and the photos to learn more about each region.

The **Arctic region** covers Nunavut and parts of the Northwest Territories and the Yukon Territory.

The **Cordillera region** is a mountainous region in British Columbia, the Yukon Territory, and parts of Alberta and the Northwest Territories.

The **Interior Plains region** covers parts of Manitoba, Saskatchewan, Alberta, British Columbia, the Northwest Territories, and the Yukon.

Regions!

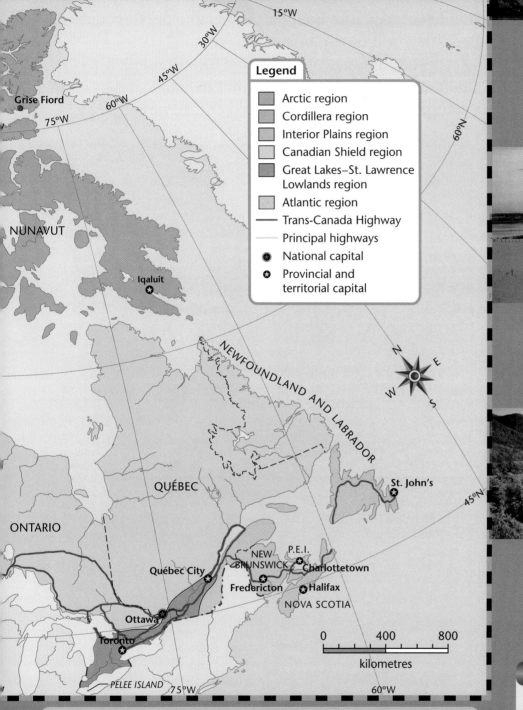

The Canadian Shield region covers Labrador, Québec, most of Ontario, northern Manitoba, and northern Saskatchewan. It also covers parts of Alberta and the Northwest Territories.

The Great Lakes–St. Lawrence Lowlands region follows the St. Lawrence River in Québec. It also extends to southern Ontario.

The Atlantic region is on the East Coast of Canada. It includes Nova Scotia, New Brunswick, Prince Edward Island, the island of Newfoundland, and parts of Québec.

Legend

- ☐ Arctic region
- ☐ Cordillera region
- ☐ Interior Plains region
- ☐ Canadian Shield region
- ☐ Great Lakes–St. Lawrence Lowlands region
- ☐ Atlantic region
- — Trans-Canada Highway
- ⋯ Principal highways
- ⊙ National capital
- ✪ Provincial and territorial capital

Thinking *It Through*

■ Read the story about Rick Hansen on pages 14–15. Then look at the map and the photos describing the regions. What important landforms did he see? Which region do you think Rick did *not* visit? What might a visitor experience in that region?

Read the story about Rick Hansen on pages 14–15.

Skill **Smart**

■ Choose a region that is not familiar to you. Write three inquiry questions about things you would like to know about that region.

17

What's My Region?

Gordie, Alistair, Sunjeet, Claire, Brianne, and Katie each live in a different region of Canada. As you explore Canada's regions, they will be exploring, too.

Read what the students say about Rick Hansen's trip across Canada. Then use the map below and the photographs on the previous pages to find out which regions they are from.

In my region, Rick travelled along highways cut into pink and grey rocks. He went by lakes and muskeg, and crossed many rivers. He might have seen a moose on the edge of the forest.

Gordie, Opaskwayak First Nation

In my region, Rick saw the Atlantic Ocean. He saw rocky cliffs and sandy beaches. He wheeled past forests and farms. I bet he had some lobster for dinner along the way.

Alistair, Old Perlican

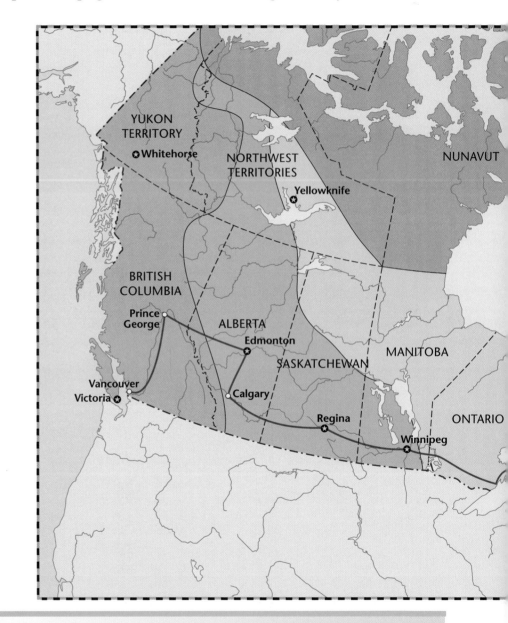

As he travelled through the valleys and mountains in my region, Rick saw heavy forests, orchards, and vineyards. He would have wheeled on high mountain roads. He ended his trip through Canada the way he began: at an ocean.

Sunjeet, Kamloops

Rick saw cities of different sizes along a large river and the Great Lakes in my region. He travelled through places where many people speak French. He also saw farms. I hope he stopped to visit Mont Royal.

Claire, Montréal

If Rick had visited my region, he might have seen snow and ice-covered land, and the beautiful northern lights. In the summer, he might have seen long days when the sun never seemed to set.

Katie, Arviat

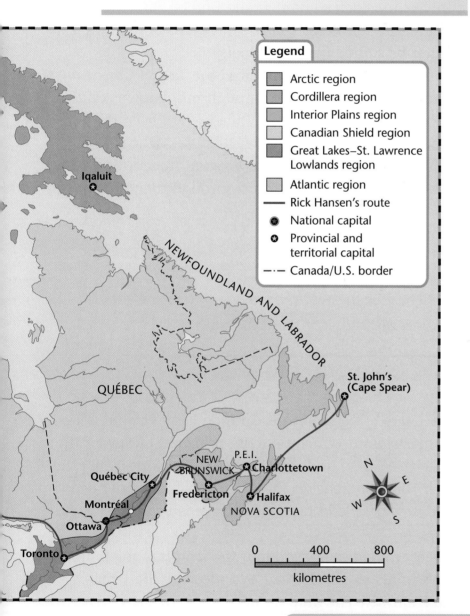

Legend

- ▨ Arctic region
- ▨ Cordillera region
- ▨ Interior Plains region
- ▢ Canadian Shield region
- ▨ Great Lakes–St. Lawrence Lowlands region
- ▢ Atlantic region
- ━ Rick Hansen's route
- ◉ National capital
- ✪ Provincial and territorial capital
- —·— Canada/U.S. border

Iqaluit

NEWFOUNDLAND AND LABRADOR

QUÉBEC

St. John's (Cape Spear)

P.E.I.
NEW BRUNSWICK
Charlottetown

Québec City

Fredericton

Montréal
Halifax
NOVA SCOTIA

Ottawa

Toronto

0   400   800
kilometres

N E W S

This is Rick Hansen's route through Canada.

When Rick wheeled across my region, he saw open plains. He saw forests and rivers, too. Then he reached the foothills of the Rocky Mountains.

Brianne, Qu'Appelle Valley

Thinking *It Through*

- Which of the six speakers describes a region in which you live? Which description sounds totally different?

The Students' Inquiry

words matter!

A **highway** is a large road that connects towns and cities. The **Trans-Canada Highway** was built so that people could travel across Canada on one highway.

Why do highway signs use symbols? Look for highways with symbols where you live. What stories do they tell? Why does this sign show a maple leaf?

The 20th anniversary of Rick Hansen's trip around the world was in 2006. Although they lived in different regions, Claire, Sunjeet, Gordie, Katie, Alistair, and Brianne each took part in projects started in their different schools that would celebrate the anniversary. Each student would find out more about Rick's route through their region. The results of their projects would later be shared among schools.

For most of his trip, Rick followed the **Trans-Canada Highway**. His route took him through many towns and cities, as well as isolated areas. While he had been through almost every region, he had not visited the Arctic region.

As they worked on their projects, each student began to wonder about how people travel through their region. They asked:

- What are the major highways in my region? How long are they?
- What would be the best route to take through my region?
- How does the landscape shape the highway?
- What are other ways to travel across Canada?
- How do people travel in regions where there are no highways?

Katie discovered that the Trans-Canada Highway did not go through her region. While there are principal highways that come into the Yukon and the Northwest Territories, only the Dempster Highway reaches the Arctic region. She decided to look into how people in her region travelled without highways.

Sunjeet wanted to know about the length of the major highways in his region. He chose to measure the Trans-Canada Highway. The map on pages 16–17 shows this highway. To measure it, Sunjeet used the scale on the map. Look at the Skill Power on the next page to learn more about scale.

SKILL POWER — Understanding Scale

Scale is a tool we use to compare the distance on a map to the actual distance on Earth's surface. By using scale, a small distance on a map can show a larger distance on Earth's surface. Look at the map of Rick's journey on pages 18–19. This map uses a bar scale.

Measuring Distance with Scale

Measure the distance of Rick's journey between Winnipeg and Calgary. First mark the locations of the two cities on the edge of a piece of paper.

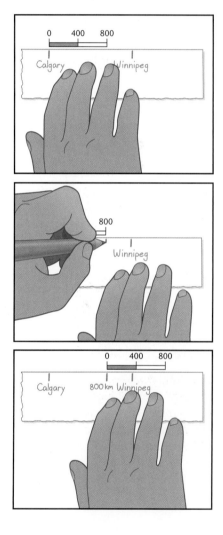

1. Place the edge of the paper against the map scale, with the first mark at zero.

2. Make a mark on the paper at the right end of the scale.

3. Move the paper so the mark lines up with 0 on the bar scale. Measure the next distance, and add the two distances together. In this example, 800 + 350 = 1150. Rick travelled 1150 km between the two cities.

Practise the Skill

Use these steps to measure the distance of Rick's journey from St. John's to Vancouver. Use the map on pages 18–19 and the bar scale to measure the distance. How many kilometres did Rick travel across Canada?

What Makes a Region?

I wonder what other physical features can be found in my region.

How would you describe the region where you live? Physical features, climate, and natural resources are things that can be used to describe each of the major regions in Canada. These things also affect how people live in each region.

A Region Shares Physical Features

The **physical features** of a region can show what a region looks like. They can also affect things like climate, and what people do for work and for fun. What physical features did Claire, Sunjeet, Alistair, Brianne, Gordie, and Katie talk about when they described their regions?

Thinking *It Through*

- Imagine that someone who has never visited your region is about to travel through the area where you live. How would you describe it to them? What physical features might they see there?

- Look at the photos on pages 16–17. Each major region in Canada has unique features. How do you think the combination of these features helps contribute to Canada's identity?

Physical features, such as the Hopewell Rocks beside the Bay of Fundy in New Brunswick, often become part of a region's identity. Features like this help people recognize a certain region. What physical features could be used to recognize your region?

A Region Shares Climate

Different regions in Canada may have different **climates**. For example, the **weather** may be muggy in the Great Lakes–St. Lawrence Lowlands region in the summer, but hot and dry in the Interior Plains region. Canada's climate is different from place to place because of different latitudes, landforms, bodies of water, and elevation.

Lines of latitude are imaginary lines around Earth. On a map, lines of latitude run from east to west. Places that are farther north are farther away from the equator. They are usually colder than places closer to the equator. Check the map on pages 16–17. Find the communities of Grise Fiord in the north and Pelee Island in the south. What do you notice about their latitudes? How do you think this affects the climate in these places?

Landforms and large **bodies of water** can also affect climate. For example, mountains can stop rain or snow from moving into or out of a region. Lakes and oceans can warm or cool an area.

Elevation is the height of the land compared to sea level or the ocean surface. Have you ever hiked up a mountain or gone up in a gondola? If you have, then you already know that the higher you go, the cooler the temperature gets.

Toronto is located on the shore of Lake Ontario. Why do you think people might want to live next to a lake?

The climate at higher elevations is good for pine forests. Why?

A Region Shares Natural Resources

words matter!

Industries are businesses that produce goods or services.

Natural resources are connected to both the physical features and the climate of a region. Each region has unique qualities that affect the kinds of natural resources found there. For example, the ocean in the Atlantic region provides fish. Animals, forests, lakes, rivers, land, minerals, and mountains are also examples of natural resources.

SOME OF CANADA'S NATURAL RESOURCES

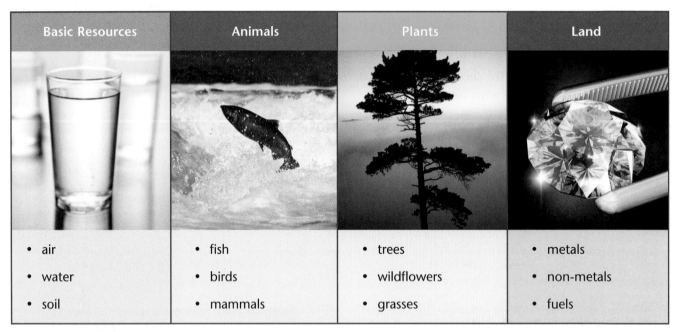

Basic Resources	Animals	Plants	Land
• air	• fish	• trees	• metals
• water	• birds	• wildflowers	• non-metals
• soil	• mammals	• grasses	• fuels

If there were a lot of one of these resources in one region, how might it affect ways of life? What if there were very few resources?

More About...

Natural Resources

Some natural resources are **renewable**, which means the resource can be replaced. Other natural resources are **non-renewable**, which means the resource can never be replaced once it is used up.

Resources and People

Natural resources are an important source of jobs in many communities. People work in different **industries** that are connected to resources. Some industries produce paper and wood products from trees. Other industries produce food, clothing, fuel, and minerals from other natural resources.

Resources are more than a source of jobs. Clean air and water are necessary for good health. Forests, rivers, animals, and plants can be enjoyed by everyone. We learn to interact with nature. We enjoy the animals and plants that are part of our environment. This enjoyment can add to our quality of life.

People Feel Connected to Regions

People often share a feeling that they are connected to their region. They work and play in their region. They enjoy the beauty of the land, and have adapted to the climate. Being from a certain region can add to their sense of identity. They can share this identity with everyone else who lives in that region.

Communities Within Regions

In each of Canada's regions, there are many sorts of communities, large and small. Each community has formed for a reason. Look at the diagram below to find out more.

I love living in the Interior Plains region. I love the open skies and the beauty of the Qu'Appelle Valley. I wonder how other people feel about where they live. I think I'll ask my cousins in British Columbia.

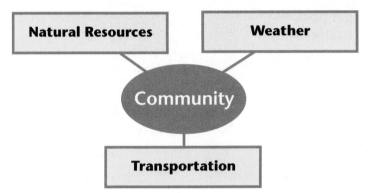

When forming communities, people look for locations with natural advantages. How might these advantages be different in the six regions?

People can feel very deeply about where they live. You might feel that you belong to the town or city in which you live. But you can also be part of a much larger picture—you can belong to Canada. What are some things that you could tell someone who asks, "What's it like to live in Canada?"

Volunteers and supporters feel that the Trans Canada Trail is creating links between Canadian communities from coast to coast, and giving Canadians a way to experience Canada's natural beauty close up.

Skill Smart

■ Research two cities in Canada. Why are these cities located where they are?

■ What things other than those listed here might help create a community? Why do you think some communities grow, while others do not?

What Do People Share in Common About the Resources in Their Region?

Many communities in Canada begin and grow as a result of natural resources. Some of these resources are renewable, but others are not. How might this affect people who depend on natural resources?

Dawson City grew very quickly when gold was discovered in the past. Prospectors once swarmed here hoping to find gold and get rich. Today, the gold is almost all gone. But the story of the Gold Rush still brings visitors to this region. I show these tourists how my ancestors used to pan for gold.

So many people in British Columbia work in the forestry industry. Most are passionate about protecting the forest and the animals that live there. We must find a balance between the environment and what people need.

In 1992, the Canadian government closed the 500-year-old cod fishery in Newfoundland. There were too few left to support the fishing industry. I decided to stay in Newfoundland and train for other work. Now I have a new job.

In the past few years, there have been many droughts in southern Saskatchewan. My family is taking part in a study on how to adapt to drought. We are planting trees and grass in some areas of our farm to protect dry soil. We really need more irrigation plans, though.

I'm helping to find ways to use renewable resources. I work on a wind farm in Murdochville, Québec. I'm glad our whole community can get together to make these decisions.

Over to **You**

1. As a group, discuss the points of view. Why do you think these people have formed their opinions?

2. Why are the resources in a region so important to the people who live there?

What Affects Life in a Region?

Skill Smart

■ Make a comparison chart to show how Canadians are the same across the country, and how they are different. Use the categories on these pages to get started.

Think about the physical features, climate, and natural resources where you live. How do they affect what you do each day? How do they affect how you dress, travel, play, and eat?

There are many ways of life across Canada, both in the past and today. Not everyone in Canada lives the same way. There are people who live on boats, people who eat whale meat, and people who travel to school on the subway. But there are things that we all have in common, too.

Look at the photos on this page. Which ones show ways of life that are similar to how *you* live?

Clothing

We live in North Bay. We have to be ready for all kinds of weather here in the Canadian Shield. That's why I wear lots of layers when we go hiking.

It can rain really suddenly in Vancouver. I almost always carry my umbrella and raincoat.

Transportation

In Igulik, more people get around on snowmobiles than in cars.

We live in Montréal. My dad works on a ship on the St. Lawrence River. It's a great way to move things from place to place.

Recreation

In Pond Inlet, we need to play inside during the coldest days of the winter.

I could spend all day sailing near Montréal.

Housing

My house is in Harling Point, on the coast of British Columbia. My friend lives on the mountain nearby.

We live in a farmhouse near Saskatoon, Saskatchewan. We can't see our neighbour's house because it is so far away.

Jobs

My uncle works on a lobster boat in West Dover. With the ocean so near, fishing is a big industry here in Nova Scotia.

There are minerals in the ground near Thunder Bay, Ontario. Many people work in the mining industry.

Exploring Canada's Peoples

More **About. . .**

Canada's Diversity

Hundreds of languages are spoken in cities like Montréal, Toronto, and Vancouver. Montréal is the second-largest French-speaking city in the world, after Paris.

Physical features, climate, and natural resources in Canada's regions affect ways of life. What else affects how people live? Think about

• the languages you speak at home and at school
• the holidays you celebrate

Part of the way you live is a reflection of your **heritage**. If your heritage is Ukrainian, your holidays might include some traditions that are different from those that someone with a Chinese heritage might celebrate. If your **ancestors** were Inuit, you might speak a different language than someone whose ancestors were Scottish.

People from many different countries have settled in Canada. This makes the population of Canada **diverse**. Different groups of people have made Canada what it is today. You will learn about the First Nations, the Métis, the Inuit, the Francophones, and the English in Canada. You will also learn about the Loyalists and people who immigrated to Western Canada.

The First Nations, Inuit, and Métis

First Nations and Inuit have always been living in the land we call Canada. You will learn about how these groups lived before contact with the Europeans, and how they live today. Look at the map on pages 336–337 of the atlas section. What does it tell you about where First Nations and Inuit lived in the different regions?

You will also learn about the Métis, who were the descendants of European and First Nations people. The Métis played an important role in the development and exploration of Canada during the fur trade.

Students use library computers in Cambridge Bay, Nunavut. How has technology changed ways of life for the Inuit?

The French and the English

The Vikings were the first Europeans to arrive in Canada. Later, European explorers from countries such as England, France, and Spain came. The French were the first to build European settlements, towns, and forts. English explorers and settlers came later. The two groups spoke different languages and had different beliefs and customs. Today, Canada is officially **bilingual**, using English and French as its official languages.

Coming to Canada

Like the English and the French, people have come to Canada from around the world. They brought with them different languages, customs, and beliefs. People continue to immigrate to Canada today.

Compare the two Voices of Canada on this page. What do they tell you about the experience of each speaker?

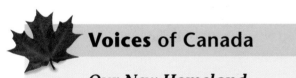

Voices of Canada

Our New Homeland

Suddenly a black stripe appeared above the fog... everyone cheered, "Land ahoy!" What was visible were dark green wooded hills. I thought I could even smell the wonderful fragrance of the distant forests. Nova Scotia, Canada, our new homeland, was spread out before our eyes in the sunshine.

Peter Hessel, German immigrant, 1952

Voices of Canada

French Settlement

From every point of view the site is fair, [and] the narrow entrance easy to defend. Upon the heights could be built a town. A very pretty place, [where] each family might in great comfort dwell and find a certain joy in life.

Sieur de Dièrville, describing Port Royal, the first permanent French settlement in New France, 1699

More About...

New France

New France was the name given to certain areas of Canada by French settlers. To them, the area was "new." The First Nations did not view the land as "New France."

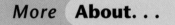

There are many bilingual signs in Canada. What does this say about Canada's identity?

Build Your Skills!

Use Scale to Explore Canada

Imagine that you are going on a tour of Canada's provincial and territorial capitals. On the map on pages 16–17, use scale to discover the distance between the capitals of each province and territory.
- Which provincial and territorial capitals are closest together?
- Which are the most isolated from other provincial and territorial capitals? How might this affect life in those cities?
- Use your findings to describe the size of Canada.

Study Ways of Life

Start a scrapbook about ways of life in Canada. You could show the different ways people play, work, and travel in each region. Begin with your own community. You can use photographs or your own drawings. Find newspaper clippings that tell you about ways of life in another region, or conduct interviews with someone you may know in another community.

Create a Display

Our identity is shaped by many things. Make a display to show how the geography of Canada's regions helps to shape the identity of Canadians. Think about Canada's
- size
- diverse landscape
- climate
- natural resources
- diverse communities

Putting It All Together

Using information in a chart is one way to present the results of an investigation of the Trans-Canada Highway. Katie's chart looked like this.

My Question	Trans-Canada Highway	Dempster Highway
How do highways affect how people live?	Connects big cities and towns and makes it easy to travel between them.	Connects some communities, such as Inuvik, with other communities in other regions. With no highways in Nunavut, people must find other ways to travel.

Review the inquiry questions for this chapter:
• What background information would Rick Hansen have to know in order to make his journey across Canada?
• Where would he look for information?

Take Time to Reflect

Think about what you have learned in this chapter. If you were to travel across Canada to raise money like Rick Hansen did, what criteria would you use to decide what your cause would be? How would you travel? Design a poster to promote your journey and describe your cause. Save your work for your Canada Collection.

Atlantic Region
Life by the Ocean

During a heavy snowstorm on January 10, 1996, the Joint Rescue Coordination Centre in Halifax, Nova Scotia, received an urgent call. Hundreds of kilometres off the shore of Newfoundland, a carrier ship, the *Amphion*, had been damaged in the storm and was about to sink. The ship's crew would die in the freezing water if they were not rescued.

Rescue teams acted quickly. A helicopter flew to the ship's location and dropped survival suits to the crew below. Then a rescue ship raced to the area. Rescuers used a smaller boat to reach the stranded crew. The rescuers had to make five trips on the cold, stormy waters to bring the crew to the rescue boat. All 24 members of the crew were saved!

The people of the Atlantic region are familiar with rescue missions like this one. Thousands of vessels have been lost in fog or have crashed on the rocky shores. Others have been lost in storms at sea. Despite the dangers, the people of this region have a deep connection to the ocean. It is a big part of life in the Atlantic region!

Canada: Our Stories Continue

Nova Scotia, New Brunswick, Prince Edward Island, the island of Newfoundland, and part of Québec are in the Atlantic region. This region is sometimes called the Appalachian region. These provinces, including Labrador, are also called the **Atlantic provinces**.

Most people in the Atlantic region live in communities close to the Atlantic Ocean. No matter where you are in this region, you are never more than 180 km from the ocean! Water is a major resource. It has provided people with food and transportation for thousands of years.

The Atlantic region receives a lot of rain, snow, and fog. Think of the story of the *Amphion*. How did the climate of this region affect the crew? How might the weather affect other people in this region?

? Critical Inquiry TIP

Planning
Before you start researching, develop a plan of action.
- Record your questions.
- Brainstorm places to find information.
- Think of ways to organize information.
- Create a schedule.

? Inquiring Minds

Here are some questions to guide your inquiry for this chapter:

- How does the ocean affect ways of life and identity in the Atlantic region?
- Even though they faced physical hardships, why was this region attractive to the Acadians and Loyalists?

More About. . .

Newfoundland and Labrador

This province includes the island of Newfoundland and part of the mainland, which is called Labrador. You will learn more about Labrador in Chapter 4, because it is part of the Canadian Shield region.

Let's Explore the Atlantic Region!

Hi! I'm Alistair MacInnis. I'm from the Atlantic region. I live in the town of Old Perlican, in Newfoundland. My house is near the ocean. Some of our neighbours catch crab or lobster for a living. My parents run a tour business. They take tourists out on a boat to see wildlife.

Lighthouses, such as this one on the coast of Newfoundland, warn ships about the rocky shores.

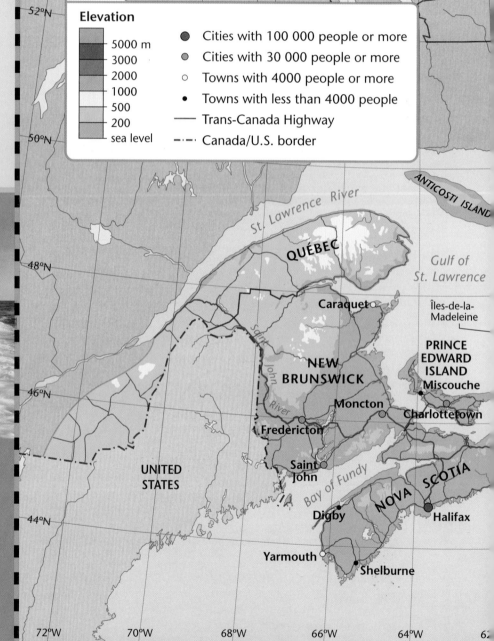

Legend

Elevation

5000 m
3000
2000
1000
500
200
sea level

● Cities with 100 000 people or more
● Cities with 30 000 people or more
○ Towns with 4000 people or more
• Towns with less than 4000 people
— Trans-Canada Highway
—·— Canada/U.S. border

St. Lawrence River

ANTICOSTI ISLAND

QUÉBEC

Gulf of St. Lawrence

Caraquet

Îles-de-la-Madeleine

PRINCE EDWARD ISLAND

NEW BRUNSWICK

Miscouche

Saint John River

Moncton

Charlottetown

Fredericton

Saint John

UNITED STATES

Bay of Fundy

NOVA SCOTIA

Digby

Halifax

Yarmouth

Shelburne

Halifax, in Nova Scotia, is the largest city in the Atlantic region. Halifax harbour is one of the most important ports in Canada. Because it never freezes, the harbour remains open year-round.

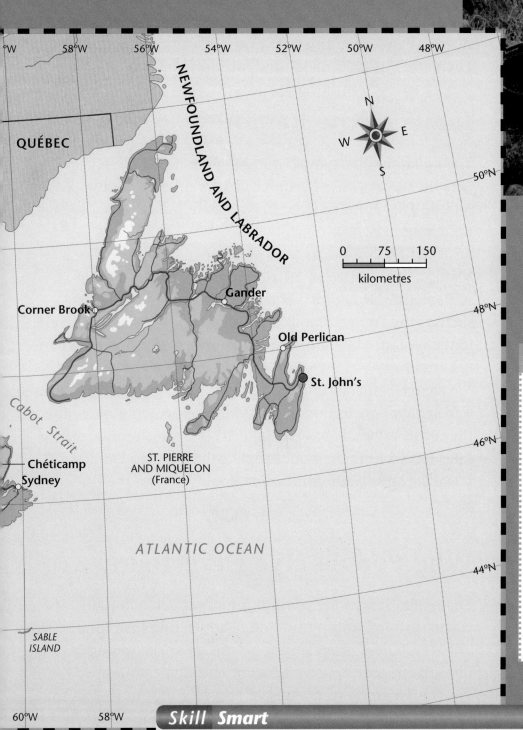

Dulse is a type of seaweed that grows along the coast. It is a traditional food for some people in this region. It was first introduced to Europeans by the First Nations.

More About. . .

Pirates!

Sailors in the Atlantic region used to have to watch out for pirates. The many bays on the coastline made great hideouts. What are some other reasons why the geography of this region would be good for this kind of activity?

Skill Smart

■ Look at the pictures on this page and read Alistair's description of his region. Use your observation skills to record details about the Atlantic region. Are these things you might see in Alberta? Write yes or no next to each observation.

The Atlantic Region

My town is called Old Perlican because a Spanish ship called the *Parlican* once visited here. Other places in my region have names like New Glasgow, Shubenacadie, and Bouctouche. I wonder why they were given those names?

The Atlantic region is next to the ocean, and many people who live in this region make their living on or next to the ocean. The region has cliffs, beaches, islands, lakes, and rivers. There are many bays and harbours along the coast. There are forests, valleys, and farmland as well.

Roots of the Region

The Mi'kmaq [meeg-mak] and Maliseet [MAH-li-seet] First Nations have always lived in this region. The Beothuk [BAY-o-thuk] First Nations lived in Newfoundland, but sadly they no longer exist.

The first Europeans to explore the region were the Vikings, who settled in Newfoundland. However, their settlements did not last. Later, other European explorers, such as the French, English, Spanish, and Portuguese, came to the region. They found that the area was a rich source of fish and furs.

French settlers were the first to establish permanent forts and settlements in the region. Many settlements were along the coast, or beside rivers. The British, Scottish, and Irish later settled in the region. People called United Empire Loyalists later came from what would become the United States.

Why People Live Here Today

The region has many natural resources, including the ocean, fish, oil and natural gas, forests, and farmland. These resources provide people with jobs. There are also jobs in tourism, government, education, and recreation.

The Mi'kmaq and Maliseet First Nations, as well as the descendants of the European settlers, continue to live in the region. People continue to immigrate to this region from places around Canada and the world.

This photo shows part of the large forests in New Brunswick. Almost 90 percent of the province is covered in forest. How might the people of this region use the forest?

What Affects Quality of Life in the Atlantic Region?

Here is how the land, water, other natural resources, and climate affect quality of life for some people in the Atlantic region.

In the 1960s, oil was discovered in the ocean floor east of Newfoundland. The Hibernia Oil Project began drilling for oil in 1997. Over 100 people work on the oil rig. Ships take the oil to a refinery in Newfoundland, and the oil is sold around the world.

The Annapolis Royal Tidal Power Station is the only saltwater power station in North America. The strong, high **tides** in the Bay of Fundy can be used to generate electricity, which provides a service to the community.

words matter!

Tides are daily changes in the level of the ocean.

Strong winds blow in from the ocean, but many people still live near the shore. Houses are built to withstand the weather.

Thinking *It Through*

- The ocean winds can affect the people in the Atlantic region. How does the weather in your community affect you? How do you feel about changes in the seasons? Share your thoughts and compare your points of view with other students in your class.

Alistair's Inquiry

Alistair's family went to visit his uncles in Halifax. One day his cousins took him to the Maritime Museum of the Atlantic.

Alistair noticed a display about shipwrecks in the Atlantic. He knew there must have been shipwrecks, but had not thought about why they might happen. What really caught his attention was a map of Sable Island.

Sable Island is a small, crescent-shaped piece of land about 300 kilometres southeast of Nova Scotia. It is called the "Graveyard of the Atlantic." The map showed where hundreds of shipwrecks had occurred around the island, all the way back to the 1500s! Alistair wondered how he could learn more about this island. He had a starting point: a map showing where Sable Island was located.

Alistair began to question many things once he saw the map.

- Why were there so many shipwrecks?
- Did the First Nations and explorers live on Sable Island?
- How do people use the ocean today?

This is an illustration of a shipwreck on Sable Island in 1854.

? Critical Inquiry TIP

Retrieving

After preparing questions, you could conduct an interview to find answers. Identify possible resources.

This is Sable Island today. I can see why ships might be wrecked here! They probably could not see it in a storm, or in fog.

Skill Smart

- What does the map on pages 36–37 make *you* question? In a small group, make a list of questions you would like to ask about the Atlantic region and the people who live there.

Latitude and Longitude

Use the map on pages 36–37 to describe the location of Sable Island. If you say "It is southeast of Nova Scotia," you are using **relative location**. Relative location means a place is somewhere close to a known place. When the crew of the *Amphion* sent a distress signal, they used **absolute location**. Absolute location describes exactly where a place is using lines of latitude and longitude. The crew of the *Amphion* used latitude and longitude to tell rescuers where they were.

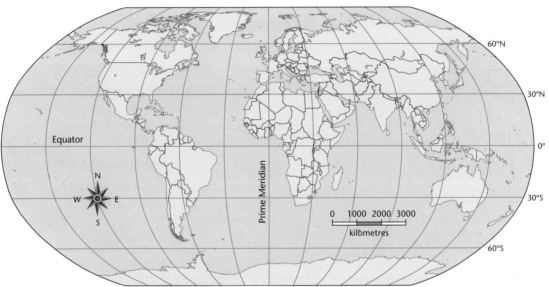

Lines of Latitude
Lines of latitude are imaginary lines that run east and west on a map or globe. These lines show distances from the **equator**. The distance is measured in degrees. The equator is the starting point for measuring latitude. (It is at 0° latitude.)

Lines of Longitude
The imaginary lines that run north and south are called **lines of longitude**. These lines show the distances from the **prime meridian**. The prime meridian is the starting point for measuring longitude. (It is at 0° longitude.)

Lines of Latitude and Longitude
Lines of latitude and longitude form a grid, or a series of lines that intersect. When you find the latitude and longitude of a place, you can create an intersection on a map and show the absolute location. For example, the city of Ottawa is at 45°N latitude by 75°W longitude.

Practise the Skill

1. Use the map on pages 36–37 to describe the absolute location and the relative location of Sable Island.

2. Using an atlas, describe the absolute and relative location of your community. Compare it to a city in the Atlantic region.

Why Did People Settle in the Atlantic Region?

The Mi'kmaq, Maliseet, and Beothuk lived by fishing, hunting, and gathering. They moved from place to place to take advantage of the seasons.

The Mi'kmaq lived along the coast for most of the year. They lived in what is now New Brunswick and Nova Scotia, but also in parts of Québec. Later, the Mi'kmaq would also live in parts of Newfoundland. They canoed on the ocean. The Maliseet lived inland and canoed along the Saint John River and the Bay of Fundy in New Brunswick. The Beothuk lived on the coast of Newfoundland in the summer and moved inland in the winter to hunt caribou. The water, and living near it, was important for all of these First Nations.

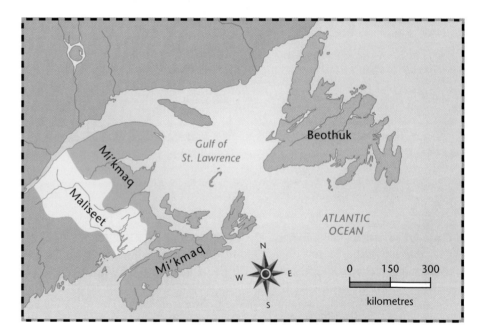

The First Nations of the Atlantic region are the Mi'kmaq, Maliseet, and Beothuk. These First Nations were the first inhabitants of this region.

Catherine Martin

Catherine Martin is a Mi'kmaq filmmaker. She made a film called *Spirit Wind*, about a Mi'kmaq group who built a traditional birchbark canoe and paddled it from Newfoundland to Nova Scotia. They worked on this project to bring their community together. Why do you think it might be important to the Mi'kmaq First Nations to have this film made?

Continuing an Ancestral Tradition

An Interview with Todd Labrador

Todd Labrador is a traditional canoe-maker and member of the Mi'kmaq First Nation.

Q. What interests you about canoes? How did you come to build them?

A. I was always fascinated by the stories my father told me about Mi'kmaq traditions and their respect for the land. My father passed on the knowledge he had received from his grandfather, who was a canoe-builder and basket-maker.

Q. How is canoe-making important to your identity as a Mi'kmaq person?

A. Building canoes is a way to bring pride back to our communities. We get our youth working with our Elders, and everybody benefits.

Q. How do you share your knowledge and traditions with others?

A. I go into the schools to teach young people about our culture. It makes them happy to know that this is the origin of the canoes people use today: it represents something that our people gave to the world.

? Critical Inquiry TIP

Creating

You can show information by creating sketches. You can draw a simple picture to share what you have learned about the First Nations of the Atlantic region on these pages.

Thinking *It Through*

■ What does Todd Labrador's personal experiences tell you about canoe-making and Mi'kmaq traditions? What else would you want to ask him?

Natural Resources

The First Nations of this region did not plant crops or keep herds of animals. They moved from camp to camp, and did not build permanent homes. The homes of the Mi'kmaq were called **wigwams**. They were made from spruce poles and birchbark. Tree roots were used for binding the poles and sewing the bark together.

Birch trees are an important resource. I wonder what other kinds of items were made from trees by the First Nations in my region.

This wigwam was built at the Bear River Mi'kmaq Interpretive Centre as part of its museum. Why did the First Nations of this region choose birchbark to build their homes?

Water, forests, and the land provided the Mi'kmaq, Maliseet, and Beothuk with what they needed. Different foods, like eggs, berries, clams, and meat, were produced in each season.

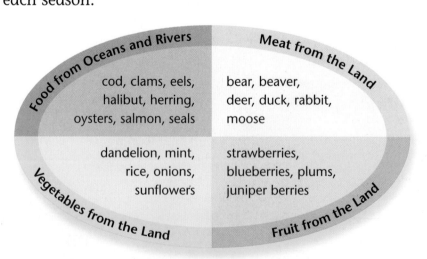

Food from Oceans and Rivers
cod, clams, eels, halibut, herring, oysters, salmon, seals

Meat from the Land
bear, beaver, deer, duck, rabbit, moose

Vegetables from the Land
dandelion, mint, rice, onions, sunflowers

Fruit from the Land
strawberries, blueberries, plums, juniper berries

How Do We Know About the Past?

How do we know about ways of life in the past? One way is from the work of **archeologists**. They study tools, clothing, and campsites from the past. Often these are the only clues we have about the ways people lived.

Another way to learn about the past is by reading journals, diaries, and letters, and by listening to oral history. Some European traders and explorers kept journals that tell about what they did and what they saw each day as they travelled.

The Beothuk

The Beothuk of Newfoundland no longer exist. Tragically, they died after Europeans arrived in Newfoundland. Many died from diseases that came with the Europeans. Some starved. Others were killed by settlers who wanted Beothuk land for themselves. We know of the Beothuk today because of archeological evidence, and also because of Shawnadithit, the last known Beothuk. She died of tuberculosis in 1829. Before she died, she told stories of the Beothuk, and drew pictures of their way of life. William Cormack, a Scottish explorer who wanted to create peace between the Beothuk and the Europeans, wrote down stories and kept pictures. With these records, the Beothuk would not be forgotten.

The petroglyphs in Kejimkujik National Park were made by the Mi'kmaq. What story do you think this petroglyph might be telling? How can you find out more?

Shawnadithit

This is a portrait of Shawnadithit, and one of her drawings. Why is it important that we preserve historical items such as Shawnadithit's drawings?

Why Did Europeans Come to the Atlantic Region?

It's amazing that so many people came from so far away to fish here. Maybe some of them settled here, in Old Perlican! I think I'll find out more about this.

Imagine something so precious that people would travel by ship for months to get it and take it back home. For Europeans living in the 1500s, this was fish—a rich, valuable resource in the Atlantic region. As soon as explorers came to the region, they discovered the amazing amount of cod that swam in the waters off Newfoundland. It is said that the fish could be caught in buckets let down over the side of ships! Soon the Spanish, Portuguese, and people from other European countries were sailing to the Atlantic region to fish for cod.

Fishing for Cod

Since cod could be preserved by drying or salting, it was possible to bring large quantities of it back to Europe. The Mi'kmaq taught the Europeans how to make racks on land for drying fish. At first, the drying stations were run only in the summer months, when the weather was good. Sometimes a few men stayed through the cold, wet winters to look after the drying racks and the docks.

Cod was still plentiful off the Grand Banks of Newfoundland in 1949.

These modern cod-drying racks in Ferryland, Newfoundland, were similar to the racks people used 500 years ago.

Trading for Fur

In 1535, a French explorer named Jacques Cartier arrived in the area that would become known as the Gaspé Peninsula. There he met several Mi'kmaq who were willing to trade furs for knives and other metal objects. Glass beads, tools, and weapons were also traded.

In Europe, beaver fur was used to trim the robes of kings and queens and other powerful people. By the early 1600s, it was being used to make hats. Word spread quickly that fur was plentiful in the newly found land. Rulers of European countries rushed to set up **colonies** in the Atlantic region to take advantage of this valuable resource.

words **matter!**

Colonies are settlements that are under the control of another country, such as Britain or France.

Artist William Eagar painted this image of Mi'kmaq people at Halifax Harbour in 1836. How might the Mi'kmaq way of life change after the arrival of Europeans? What can be learned from this painting, done by a European artist?

Thinking *It Through*

- Having a settlement allowed Europeans to stay all year and take part in the fur trade. Why would they do this?

The Mi'kmaq used porcupine quills for decoration, such as on this box (above left). The second box is Maliseet, and European materials such as velvet and glass beads were used. Both boxes were made in the late 1800s.

The First French Settlements

This is Île Sainte-Croix. Why do you think the colonists thought an island might be a good place to settle?

Thinking It Through

- To help the colonists get through the long, cold winter, Champlain created the Ordre de bon temps (the Order of Good Cheer). Everyone would gather together and share a meal every day, with colonists taking turns to provide food and entertainment. How might this have helped the colonists survive the winter?

In 1604, the King of France sent Pierre Du Gua de Monts to set up a fur-trading colony in the Atlantic region. De Monts hired explorer and mapmaker Samuel de Champlain, and about 100 male colonists to travel to the "New World."

When the group sailed into the Bay of Fundy, they settled on what they called Île Sainte-Croix, in the mouth of a river that flowed into the bay.

Port Royal

Champlain and the colonists were not prepared for the cold climate at Île Sainte-Croix. The colonists ran out of food, firewood, and water. During the first winter, at least a third of the colonists died, many from **scurvy**.

The next year, Champlain and the survivors left Île Sainte-Croix. They built a settlement in what would be called Nova Scotia. They called the settlement Port Royal. The site had access to the ocean, rich soil, and abundant fish and wildlife. Relations with the Mi'kmaq who lived nearby were very friendly. The French colonists may not have survived if it hadn't been for their relationship with the Mi'kmaq, who helped them by providing food and medicine and by sharing knowledge of the land.

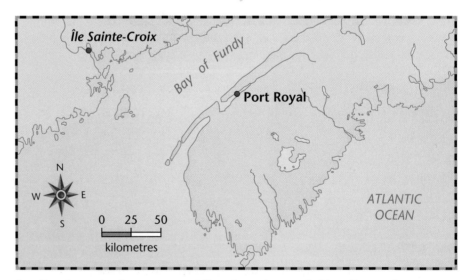

Port Royal was the first permanent French settlement in New France. As more French settlers came, they spread out into an area they called Acadie [a-ka-DEE]. Acadie grew to include areas such as Île Saint-Jean, known today as Prince Edward Island.

Life in Acadie

Port Royal was a better site than Île Sainte-Croix, but Champlain and others left for the St. Lawrence River area. Some settlers remained in what they called Acadie. Families began to arrive from France. These French settlers became known as Acadians. The Acadians were the first European settlers in North America to have their own name and identity. What do the Voices of Canada on this page tell about life in Acadie?

This painting was made in the early 1980s by an Acadian artist named Azor Vienneau. What does it show about life in historic Acadie?

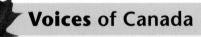

Voices of Canada

The Climate of Acadie

The summer is as warm [as in France], but the winter is colder— it snows almost continuously in this season, and the winds are so cold that they freeze one's face.

Sieur de Dièrville, Acadie, 1699

Conflict Between the British and the French

For decades, England and France fought over the Atlantic region. Each country wanted control of the territory for fishing and the fur trade.

After a war in 1713, **treaties** were made between France and England. Now all of the Atlantic region, except Cape Breton Island, would be British territory. The British now controlled Acadie. British laws were used, and more British settlers arrived to make their home in the Atlantic region.

The British wanted the Acadians to swear an oath of **allegiance** to Britain. Part of the oath included a promise to fight against the French and the Mi'kmaq if the British asked them to. If they did not agree, they would have to leave. The Acadians refused to sign.

Voices of Canada

Help of the Mi'kmaq

Our first experience of the newcomers was based on sharing and caring, and established the parameters of the relationship. Mi'kmaq values of sharing and helping ensured that the French would be welcomed here.

Patricia Doyle-Bedwell, Mi'kmaq First Nation, 2004

words matter!

A **treaty** is an agreement between countries. It is also an agreement between the government and First Nations people.

Allegiance means loyalty to a nation or country.

In 1884, the Acadians created their own flag. How do you think the flag contributes to the Acadians' identity?

Le Grand Dérangement

In 1755, the British forced the Acadians to leave because they would not swear allegiance to Britain. Most Acadians went south, to what is now the United States. Others went to France. Some journeyed to Québec. This deportation continued until 1762. More than ten thousand Acadians were forced away. They called it **le Grand Dérangement** [le grawn day-rawnge-maw], or "the Great Upheaval."

What Happened to the Acadians?

Years later, many Acadians made their way back to the Atlantic region. The returning Acadians started new Francophone communities in what would become New Brunswick, Prince Edward Island, and Nova Scotia.

Slowly, the Acadian community was rebuilt. In 1881, Acadian leaders had a meeting in Memramcook, New Brunswick. The Acadians chose a date, August 15, which would become their yearly celebration of Acadian identity. In 2003, that date was declared National Acadian Day by the Canadian government.

Today there are more than 300 000 Francophone Acadians living in the Atlantic region. New Brunswick is the only officially bilingual province in Canada.

More About. . .

Acadian Communities

Some modern Acadian communities include
- Caraquet, New Brunswick
- Chéticamp, Nova Scotia
- Miscouche, Prince Edward Island

Find information about these communities.

Voices of Canada

What does this quote tell about keeping the Acadian identity?

Remembering the Past

We need to know both the positive and negative parts of our history. We need to understand our roots. Knowing about the Great Upheaval is an important part of understanding Acadia's history.

Barbara LeBlanc, Saulnierville, Nova Scotia, 2005

Tantramar Marshes today

The Trans Canada Trail in New Brunswick goes around the Tantramar Marshes, which are the largest diked marshlands in North America. These dikes are the remains of old Acadian dikes.

Who Were the Loyalists?

In 1776, the Thirteen Colonies, in what would become part of the United States, declared independence from Britain. They wanted to form their own country, free of British rule. But some of the people living in the Colonies wanted to remain part of the British Empire and were loyal to the British king. They became known as United Empire Loyalists. Many Loyalists left the Thirteen Colonies during the American War of Independence. Some went north, to what had become **British North America**.

words matter!

British North America is the term for the British colonies in North America after the United States became independent from Britain.

Loyalists settled in places such as Shelburne and Digby, in Nova Scotia. One of the largest Loyalist settlements was in Saint John, New Brunswick. This is Loyalist House, built in 1811. It is now a National Historic Site. How does this house compare to the story told in the Voices of Canada on this page?

Coming to a New Land

In what would become Canada, Britain promised free land to the Loyalists. Most arrived with little money and few supplies. Some had been doctors. Others had worked as carpenters, farmers, or soldiers. Now they had to start over.

The Loyalists lived in tents during their first winter. In order to receive the free land they were promised, they had to build homes and start farms. It took months to clear trees and rocks from the land before crops could be planted.

Skill Smart

- Imagine that you are a reporter writing about the United Empire Loyalists in the Atlantic region. Use the Voices of Canada on this page to form some questions that you might ask Hannah Ingraham about her experiences. What else would you like to know?

Voices of Canada

A Loyalist Home

When we woke, we found the snow lying deep around us and father told us the house was ready. There was a floor laid, no windows, no chimney, no door but we had a roof at least. A good fire was blazing and mother had a big loaf of bread and she boiled a kettle of water. We toasted the bread and ate our breakfast, and mother said, "This is the sweetest meal I have tasted for many a day."

Hannah Ingraham, Loyalist daughter, age 11

I'd like to know more about the Loyalist communities in my region. I have a pen pal in Saint John. She says that many Loyalists settled there. They even have a special celebration called Loyalist Day! I think I'll write to her to find out more.

The United Empire Loyalists who came to British North America were a diverse group. They helped to build new communities. The Loyalists included

- many nationalities: African, English, Irish, Scottish, German, and Dutch
- many religions: Presbyterian, Anglican, Roman Catholic, Methodist, Mennonite, and Quaker
- many backgrounds: farmers, carpenters, domestic workers, lawyers, and ministers

The arrival of the Loyalists changed the region in many ways. The population of the Atlantic region was now much greater and more diverse, with people from many different backgrounds. The Loyalists also brought their beliefs and ways of life with them.

The Black Loyalists

More than 3000 of the Loyalists who came to Nova Scotia were Black Loyalists. The Black Loyalists were not given an equal share of the free land promised to them by the British. Much of the land given to them was rocky and bad for farming. As a result, 1196 Black Loyalists left Canada for Sierra Leone, a British colony in Africa. Thousands stayed in Nova Scotia.

This 1835 painting by Robert Petley shows a family of Black Loyalists on a road near Halifax. The Black Loyalists who did not move to Sierra Leone would settle in more than 40 communities in Nova Scotia.

Africville

Some Black Loyalists settled in Halifax. In 1885, the community adopted the name Africville when they named their church the Africville United Baptist Church.

While many people called Africville home, the city of Halifax had placed a prison, a dump, and a slaughterhouse in the area. It did not give the Africville community services such as lights, sewers, water, or fire and police protection.

In 1964, the city of Halifax decided to use the area of Africville as the location for a new bridge crossing Halifax Harbour. The residents of Africville were given homes in other parts of the city and Africville was demolished. Today, Africville is a national historic site, and many former residents of Africville and their descendants continue to come together as a community, in reunions.

Voices of Canada

A Strong Spirit

Those who refused or were slow to leave often found themselves scrambling out the back door with their belongings as the bulldozers were coming in the front. Yet in spite of all this, the spirit of Africville remains alive and strong.

Joe Sealy

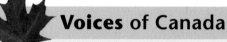

Voices of Canada

Staying Together

The reunion is important to the descendants because it gives them a place to come back to and remember. It's important to teach the children. We hope they can learn from what happened.

Former Africville resident

THEN AND NOW

Africville

This photo was taken just before Africville was destroyed.

Today, the land where Africville stood is called Seaview Memorial Park. A monument for Africville was created in the 1980s.

Did Quality of Life Change in the Atlantic Region?

I wonder how the chiefs of the Mi'kmaq Nation felt when they wrote this letter to the governor.

Between the 1500s and the 1800s, people came to the Atlantic region from France, England, Scotland, and Ireland. The discovery of rich natural resources and the beginning of settlements meant that life was changing in the region.

The First Nations

The newcomers to the Atlantic region had an impact on the First Nations of the area. In the 1800s, ten chiefs of the Mi'kmaq First Nation decided to talk to the governor of Nova Scotia. Here is their letter to him. What does the letter tell you about changes in their quality of life?

This Maliseet man worked as a guide in 1899. How else might the First Nations people of this region have adapted their traditional ways of life?

> February 1840
> To His Excellency John Harvey,
>
> Good and Honourable Governor, be not offended at what we say... [But] you have taken from us our lands and trees and have destroyed our game. The moose yards of our fathers, where are they? You have put ships and steamboats upon the waters and they scare away the fish.
> In old times our wigwams stood in the pleasant places along the sides of the rivers. These places are now taken from us, and we are told to go away...
>
> **Signed: Pelancea Paul, Colum Paul, Pierre Antoine, Louis Paul, Gabriel Boonus, James Mius, Louis Alexis, Savier Paul, Pierre Morris, François Paul**

Skill Smart

- Skim this chapter to review how the early explorers, fishers, and fur traders changed the ways of life of the First Nations in the Atlantic region. Begin with the letter on this page. Make a three-column chart with the headings "Changes in Ways of Life," "Effect on the First Nations," and "Positive or Negative."

Changing Industries

The diverse groups of people who settled in the Atlantic region helped develop many industries. Some of these industries would be changed by new technology or the loss of natural resources. This affected the way people lived in the region.

Building Wooden Ships

Large forests and access to the ocean meant that shipbuilding was a major industry in the Atlantic region. Many people were employed in this industry—from the forestry workers who harvested and cut the timber, to the craftspeople who built the ships.

Gradually, new steel ships powered by steam engines replaced wooden ships. Many shipbuilders had to find new work. Today, some wooden ships are still made, and shipbuilding is part of the region's heritage.

Railways and Harbours

The first part of the Dominion Atlantic Railway opened in 1856. Trains carried products to and from the region. Farmers, forestry companies, and mining companies could now send their products to other parts of the region. Later, the railways in the region would connect to those in Canada and the United States.

Harbours remained an important hub of activity. Ships came from around the world to pick up and deliver products and people. As a result, communities like Halifax, Saint John, and St. John's would grow into major port cities where people could live and work.

English and Scottish settlers found rich red soil in Prince Edward Island. Soon the island would be well known for producing potatoes. Today, McCain Foods Limited, based in New Brunswick, uses PEI potatoes to make frozen french fries.

More About...

The *Bluenose*

The *Bluenose* was a famous wooden ship built in Lunenburg, Nova Scotia. It was used for fishing and for races. It was the fastest ship in the world for many years. Today, we can still see the *Bluenose*—on a Canadian dime!

Mining

People settling in parts of Nova Scotia quickly found coal, a valuable fossil fuel. Coal mining in Nova Scotia began when France controlled the area. Eventually it became a large industry. In 1873, there were eight coal companies operating in Cape Breton.

The Men of the Deeps is North America's only coal miners' choir. It is based in Cape Breton, Nova Scotia. Although the coal mining industry has come to an end, the choir keeps part of their community's history alive by singing traditional mining songs.

For the miners who worked far beneath the ground, coal mining was dirty and very dangerous. However, coal was important. It fuelled furnaces and engines and created a new way of life for everybody in the region. If an accident happened, everyone gathered together to support each other.

By 2001, coal mining came to an end in Nova Scotia. This placed many families out of work, and ended a way of life that many generations had experienced. What do the following Voices of Canada tell you about this changing way of life?

Voices of Canada

A Coal Miner's Life

These miners all worked in the coal mines of Cape Breton. How could the closure of the mines affect their identities?

I'm a coal miner. I'm proud to be one. That's all I've ever done.

Terry McVarish, 2000

Coal is the reason our families came here. It is who we are—it's our identity.

Steve Woods, 2001

I was always proud to be a miner. It made me feel good to know that we put the lights on in Nova Scotia.

Leo Scott, 2001

It's a sad thing to be part of a dying breed.

Ron Henessey, 2001

The Loss of the Cod Fishery

From the 1500s to the 1900s, cod fishing remained an important Atlantic industry. For generations, "fishing families" lived through hard winters in hope of the big summer catch.

Voices of Canada

Remembering How It Used to Be

Often we didn't have room for the fish on the flacks [the drying racks] and it had to be dried on the rocks and we would be called in the morning to go over and spread that fish. We would have to protect it from the rain. We'd get birchbark, the rinds of the birch to put over that fish.

Stella Bury, Greenspond Island, Newfoundland

A Way of Life Is Changed

In 1992, the Canadian government stopped the cod fishery. Years of overfishing by Canada and other countries had reduced the numbers of cod in the ocean. People believed that stopping the fishery would let the cod recover in numbers.

This was a serious blow to the thousands of people who worked in the fishing industry. Generations of families had fished for cod. Fishing was a part of their identity. Fishing was the only job that many had ever had. It would be hard to find other work or learn to do something else. Hundreds of people moved away from the region, leaving their families and friends. Others stayed and trained for other types of work.

When fishing ended, my dad started doing boat tours. But sometimes he says, "It's a good day for flounder." I know he misses fishing. I wonder when he will be able to do it again.

Thinking It Through

■ Evaluate the song "Goin' Up with Brudder." What is the mood of the singer? Why might writing a song be a good way to express feelings?

■ How does this song reflect ways of life in this region? What other songs can you find that might help you learn more about this region?

Goin' Up with Brudder
–by Buddy Wasisname and the Other Fellers

I went out to haul me trawl.
All I got was nothing at all.
I'm packing up and I'm moving out.
Going to McMurray.

I'll say goodbye to all me friends
With hopes that I'll be back again.
There's nothing more that I can do.
I'm going up with me brudder.

brudder: brother   **trawl:** a strong fishing net   **McMurray:** Fort McMurray, Alberta

What Jobs Do People Have in the Atlantic Region Today?

words **matter!**

Aquaculture is raising fish in protected areas until they are big enough to harvest for human consumption.

? **Critical Inquiry TIP**

Keep a section in your notebook to record new words. Try using jot notes and pictures to remember what the word means.

Today in the Atlantic region, jobs can be found in manufacturing, **aquaculture**, and in service industries. There are universities, call centres, ocean research centres, and oil refineries. There is oil and gas development. An offshore oil field, called Hibernia, has been developed on the Grand Banks.

Fruit and potatoes are farmed in the region and sent around the world. The region's forests still provide trees for lumber, and there are pulp and paper mills in New Brunswick.

In the Atlantic region, more than 85 000 people work in the tourism industry. The beauty and history of the region attract visitors from all over the world.

Making *a Difference*

Moira Brown: Saving the Northern Right Whale

The northern right whale is the world's most endangered whale. Only a few hundred remain. Every summer, the Bay of Fundy is a feeding ground for many of these whales. But the Bay of Fundy is also a busy shipping area. Huge supertankers carry oil through the bay, to and from the port of Saint John.

Moira Brown is a whale researcher. She realized that the ships were taking a route that ran straight through the whales' feeding area. Whales could easily be killed if a ship hit them.

Moira asked the government to change the route taken by the supertankers. After four years of talks, the government ordered that the ships should travel on a route that avoids the feeding ground.

Moira's determination to change the shipping lanes will help the right whale survive!

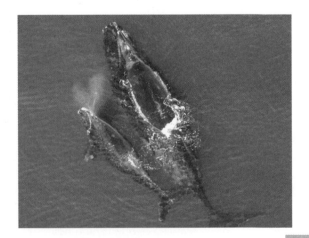

Watching the Weather

Some jobs in the Atlantic region are centred on the region's climate. The weather affects how people live and work. Ships like the *Amphion* are in danger when there are storms at sea. People cannot cross the Confederation Bridge between Prince Edward Island and New Brunswick when the winds are too strong.

Weather centres, like the Canadian Hurricane Centre in Dartmouth, Nova Scotia, are used to track the weather. Scientists and meteorologists work in all parts of the region—even on islands like Sable Island!

The weather can really affect what we do every day. We check the weather reports every morning on the radio. We also have emergency supplies to use when bad storms happen.

Waves of Disaster

The Atlantic region experiences some terrible storms. **Gales** are fierce windstorms. On the sea, gale-force winds create huge waves. The wind, waves, and rain can cause shipwrecks.

Large storms called **hurricanes** form over the ocean. Every year, hurricanes hit the Atlantic region. When there is a hurricane, people near the coastline must take cover or move inland to safer areas.

A **tsunami** is an ocean wave produced by an underwater earthquake. On November 18, 1929, a tsunami hit the southern part of the coast of Newfoundland. The water raced to the coast at a speed of 70 kilometres an hour. Waves as high as 27 metres crashed onto the shore, destroying houses, fishing boats, stores, and roads.

This is a spring flood in Moncton, New Brunswick, in 2002. Why do you think predicting the weather might be important in any region of Canada?

Voices of Canada

The Destruction Caused by the Wave

All the people had their winter provisions, fuel, traps, and gear of every description in their stores. Everything is gone. I visited them today. There is great distress. It is imperative that something be done at once to help… I shall have to get food, clothing, and coal to many families.

Magistrate Hollett, in a letter to the prime minister, November 20, 1929

Viewpoints

If the Numbers of Cod Increased, Should the Cod Fishery Re-open?

When the Canadian government ended commercial cod fishing, more than 40 000 people in the Atlantic region lost their way of life. People in Newfoundland were hit the hardest. Coastal towns that had depended on fishing for generations were faced with unemployment. Losing their way of life was devastating to families.

Some people were trained to do other jobs, and worked in call centres that provided customer service to people all over Canada. Others left the province, going to places like Fort McMurray, where people were needed to work in the oil industry. Many small communities were left almost empty when so many people moved away.

The industry was closed because people were afraid the cod would be harvested to extinction.

This stamp from 1941 calls codfish "Newfoundland currency." Why do you think this stamp was made?

The numbers of cod are not getting any better. Other areas in the world are also showing signs that cod are disappearing. We need to work with these governments to ensure the same mistakes made in Canada are not repeated.

It's very sad to be sitting here, looking out at the sea, yearning to fish again. I am 57 years old and I don't know if the fishery will open before I'm too old to fish. There is a call centre opening in Little Rapids. I could sit at a desk and take customer service calls. But I'm used to being my own boss and living off the sea—not working for some big company.

Large deep-sea trawlers came from countries such as Spain and Portugal to fish for cod off the coast of Newfoundland. They used huge nets that caught large numbers of fish.

NEW MARINE PROTECTED AREAS OFF NEWFOUNDLAND AND LABRADOR
Public give opinions on cod recovery

The Mi'kmaq people have always fished in this region. There was always lots of fish, lobster, and eels for everyone. Then people began catching many fish. They had nets and boats that just kept getting bigger. I think that's why the codfish are almost gone now. People should never fish with such big nets again.

Over to You

1. As a group, discuss the different points of view. Take a class vote to decide whether the cod fishery should be re-opened if the numbers of cod increase.

2. How do you think the Atlantic cod should be protected? For example, how should laws be used to control the industry? Brainstorm some ideas in your group.

3. If the oil industry in Alberta closed, how might that affect the people?

Build Your Skills!

Use Absolute and Relative Location

- Write the latitude and longitude of two communities in the Atlantic region and two communities in your own region. Then write the relative location of these communities. Give these clues to a partner and, using an atlas, have them find out the names of the communities.
- Find another community near the same line of latitude as your community. Then find another community near the same line of longitude as your community.
- When do you think it is best to use relative location? When do you think it is best to use absolute location?

Research a Settlement

What features would help Loyalist, Acadian, Scottish, or British settlers decide where to build a new settlement?

- Research a community in the Atlantic region that was founded by one of the groups listed above.
- Why did they settle there?
- Compare the community with your community. Are there any similarities? Are there any differences?

Develop a Web

A "trigger industry" is an industry that causes many other businesses to begin. For example, a company may be created to ship and deliver fish that is caught by other people. Develop a web to show the connections between industries that began because of fishing in the Atlantic region. Explain how the loss of the fishing industry would impact this region.

Putting It All Together

Alistair used a web to organize his inquiry about shipwrecks and Sable Island.

There was no lighthouse on the island in the past.

Ships would have to pass close to Sable Island on their way to Nova Scotia.

Why were there shipwrecks on Sable Island?

Ships in the past did not have technology, such as GPS, to help guide them safely around the island.

Sable Island is dangerous because it is a low sandbar and is hard to see.

Review the inquiry questions for this chapter:
- How does the ocean affect ways of life and identity in the Atlantic region?
- Even though they faced physical hardships, why was this region attractive to the Acadians and Loyalists?

Take Time to Reflect

Before you go on to the next chapter, think about what you have learned in this one. Write a short story about a sea rescue. Put yourself into the story. Keep your work for your Canada Collection.

CHAPTER 3

Great Lakes–St. Lawrence Lowlands

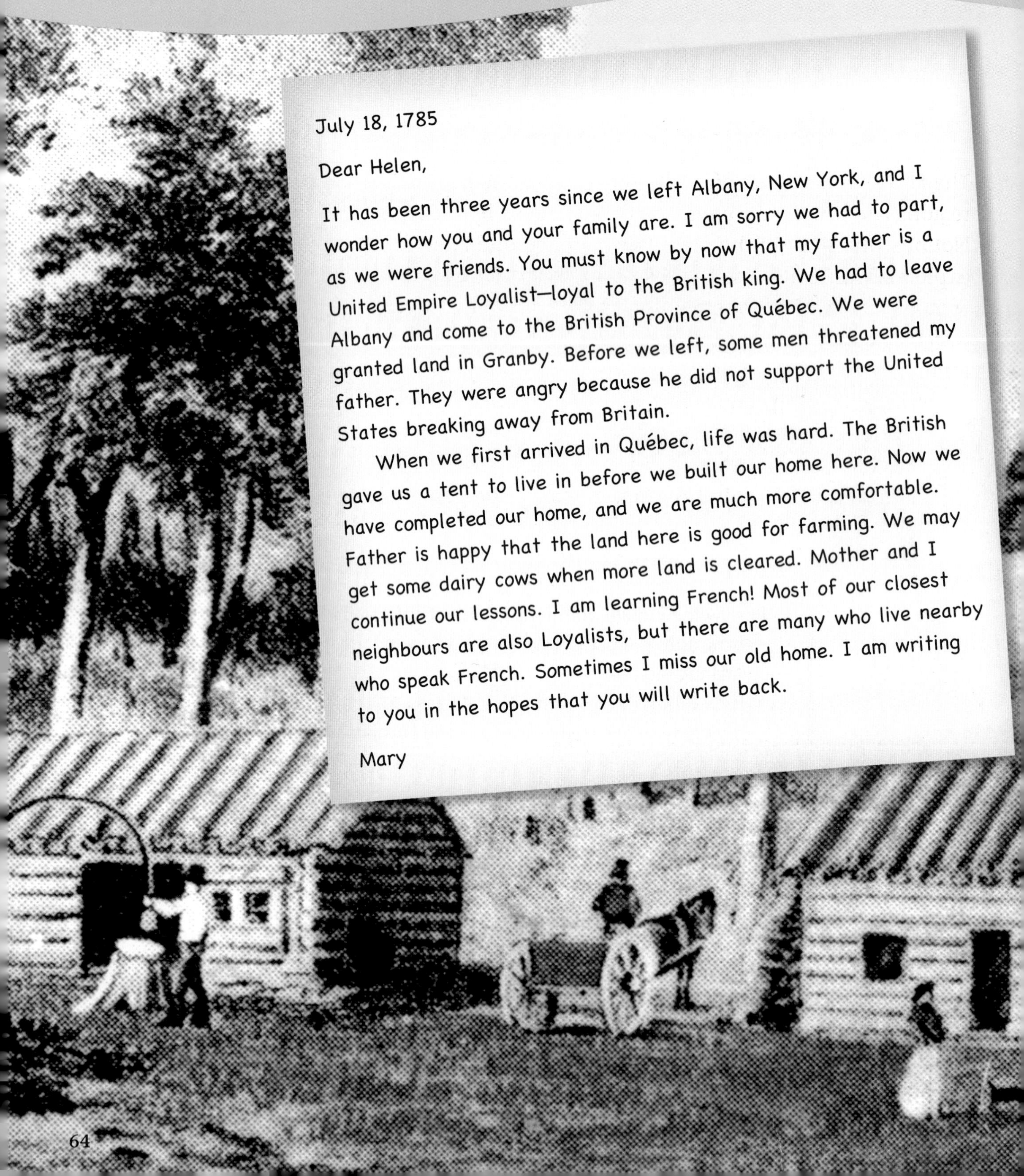

July 18, 1785

Dear Helen,

It has been three years since we left Albany, New York, and I wonder how you and your family are. I am sorry we had to part, as we were friends. You must know by now that my father is a United Empire Loyalist—loyal to the British king. We had to leave Albany and come to the British Province of Québec. We were granted land in Granby. Before we left, some men threatened my father. They were angry because he did not support the United States breaking away from Britain.

When we first arrived in Québec, life was hard. The British gave us a tent to live in before we built our home here. Now we have completed our home, and we are much more comfortable. Father is happy that the land here is good for farming. We may get some dairy cows when more land is cleared. Mother and I continue our lessons. I am learning French! Most of our closest neighbours are also Loyalists, but there are many who live nearby who speak French. Sometimes I miss our old home. I am writing to you in the hopes that you will write back.

Mary

Canada: Our Stories Continue

The St. Lawrence River affects how many people live in this region. The waterways have always been used by the First Nations who lived in the area. Later, French and English explorers would also use the rivers and lakes to travel. The French were the first to settle along the St. Lawrence River, which was originally called the Fleuve St-Laurent. Loyalist families, such as Mary's family, came later. Today, ships bring people and goods into the region from around the world. Communities have developed along the river and the lakes. Although this region is one of the smallest regions in Canada, it has a huge population.

? Critical Inquiry TIP

Planning

A good plan includes your own inquiry questions. Think about what you already know about the Great Lakes–St. Lawrence Lowlands. Then brainstorm inquiry questions with a partner.

This painting from the mid-1800s shows a manor next to the St. Lawrence.

? Inquiring Minds

Here are some questions to guide your inquiry for this chapter:

- How does the St. Lawrence River affect ways of life in this region?
- Why are First Nations and Francophones so important to the identity of this region?

Let's Explore the Great St. Lawrence Lowlands!

Bonjour! My name is Claire Martineau. I live in Montréal, Québec, on the St. Lawrence River. Montréal is the second-largest city in Canada. It is also the second-largest French-speaking city in the world!

The city of Montréal is on an island in the St. Lawrence River. It is one of the largest ports in the world.

Lakes–

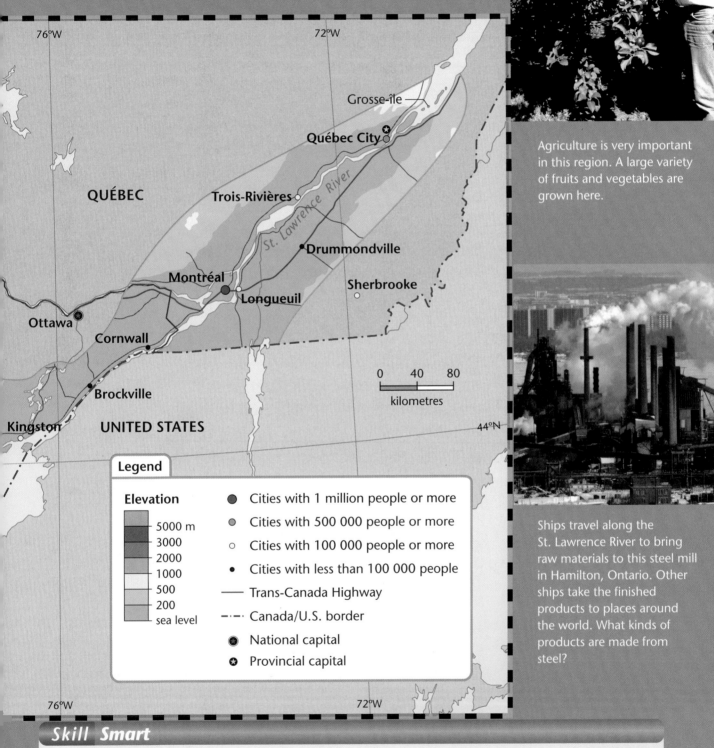

76°W   72°W

Grosse-île

Québec City

QUÉBEC

Trois-Rivières

St. Lawrence River

Drummondville

Montréal

Longueuil

Sherbrooke

Ottawa

Cornwall

Brockville

Kingston   UNITED STATES

44°N

0   40   80

kilometres

Legend

Elevation

5000 m	
3000	
2000	
1000	
500	
200	
sea level	

⬤ Cities with 1 million people or more

◯ Cities with 500 000 people or more

○ Cities with 100 000 people or more

• Cities with less than 100 000 people

— Trans-Canada Highway

–·–· Canada/U.S. border

◉ National capital

✪ Provincial capital

Agriculture is very important in this region. A large variety of fruits and vegetables are grown here.

Ships travel along the St. Lawrence River to bring raw materials to this steel mill in Hamilton, Ontario. Other ships take the finished products to places around the world. What kinds of products are made from steel?

Skill Smart

■ Make a chart like this one. Use latitude and longitude to describe the location of each place. Then use scale to measure the distance from Claire's city to the other communities.

City	Latitude, Longitude	Distance from Montréal
Québec City		
Toronto		
Windsor		

The Great Lakes–St. Lawrence Lowlands

I love going for a picnic with my family at Parc du Mont-Royal. We take the Métro—that's our subway.

Québec City is one of the oldest cities in Canada. How does closeness to a river help a city grow?

The Lowlands are low, flat lands with gently rolling hills in southern Québec and southern Ontario. This region follows the path of the St. Lawrence River, as far as the western end of Lake Erie. Many of the cities, towns, and villages of this region have developed along this river and beside Lake Ontario, Lake Huron, and Lake Erie.

Roots of the Region

First Nations people have always travelled along the river to trade with other groups. Several groups within the Haudenosaunee [how-den-o-show-nee], or nations within the **Iroquois Confederacy**, live in this region. The Ouendat [wen-dat], also known as the Huron, live in the region as well.

In 1608, Samuel de Champlain founded the settlement of Québec. As more French settlers, explorers, and fur traders came, they used the St. Lawrence River to explore further inland. Their **Canadien** descendants farmed the land along the river. United Empire Loyalists came to the region in the late 1700s. In the mid 1800s, many Scottish and Irish people came to live and work in the region.

Why People Live Here Today

First Nations people continue to live in the region, as do the descendants of the French settlers and the Loyalists. People have also come from countries around the world to live in this region. They continue to come here today.

The Great Lakes–St. Lawrence Lowlands is **fertile**. A long growing season provides many people with work in the agricultural industry. Manufacturing is also an important industry here. Tourism and outdoor activities also bring people to this region.

What Affects Quality of Life in the Great Lakes–St. Lawrence Lowlands?

Look at these photos and read the point of view each person expresses. Decide how land, water, and climate affect people in the region.

In Picton, Ontario, you can get ice cream that is made from the milk from a nearby dairy farm. There are over 9000 dairy farms in Ontario.

This region gets a lot of snow in the winter, although temperatures are usually mild. This makes great weather for outdoor activities such as skiing, skating, and snowshoeing.

Hours can be spent in Montréal's RÉSO, or the "Indoor City," especially in the winter, when it's really cold. People can shop there, or see a hockey game.

Thinking *It Through*

- How do natural resources and climate affect quality of life for the people in these pictures?

- Are there any parks, lakes, or rivers that you go to in your community? If so, which ones? How do you think this affects the quality of life where you live?

Claire's Inquiry

My brother and I visited our cousins' farm in Trois-Rivières. While we were there, we saw an old stone foundation near the river. My cousin Guy told us that it was from an old flour mill. I asked:

- Why would the flour mill be here?
- Who would have used the mill?
- Why was there only a foundation left?

I saw this photo from 1897 of a Québec flour mill. Maybe this is what the building near the farm looked like!

Back at my cousins' house, I noticed they had some old paintings and furniture. There were some bowls and tools, too. I asked my cousin Sophie why her family kept these things. She said that having them helps them remember their family history.

The next day, Guy took my brother and me to the Musée québécois de culture populaire (the Québec Museum of Popular Culture) in Trois-Rivières. There, we found out that the flour mill would have been very important to the habitants in the past. Farmers in the area needed a mill to grind grain into flour. I decided to go to the McCord Museum when I got home. It is in Montréal. It is a great place to find out more information about the past. Maybe I'll learn more about my family history, too!

❓ Critical Inquiry TIP

Processing

Visiting museums is a great way to find information. Museums might have tools, clothes, or other objects from the past. There might be old photos, newspapers, record books, or people's diaries. Information at museums can give you an idea of what life was like in the past.

Skill Smart

- Choose an item in your home that is important to your family. Explain why it is significant.

Using Historical Resources

When Claire wanted to find out more about the mill near her cousins' farm, she went to the local museum for information. There, she looked at maps, documents, photographs, art, posters, and objects. The museum also had sound and film recordings. All of these resources tell stories and give evidence about the past. By examining them carefully, Claire could start finding the answers she wanted. For example, she found the photograph of a mill from 1897. She also found a letter from a habitant describing the flour mill close to his home.

Here are some ways Claire examined the resources at the museum and at her cousins' farm.

Document	Object	Map	Film/Sound	Photo/Art
• Who wrote it? • When was it written? • What was the author saying?	• What is it made of? • What was it used for? • Who might have used it?	• Who made it? • When was it made? • Are there differences between this map and a contemporary one?	• Who is on the recording? • Why were they interviewed? • What audience was the film made for?	• What does it show? • Who was the artist or photographer? • What can I learn from this photo or drawing?

Practise the Skill

1. Find a historical resource that tells something about your community's past.

2. Using the table above as a guide, write a description of the resource.

3. What is the most important thing the resource shows about the history of your community?

How Did the First Nations Live on the Land?

More About. . .

The Canadian Canoe Museum

This museum opened in Peterborough, Ontario, in 1997. It has a collection of more than 600 canoes and kayaks taken from all over Canada. First Nations, Métis, and historical experts contributed to the design of the museum. The museum also teaches visitors in an outdoor paddling centre. Why do you think an entire museum could be dedicated to the canoe?

Long ago, different First Nations invented various kinds of canoes. Some were small, light, and easy to carry. Others were sturdy and could hold many people. French and British explorers quickly learned that canoeing was the best way to travel along Canada's waterways. This canoe was made in 1900.

Many First Nations have always lived in the Great Lakes–St. Lawrence Lowlands. The landscape and natural resources shaped different ways of life.

The Rivers and Lakes

Rivers and lakes in the region were very important to the First Nations who lived there. For example, being close to a river or lake gave the Ouendat access to food and water. They could travel long distances along the connected waterways. The Ouendat and the Haudenosaunee could load their canoes with food and goods to trade with other First Nations. Later, they traded with the French and the British.

What can you tell about travelling on rivers by reading the poem below?

Voices of Canada

The Song My Paddles Sings

Be strong, O paddle! be brave, canoe!
The reckless waves you must plunge into.
Reel, reel,
On your trembling keel,
But never a fear my craft will feel.

We've raced the rapid, we're far ahead!
The river slips through its silent bed.
Sway, sway,
As the bubbles spray
And fall in tinkling tunes away.

Pauline E. Johnson, Six Nations of the Grand River

The Forests

Much of the Lowlands was once covered with mixed forests. The animals found in these forests included deer, rabbits, moose, bears, and birds. These animals provided food and materials for clothing, shelter, and tools for the Ouendat and Haudenosaunee.

The trees of the forests were also useful. For example, birch, cedar, and elm were used to make canoes.

The Haudenosaunee were the first to collect and use maple syrup.

Voices of Canada

Medicine Plants

To the Haudenosaunee, plants were also used for medicine. Medicines not only healed people when they were sick, but kept them healthy at all times.

Medicines grow all over. They can be found in the forest. They are in the meadows, in water, on the shore. People who work with medicines teach us to walk gently on the earth, and to take only what we need. Learning the right ways of gathering and caring for medicine plants is a lesson in an entire way of living.

Suzanne Brant, Mohawk First Nations

The white-tailed deer and the black bear were the most important animals to the Haudenosaunee. They provided food and clothing. Why else were they important?

Thinking *It Through*

- Today, much of the forest in the Lowlands region has been cut down to make room for farms and communities. What do you think would be the most significant changes to First Nations' ways of life?

The Farmland

The Haudenosaunee and the Ouendat have always farmed in the Great Lakes–St. Lawrence Lowlands. The soil is rich, and the growing season is long because there are many warm days throughout the year. Most of the Haudenosaunee villages were located south of the St. Lawrence River, but their hunting territory stretched north of the river into Ontario and Québec. The Ouendat nations lived along Georgian Bay and Lake Huron.

Just as First Nations hunters have great respect for the animals of the forests and lakes, First Nations farmers respect the land. The Haudenosaunee give thanks to the food plants they harvest.

I've read that the Ouendat showed the Europeans how to make popcorn! I wonder what else European settlers learned from First Nations about farming in my region.

 Critical Inquiry TIP

Retrieving

It is important to save and organize the information you find. You can write headings in your notebook and jot down brief notes beneath them as you read this text and do other research.

Voices of Canada

The Three Sisters

In late spring, we plant the corn and beans and squash. They're not just plants—we call them the three sisters. We plant them together, three kinds of seeds in one hole. They want to be together with each other, just as we want to be together with each other. So long as the three sisters are with us we know we will never starve. The Creator sends them to us each year. We celebrate them now. We thank Him for the gift He gives us today and every day.

Chief Louis Farmer, Onondaga First Nation

This sculpture by Haudenosaunee sculptor Stanley Hill shows the three sisters—corn, beans, and squash. They are also called the "life supporters." Are there similarly important crops grown in Alberta? Why are they important?

What Were First Nations Communities Like?

The Ouendat and Haudenosaunee formed villages near the fields where their crops grew. The oldest woman of each Haudenosaunee group was called the Clan Mother. This was an important position, as she was responsible for the welfare of the entire clan.

The villages were made of groups of **longhouses**. Longhouses were one long house where several related Ouendat or Haudenosaunee families lived. Down the middle of the building was a long row of fires. Along the sides were platforms for sleeping and storage. Look at the picture below. What do the items in this longhouse tell you about how the Haudenosaunee and the Ouendat lived?

The longhouse has always been important to these First Nations. It is where families lived, worked, and celebrated together. Today, it is a spiritual symbol for some of the Haudenosaunee, whose name means "people of the longhouse."

More **About. . .**

Matriarchal Societies

Longhouses were permanent homes built of wood. Each housed several families within the same First Nation. Every family traced their ancestry through their mothers and grandmothers. The Clan Mother was in charge of daily life. Families that are identified through their mothers are called matriarchal societies.

Voices of Canada

Listen to Us

What does this quote tell about the position of women in Haudenosaunee communities?

You ought to hear and listen to what we, women, shall speak, as well as the [chiefs], for we are the owners of this land—and it is ours. It is we that plant it for our use.

Haudenosaunee women in council with Colonel Proctor, a British soldier, 1791

1 fire in the middle
2 platforms for sleeping and storage
3 bark and branch construction
4 bucket with scoop
5 pottery
6 squash
7 drying fish
8 drying skins
9 snowshoes

What would it be like for many families to live together in a longhouse? If you lived in a longhouse, what rules would you make?

Who Were the First Europeans to Come to the Lowlands?

I learned that the French were the first Europeans to settle in the Lowlands.

In 1534, the king of France sent Jacques Cartier to find a sea route to China. On his first voyage across the ocean, Cartier reached the Gaspé Peninsula. He found well-developed communities where the Haudenosaunee were living. However, many years would pass before settlers would come from France to begin a colony.

The Colony of New France

In 1608, Samuel de Champlain founded the settlement of Québec. French settlers were soon clearing the land and building homes. Champlain also made trade agreements with the First Nations. He sent French explorers to live among the Ouendat and learn their language. Although life was hard for the settlers, the colony gradually began to grow. Champlain was named governor of the colony of New France.

One hundred years later, New France included parts of what are now Atlantic Canada, Québec, Ontario, and the United States.

This modern painting by J.D. Kelley shows what Champlain may have looked like in 1615. Why do you think Champlain is called the "father of New France"?

What parts of modern-day Canada were covered by New France? Use an atlas and this map to identify the areas and to name the main waterways and lakes within New France.

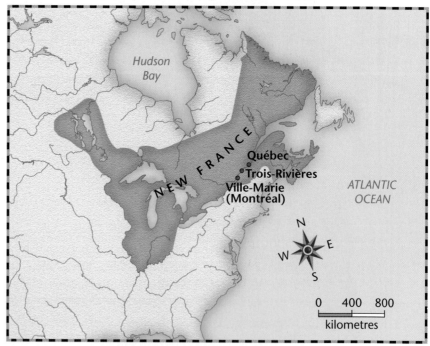

New France, About 1712

Hudson Bay

NEW FRANCE

Québec
Trois-Rivières
Ville-Marie
(Montréal)

ATLANTIC OCEAN

0 400 800
kilometres

The First Settlers of New France

In 1617, Louis Hébert sold his house and garden in Paris, France. He and his wife, Marie Rollet, took their three children on the greatest adventure of their lives. They were moving to New France to farm a piece of land beside the St. Lawrence River, which Champlain had promised them. Louis' goal was to build a farm that could support the family.

In their new country, Louis and Marie cleared land to grow grain and vegetables. They were the first wheat farmers in Canada. They also cleared land to raise chickens and pigs. They planted an orchard with apples they had brought from France. Louis also made and sold medicine. After a lot of hard work, the Hébert family became successful settlers in New France.

The Louis Hébert Café is a restaurant in Montréal. There is also a street and an area of Québec City named after the Héberts. How is the past a part of who Canadians are today?

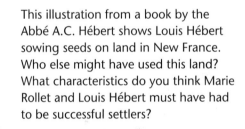

This illustration from a book by the Abbé A.C. Hébert shows Louis Hébert sowing seeds on land in New France. Who else might have used this land? What characteristics do you think Marie Rollet and Louis Hébert must have had to be successful settlers?

The Trans Canada Trail passes by a natural wonder at Montmorency Falls, near Québec City. Located at the mouth of Rivière Montmorency, the falls were named after Henri II of France by Champlain in 1603. In winter, the icy water of the falls creates a huge cone of ice and snow, where people can ice climb or ski.

Seigneurs were land owners in New France who rented out pieces of land to habitants.

Habitants were French settlers in New France who cleared and farmed the land.

Ways of Life in New France

As more settlers arrived, life was centred on farming and trade. The land in New France was owned and controlled by wealthy men called **seigneurs** [san-YEUR]. **Habitants** [a-bee-tawn] paid the seigneurs with part of their harvest in exchange for being allowed to live on and farm the seigneurs' land.

THEN AND NOW

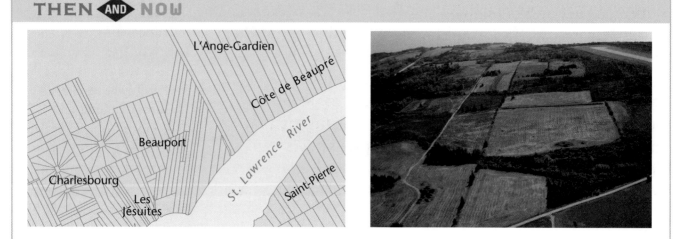

Under the seigneurial system, the land was divided into long, narrow strips. Compare the map to the photo. How do these farmlots compare to farms in Alberta? What might have been some advantages to the seigneurial system? Disadvantages?

Les Filles du Roi

Filles du roi [fee-doo-RWAW] means "daughters of the king." This was the name given to hundreds of young women from France. Encouraged by the French king, they sailed to New France during the mid-1600s to marry male settlers and build families to work on the farms. Many people now living in Québec have ancestors who were filles du roi.

Thinking It Through

■ Read the Voices of Canada. How might the move have affected Marie-Claude's way of life? How does it compare to Mary's experiences, told in the letter on page 64?

🍁 Voices of Canada

A Long Voyage

This is a diary note by a young fille du roi.

I was chosen to join the women heading for New France… I preferred to give up my homeland, make a [long] voyage and arrive in a new world. I remained there in silence, far from my country, without friends, or support of any kind…

From the journal of 14-year-old Marie-Claude Chamois, 1670

Missionaries in the Lowlands

For many Francophone settlers, practising the Catholic religion was important. Champlain invited priests from France. They provided religious services for the settlers and later ran schools for the children. The priests also wanted to teach the First Nations people about the Catholic faith. They travelled throughout New France to achieve this goal. Many were Jesuits. The Jesuits often noted their observations in letters and diaries. This vast collection became known as *The Jesuit Relations*. What they thought at this time can be learned from their observations.

As more priests and nuns came from France, they began to build their own settlements, called missions. Montréal began as Ville-Marie, a mission that had the first hospital in New France. It was in these missions that settlers and First Nations could seek help in times of need. Food, clothing, and medical help were provided by the priests and nuns year-round.

The reconstructed mission of Sainte-Marie Among the Hurons can be found on the shores of Georgian Bay. How were the missionaries important to the development of New France?

More About. . .

Marguerite Bourgeoys

Marguerite Bourgeoys came to Ville-Marie from France in 1653. She taught young women the skills they needed to make a life in New France, and helped welcome the filles du roi. In 1658, she created the Congrégation Notre-Dame, a religious organization of women who worked as teachers. The Congrégation still exists today. Its members work around the world as teachers, missionaries, and social workers.

Voices of Canada

A Missionary's Life

What point of view does this quote represent? Would everyone on this journey have thought this way?

During the day, the sun burns you. During the night, you run the risks of... mosquitoes. You sometimes [go up] five or six rapids in a day; in the evening the only refreshment is a little corn; the only bed is the earth...

The Jesuit Relations

I can understand why French is an official language of Canada. Why did English become the other official language?

A Canadien Petition

...[end] these fears and this uneasiness, by restoring to us our ancient laws and customs. Then our fears will be removed, and we shall pass our lives in happiness...

From a petition brought to London by merchant François Baby, 1770

Gaining Religious Rights

Religion is perfectly free. I can exercise my ministry without any restriction.

Bishop Jean-Olivier Brand, 1775

In 1764, British military commander James Murray became the first British governor of Québec. He was sympathetic to the Canadiens and allowed French civil laws to continue. Many British settlers did not like this policy, but it did help lead to the creation of the Québec Act.

Why Was the Québec Act Passed?

For many years, France and Britain fought for control over North America. Both countries had established colonies, which were sources of great wealth because of the fur trade and other resources. In 1759, the British attacked Québec, and by the next year the British had taken control of New France. Later, they renamed the land along the St. Lawrence River the "Province of Québec." They also created British laws that took rights away from Canadiens.

At this time, there were over 70 000 Canadiens living in the Province of Québec. Many feared the changes brought by the new British government. Merchants such as François Baby brought petitions to the British in London to protest the loss of Canadien rights. At the same time, British settlers living in the Thirteen Colonies were preparing to rebel against the British. Britain feared that the Canadiens would join in the rebellion. To help guarantee the loyalty of the Canadiens, the Québec Act was passed in 1774. It said that the Canadiens would be able to keep their land and the seigneurial system. They would be able to practise their religion freely, speak their language, and keep their civil laws.

As a result of the Québec Act, the majority of Canadiens remained neutral during the American Revolution. The rights in the Act guaranteed that they would be able to maintain their language and identity. The Québec Act was the first step towards bilingualism in Canada.

When Did the Loyalists Arrive?

After the American Revolution began in 1776, thousands of United Empire Loyalists moved north. Like Mary's family, they were loyal to the British king. Many of them spoke English and wanted to live under British rule. Most of the Loyalists went to communities in Nova Scotia and New Brunswick. Others came to the Great Lakes–St. Lawrence Lowlands.

However, the Loyalists were uncomfortable with the ways of life that had been guaranteed in the Province of Québec by the Québec Act:

- They didn't like the seigneurial system. They wanted to own land themselves.
- They wanted the official language to be English.
- They wanted to practise their own religion.
- They wanted to have British laws.

The British government wanted to satisfy everyone. In 1791, it divided the colony into two parts: Upper Canada and Lower Canada. This way, each group could keep its language, its religion, and its way of life.

Upper and Lower Canada, 1791

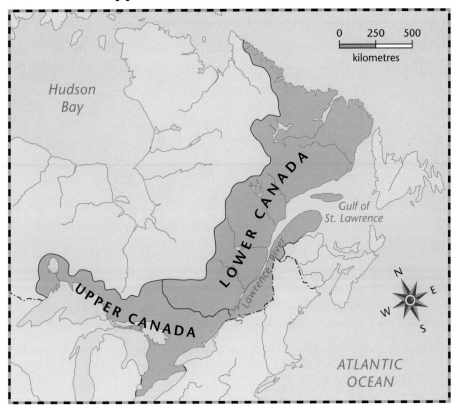

Thinking *It Through*

- How would the giving of land grants to the Loyalists affect the people already living on the land?

? Critical Inquiry TIP

Planning

Ask your teacher to help you find information on the Internet. Many Web sites have useful information and images. But remember that not all Web sites are reliable. Make sure to use a variety of sources and compare the information they offer.

The names of Upper and Lower Canada were chosen because of the position of the areas next to the St. Lawrence River, which flows downstream to the Gulf of St. Lawrence. Upper Canada was upstream, and Lower Canada was on the lower end of the river.

I want to look at a historical map that shows where the first United Empire Loyalist settlements were in my region. I'll compare it with a modern map to see if there are any connections from past to present.

Stories of the Loyalists

When the Loyalists first came to the Great Lakes–St. Lawrence Lowlands, they often had difficulty finding good land. The Canadiens were already occupying the best lands in the Province of Québec. Many of the Loyalists settled farther west, in present-day southern Ontario. How did this contribute to the division of Upper and Lower Canada?

Voices of Canada

The Land Changes

I can never forget the impression I felt in contemplating these thousands [of people] in the midst of forests that had never been cleared for shelter until the log hut was fashioned... I am told now you can travel from Montréal to Ontario and Erie, through cultivated farms and good roads and that the wilderness has been converted into a paradise of plenty, and all this within 33 years.

Joseph Hadfield, 1785

Voices of Canada

Hardships

None of us had any shoes or stockings, winter or summer, as those we brought with us were soon worn out. At length my father tanned some leather, and I recollect the first pair of shoes he made which fell to my lot, I greased and putting them too near the fire, on returning to my grief found that my shoes were all shrivelled up, so that I could never wear them. It was twelve months before I obtained another pair.

James Dittrick, a United Empire Loyalist child

This sketch shows what the inside of a Loyalist farmhouse might have looked like once the Loyalists had built their new homes. How can you find out if this type of scene really happened?

Joseph Brant

Not all the Loyalists were British. Many were members of First Nations. Joseph Brant, or Thayendanegea [tai-yen-da-nay-geh], was a Mohawk leader born in Ohio. He was worried that if the Americans won the war in 1776, they would take more Mohawk traditional land in that area. Brant wanted to fight with the British against the Americans, but at first they would not let him. So he sailed to England and told the king: "The Mohawks have on all occasions shown their... loyalty to the Great King." Brant did fight with the British—in fact, he became an officer in the army.

The American colonists won the war and took the Mohawk land as Brant had feared. Brant was able to convince the British government to set aside land for the Mohawk along the Grand River in Ontario. He then led almost 2000 Mohawks there from New York State. For the next 20 years, Brant worked to protect the land for his people.

This statue of Joseph Brant can be found in the city of Brantford. The city is on the land he negotiated with the British and is named after him. What does Brant's leadership show about his commitment to his communitiy?

An Interview with Brant's Descendant

David Kanowakeron Hill Morrison UE is a descendant of Joseph Thayendanegea Brant. David is a member of the Six Nations of the Grand River.

What makes you most proud of your family's Loyalist history?

I'm proud of [Brant's] foresight and his courage... leaving a place which has been called home for a hundred years is different than leaving a place called home for thousands of years.

Where did your family members arrive in Canada?

My ancestors gathered at Fort Niagara and crossed the Niagara River on their way to their new homelands along the Grand River. They settled in an area where the city of Brantford, Ontario, is today.

What did your family members do when they arrived in Upper Canada?

Most of the Six Nations people became farmers and hunters. The move to the Grand River area wasn't that much different from the climate and the environment they had lived in...

David Kanowakeron Hill Morrison UE includes the letters "UE" in his name. They stand for "Unity of the Empire." Why might a person living today identify himself with the Loyalists?

What Was the Underground Railroad?

Voices of Canada

A Duty to Help

To me it was a command; and a settled conviction took possession of my mind that it was my duty to help the oppressed to freedom...

Alexander Ross, a Canadian who helped slaves find their way to Canada, around 1855

words matter!

Slaves are people who are owned by another person and made to work for little or no money. Parts of the Thirteen Colonies, and later, part of the United States, forced Black people to work as slaves for almost 200 years.

Josiah Henson 1789-1883   postage/postes

This stamp was designed to remember Josiah Henson. He settled in Dresden, Ontario. He helped other escaped slaves learn how to farm. What are other ways he contributed to his community?

In 1830, a man named Josiah Henson landed on a beach in Fort Erie, Ontario. He had just crossed the Niagara River at night in a boat. Later, Josiah wrote:

> When my feet first touched the Canada shore, I threw myself on the ground, rolled in the sand, seized handfuls of it and kissed them and danced around...

Josiah Henson and thousands of other **slaves** escaped to freedom using the "Underground Railroad," which was not a railway at all. It was the name for the people who worked secretly to help slaves reach Upper Canada safely. Some people helped the runaways move from one safe place to another. Others offered their houses to sleep in and hot meals to eat. For some escaped slaves, the journey could take as long as a year. For many, the destination was the Lowlands.

Black Settlements in Upper Canada, 1835–1870

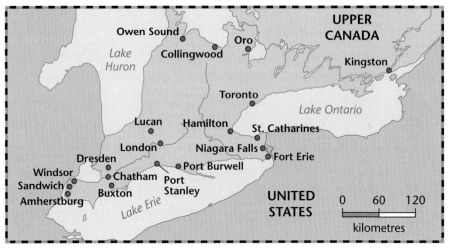

This map shows the communities where many escaped slaves settled when they reached Upper Canada. Find Owen Sound on the map. How can you find out more about the Black people who settled there? What did they do when they came to the community?

Thinking *It Through*

■ Today, many people from around the world seek safety, or asylum, in Canada. Are their reasons for coming the same as in the past or are they different?

How Did the Great Migration Change the Lowlands?

About 8 million immigrants, mostly from Britain, Scotland, and Ireland, came to the British colonies in Canada between 1815 and 1850. This was called the **Great Migration**. These immigrants faced many hardships aboard ship and once they arrived. Thousands of British and Irish people settled in the Great Lakes–St. Lawrence Lowlands. For many, this was a chance to start a new life. Read these stories to find out more about why they came and about their lives in the new land.

My friend Marc says that his ancestors were Irish people who came to Québec during this time. How can I trace my own ancestry?

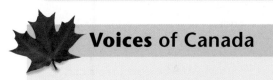

Voices of Canada

The Irish in Québec

Irish newcomers to Québec found themselves in a place where they did not speak the common language, French. However, many remained happy that they had come.

Whenever an Irish [person] told me of his hard up-hill fight, he was sure to add: "The laws are good and just, and we enjoy everything we have a right to hope for. We have nothing to complain of here, and we all wish that you were as well off at home."

John Frances Maguire, 1868

Voices of Canada

A Canadian Song

Come, launch the light canoe!
The breeze is fresh and strong;
The summer skies are blue,
And 'tis a joy to float along.
Away o'er the waters!
The bright-glancing waters,
The many-voiced waters,
As they dance in light and song.

Susanna Moodie

Susanna Moodie came from England. She and her family settled in Upper Canada in 1832. Moodie published many writings about her life as a settler. What does this poem show about her character and her life? What can you find out about how her life changed when she came to Upper Canada?

Stopping at Grosse-Île

Many ships with immigrants from Europe were overcrowded, and often there was not enough food and water. Terrible diseases spread among the passengers, many of whom died before they arrived in Canada.

To make sure that diseases did not spread throughout Lowlands communities, all ships had to stop at Grosse-Île. Grosse-Île is an island in the St. Lawrence River, not far from Québec City. There, doctors tried to cure as many people as they could before letting them onto the mainland. Despite their attempts, thousands of people died on Grosse-Île.

Grosse-Île

Catherine Parr Traill travelled by ship from England and landed at Grosse-Île. She was Susanna Moodie's sister. This is what she wrote in her journal:

August 12, 1832. We reached Grosse-Île yesterday evening. There are several vessels lying at anchor close to the shore; one bears the melancholy symbol of disease, the yellow flag; she is a passenger-ship, and has the smallpox and measles among her crew.

Catherine Parr Traill

More **About. . .**

Irish in Québec

Many children were left orphans after their parents died on Grosse-Île. Patrick and Thomas Quinn were adopted by a Francophone named George Bourke. With him, they learned French and adopted a Francophone identity. Today, there are many Francophone families in Québec with Irish last names.

Skill Smart

- Prepare a tour guide script that explains the importance of the Grosse-Île site.

This memorial was built on Grosse-Île in 1909. It is dedicated to the memory of the Irish people who died on the island. Is this memorial still in place today?

Contributions of the People

Did you ever wonder why we celebrate St. Patrick's Day? St. Patrick is the patron saint of Ireland, not Canada. But when Irish immigrants came to Canada, they brought their celebrations, traditions, and ways of life with them. Scottish and English immigrants did the same thing.

Immigrants from Scotland, Ireland, and England contributed more than just holidays and games to their new country. They worked as teachers, priests and nuns, politicians, farmers, engineers, explorers, and artists. Their work helped shape our schools, churches, communities, and government. Today, the descendants of these immigrants form a large part of Canada's population. In 2001, more than 3 million people living in Canada identified themselves as being of Irish ancestry. More than 4 million were Scottish, and over 5 million English.

Critical Inquiry TIP

Creating

A poster is one way you might present information about different traditions and celebrations in Canada.

Curling was probably invented in Scotland. The first curling club in Canada began in Montréal on the St. Lawrence River.

Egerton Ryerson was the son of British loyalists. He was born in Upper Canada in 1803. Ryerson helped found the Upper Canada Academy. In 1844, he became the Superintendent of Education in Upper Canada and would leave a lasting mark on the education system. He put libraries in all schools, and started a textbook publishing press. A school he founded in Toronto would later become Ryerson University.

Tommy Douglas (1904–1986) was born in Scotland, but grew up in Winnipeg. A preacher, social activist, and politician, Douglas was premiere of Saskatchewan and the leader of the NDP. He led the creation of Medicare, a system which gives all Canadians access to free medical care. In 2004, he was voted "The Greatest Canadian".

How Has the Region Changed?

Can you imagine trying to paddle through the Lachine Rapids?

This lock is near Montréal.

The Lowlands does not look the same as it did 300 years ago. Over time, more and more people have come to the region. Newcomers often changed the land to fit their needs.

Creating the St. Lawrence Seaway

Today, ships can travel on the St. Lawrence River from the Atlantic Ocean to Lake Superior. In the past, people had to portage around rapids, such as the Lachine Rapids near Montréal. The rapids prevented larger ships from travelling on the river.

Over the years, people built canals and locks. Canals are long, narrow strips dug out of the land and filled with water. They are used to join two bodies of water. Built into the canals are locks. Locks act like staircases or elevators for ships. Using canals and locks, workers connected the St. Lawrence River, the Great Lakes, and other rivers and lakes. This system is called the St. Lawrence Seaway.

The St. Lawrence Seaway

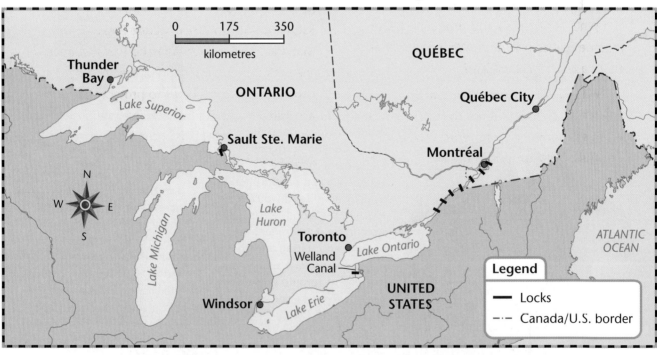

Effects of the Seaway

In order to build the St. Lawrence Seaway, more than 6500 people had to move to new towns. Ten villages were flooded. They became known as the "Lost Villages." How might you feel if you were forced to move or your community was destroyed? How do these two people feel?

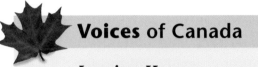

Voices of Canada

Leaving Home

Three years before the flooding, this farmer spoke of how he felt about moving away from his farm.

It's a really hard thing to do after 23 years because I'm very much attached to [my farm]. It's hard leaving orchards... you can't take them with you.

W.J. Kirkwood, Aultsville, Ontario

Voices of Canada

Prosperity

The mayor of Cornwall thought that the new Seaway would bring prosperity to his city.

We in Cornwall are very happy [about] the St. Lawrence development. It will bring industry to Cornwall. Cornwall will be a prosperous little city for the next few years. And I daresay it will be one of the largest cities in eastern Ontario.

Mayor Horowitz, 1954

Making a Difference

After the Seaway was built, shipping activity on the St. Lawrence River increased. Factories were built close to the river and the Great Lakes, because the Seaway allowed for easier shipping of materials and products. These factories cause pollution. What effect does that have on local wildlife?

Beluga whales live in parts of the St. Lawrence. Pollution in the river has made them sick and unable to reproduce. Today, environmental groups in the area monitor the condition of the river and campaign to reduce pollution.

An important result of the campaign to help the beluga was the creation of the Saguenay–St. Lawrence Marine Park. Managed by Parks Canada and Parcs Québec, the park protects a section of the St. Lawrence. The park helps to protect the ecosystem where the whales live, and also educates the public about the importance of protecting the fragile marine environment.

Viewpoints

Should We Control How Big Our Cities Get?

When cities spread quickly, more land is used than people need. This is called **urban sprawl**. Cities often grow so big that they join up with other cities. Farmland in between the cities is used to build new homes, schools, libraries, and stores.

Toronto: A Century of Changes

More than 1000 years ago, people began settling in the area known today as Toronto. The area was a meeting place between lakes Ontario and Huron. Today, people from many countries still come to make their home in Toronto. The Greater Toronto Area (GTA) is the City of Toronto plus the surrounding areas. The GTA has more than 4.5 million people.

The picture on the left shows Yonge Street in Toronto in 1907. Today, Toronto is one of the most culturally diverse cities in the world.

Read the following views to learn more about what different people think about urban sprawl.

There is so much building going on that I have my choice of jobs. It's great for my family. We can live near my work, and I'm making good money.

Green areas need to be preserved in our city. Parks keep cities healthy.

Wildlife used to live in the forests and along the rivers in my area. But as the city grew, the animals and birds lost their homes. We have all lost something very valuable now.

I love my new house! We live near a park where I can play with my friends. My parents drive to work on the nearby highway.

Over to **You**

1. Discuss each point of view. How many different points of view are presented?

2. Do the points of view represent an individual or a group? What to they have in common?

3. Do you live in or near a large community in Alberta? How do you think urban sprawl might affect you? How might it affect you if you lived far away from a large community?

Discuss a Historical Resource

Choose an example of a historical resource from this chapter. It could be a photograph, a map, an interview, an object, or a story, such as a Voices of Canada. Discuss why this resource could be used to illustrate the past in the Great Lakes–St. Lawrence Lowlands.

Research a Community

Find out more about a city or a town in the Great Lakes–St. Lawrence Lowlands.

- How did it start? How did the community get its name?
- What are some historical sites in the community?

Use your information to create a newsletter to tell the story of the community. Include ways people can help preserve and remember the history of the community. Try using technology to make your newsletter.

Design a Licence Plate

This is a licence plate from Québec. "Je me souviens" is French for "I remember."

- Create a design for a licence plate for your family, school, or region. You can include symbols that bring more meaning to the design. Explain your idea.
- Why did Québec choose "Je me souviens" as its motto? How does the motto represent the province?

Putting It All Together

During her inquiry, Claire discovered that museums were an important source of information about the past. While she was researching, she realized that she could organize the museums she found to keep track of what kind of information they offered. This made her research easier. This is what part of her tracking chart looked like:

Name of Museum	Where it is located	Web site	Information
McCord Museum of Canadian History	Montréal	http://www.mccord-museum.qc.ca/en	History of Montréal
Marguerite Bourgeoys Museum	Montréal	http://www.marguerite-bourgeoys.com	History of Marguerite Bourgeoys and the Notre-Dame-de-Bon-Secours Chapel

Review the inquiry questions for this chapter:
- How does the St. Lawrence River affect ways of life in this region?
- Why are First Nations and Francophones so important to the identity of this region?

Take Time to Reflect

What happens when someone moves to a new place? Think about the Loyalists when they first came to this region. Conduct an interview with someone in your school or community who has recently come from a different place. What effects did this have on the person? Write or record your interview. Save your work for your Canada Collection.

Canadian Shield
Muskeg, Moose, and Minerals

September 12, 2005

Day 140: North Bay, Ontario

...The next morning, we set out into Georgian Bay with hopes of making it to the mouth of the French River. The wind proved too difficult on this day and after paddling about 30 km we were forced to pull onto shore. The next morning we paddled up the Voyageur Channel of the river, only to find it full of high reeds and very little water. We pushed on and after a few unmarked portages we were finally on the French River. As we emerged from the French River into Lake Nipissing, we were again hit with rough winds and steep waves and had to take refuge in the protection of a small bay...

Can you imagine spending five months in a canoe? That is just what Drew Osborne and Clare Cayley did when they followed the traditional fur trade route through the Canadian Shield. They travelled on rivers and lakes, from Rocky Mountain House, Alberta, to Montréal, Québec. They woke with the sun, paddled all day, and camped in the wilderness at night. They saw moose and bears, and the insects were so fierce that they had to wear bug jackets for protection.

Luckily, Drew and Clare met many helpful people along the way. There were cities and towns where they could find food and shelter when they needed it. Read Drew and Clare's journal entry again. What do you think the fur traders might have done hundreds of years ago, when faced with the same conditions in the Canadian Shield?

Canada: Our Stories Continue

In the last chapter, you read about how the St. Lawrence River is like a highway. People have built communities along the river and use ships to transport goods within the region and around the world. Drew and Clare also used lakes and rivers as they crossed almost half the country. Much of their trip was through one region, the Canadian Shield. The Shield is the largest region in Canada, covering parts of five provinces and two territories. There are countless lakes and rivers, animals, abundant rocks, and vast forests.

? Critical Inquiry TIP

Retrieving

Good researchers keep track of where they find information. Use a section in your notebook to record book titles, authors, page numbers, and any Internet sites you use.

? Inquiring Minds

Here are some questions to guide your inquiry for this chapter:

- What would Drew and Clare have to know about the geography and climate of this region in order to have a successful journey?
- List the factors that drew Europeans to explore this region.

Let's Explore the Canadian

Hi! My name is Gordie McGillivary. I live in the Opaskwayak [o-PASS-kwee-ak] First Nation community. It's across from The Pas in northern Manitoba.

Algonquin Park is one of many wilderness areas in the Shield region. Visitors can camp, canoe, and hike. It's also a great place to see a moose!

The forestry industry provides many jobs for people in the Shield.

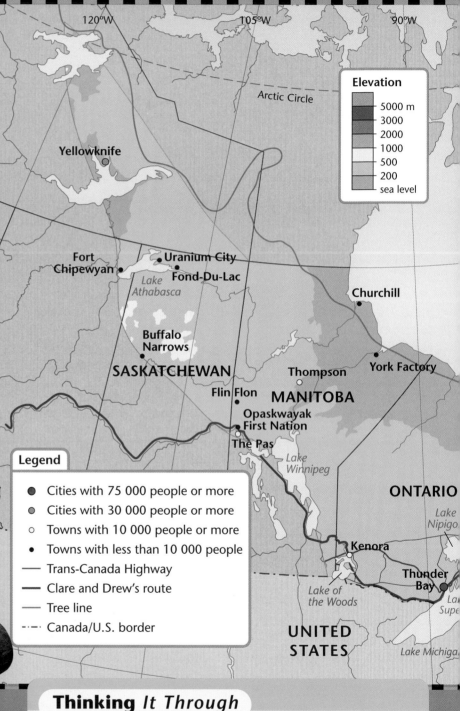

Elevation

5000 m
3000
2000
1000
500
200
sea level

Arctic Circle

Yellowknife

Fort Chipewyan
Uranium City
Fond-Du-Lac
Lake Athabasca

Churchill

Buffalo Narrows

SASKATCHEWAN

Thompson

York Factory

Flin Flon

MANITOBA

Opaskwayak First Nation

The Pas

Lake Winnipeg

ONTARIO

Lake Nipigo

Kenora

Thunder Bay

Lake of the Woods

La Supe

UNITED STATES

Lake Michiga

Legend

● Cities with 75 000 people or more
● Cities with 30 000 people or more
○ Towns with 10 000 people or more
• Towns with less than 10 000 people
— Trans-Canada Highway
— Clare and Drew's route
— Tree line
-·-· Canada/U.S. border

Thinking *It Through*

■ Where are the largest cities in this region located?

■ What types of jobs do you think the people of the Shield might have?

Shield!

Chicoutimi, Québec, was originally settled in 1676 when a fur trading post was built there by the French.

Moose Factory, Ontario, is the home of the Moose Cree First Nation. The Hudson's Bay Company set up a trading post here in 1673.

Skill Smart

■ On the map, locate Gordie's community, Algonquin Provincial Park, and Moose Factory. Give the absolute and relative location for each place.

The Canadian Shield

words matter!

Muskeg is a swamp or bog formed from the buildup of moss, leaves, and other plants.

Waterways are rivers and lakes that can be used by people as highways for travel.

Millions of years ago, this region had many mountains. Geologists say that over a very long time the movement of thick ice wore the mountains down, leaving behind thin, rocky soil. The region is home to many bogs called **muskeg**. There are also rich mineral deposits of nickel, gold, silver, and copper. Many cities and towns have developed throughout this region.

Roots of the Region

The Woodland Cree, the Anishinabé, and the Innu were the first people to live in this region. They depended on the animals, plants, and rivers. French and English fur traders came into the Canadian Shield region to trade with the First Nations. They set up trading posts, and many of these trading posts became larger communities.

The **waterways** made travelling possible for First Nations people, Métis, explorers, and traders. French and English explorers came to the region and mapped the many rivers, lakes, and bays.

Why People Live Here Today

First Nations people continue to live in the region. Some live in First Nations communities, and some live in towns and cities. Descendants of the French, English, Métis, and other people also live in the region.

The region has many valuable natural resources, such as lumber, water, and minerals. Many people work in the forestry, mining, and hydroelectric industries, too.

Kakabeka Falls is near the city of Thunder Bay.

The Churchill Falls hydroelectric plant, in Labrador, is one of the largest of its kind in North America. Find Churchill Falls on the map on pages 96–97. What do you notice about its location?

What Affects Quality of Life?

Here is how the land, water, and climate affect quality of life for some people in the Canadian Shield. Recreation is one aspect of quality of life.

In Churchill, the snow is so high that sometimes people have to dig out the snow before they can open their door. The snow is also high enough to make great snow forts.

To build this highway in Algonquin Park, workers had to cut through the rock of the Canadian Shield. It was dangerous work, but the roads provided transportation routes. They allow visitors to see the beauty of the park.

Tourists come to the region to enjoy fishing and boating on beautiful lakes, such as Rock Lake. They can catch walleye, bass, and lake trout.

Thinking *It Through*

■ How does the land, water, and other natural resources contribute to recreational activities in this region?

Georgian Bay is part of Lake Huron. The area is popular with hikers and cottagers.

Gordie's Inquiry

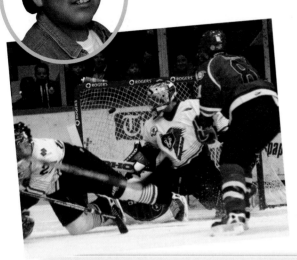

My brother, Matt, played hockey for the OCN (Opaskwayak Cree Nation) Blizzard last year. This year he is a defenceman for the Rouyn-Noranda Huskies, in Québec. Matt had to move away from home to play on his new hockey team. I wonder what Rouyn-Noranda is like? I think I'll send Matt an e-mail to find out more. Maybe he can even help me with my school research project.

| From | Contains | Search |

Newest on top ▼

12:48 PM

12:15 PM

Mon 12:36 AM

Sat 1:30 PM

Sat 2:16 AM

Fri 5:12 PM

Fri 5:09 PM

Fri 4:51 PM

Fri 3:51 PM

Fri 12:07 PM

To: Matt McGillivary
From: Gordie McGillivary
Re: Research Project

Hi Matt,

How do you like Rouyn-Noranda? It is a city with a funny name. I used to think The Pas was an odd name, too, until I learned more about it. I want to find out more about Rouyn-Noranda and the rest of the Canadian Shield. I've thought of some questions:

- Who lived there first? What did they do? How did the city get its name?
- What other groups of people moved to the region long ago? Why?
- Why do people live in the Canadian Shield today?
- Why do many people speak French in the region?

I'll look for some answers on the Internet, in books, and by talking to people. To help me, could you interview some people in Rouyn-Noranda and Val-d'Or? Ask them what they do for work and for play. Why do they live in the Canadian Shield? Where did their ancestors come from?

I'll keep you posted on the research I do here.

Skill Smart

■ Make a list of three questions you want answers to about this region. Look for answers in this chapter and in other sources.

SKILL POWER — Using Information on a Chart

In an inquiry, you sometimes need to analyze information on a chart. Gordie knew that Rouyn-Noranda and Val-d'Or are in the Canadian Shield and that some of the other hockey communities Matt would be visiting are in the Great Lakes–St. Lawrence Lowlands. Gordie wanted to know how each community compared with The Pas. He did some research and organized his findings in the chart below.

Town	Total Population (2001)	Population Increasing (+) or Decreasing (−)	% of Jobs with Natural Resources	% of Jobs in Factories
The Pas	6000	−	4	16
Rouyn-Noranda	27 000	−	10.5	12
Val-d'Or	28 000	−	13	13
Gatineau	103 000	+	1	12
Drummondville	46 600	+	2	33
Shawinigan	17 535	−	3	28
Québec City	683 000	+	1	11

☐ Shield communities
☐ Lowlands communities

Practise the Skill

Use the chart above to answer these questions:

1. How does the population of The Pas compare with that of Rouyn-Noranda? With that of Val-d'Or? Québec City?

2. Look at the middle column. Which towns are increasing in population? Are they in the Lowlands or the Shield? What factors might affect population in these communities?

3. For each of the towns in the Shield, add the numbers in the last two columns. This will tell you how much of the industry in these towns is related to resources and factories. Next, do the same for the towns in the Lowlands. What does this information tell you about how ways of life in the Shield compare with the Lowlands?

Who First Lived in the Canadian Shield?

What do these two quotes tell about the traditional ways of life of the Innu and Anishinabé people in this region?

Respect for Animals

Respect for the animals is very important in our culture. When a caribou is killed, the antlers should be well taken care of. Always respect the bones of the animal you kill.

Pien Penashue, Innu Elder

[We] never wasted even a bit of [a porcupine]. We'd use the quills and hair in our crafts, and when we'd eaten we'd put the bones into the fire as an offering of thanks to the **Creator**.

Freda McDonald, Anishinabé Elder

---

words matter!

Creator is a word used by some First Nations to refer to Great Spirit.

The Woodland Cree, the Anishinabé, and the Innu have always lived in the Canadian Shield. Traditionally, the Anishinabé lived in the southern part of the Shield, around Lake Superior. The Woodland Cree lived in more northern areas, closer to Hudson Bay. The Innu lived in what is now Québec and Labrador. There were also Inuit living on the northern coast of Labrador and Québec.

These Cree children in northern Québec are learning how to make snowshoes. How were snowshoes traditionally made? How are they made today?

Connection to the Land

The First Nations of the Shield region used all the resources of the land and followed the cycle of the seasons. In the spring and summer, the Woodland Cree and Anishinabé fished and hunted ducks and geese using bows and arrows. They gathered berries and other plants. In the fall, they harvested wild rice. They also hunted animals such as deer, moose, caribou, and rabbits using snares, traps, and pens.

The Innu travelled throughout their lands, camping in the best hunting lands, often journeying farther in search of caribou. They developed technology to travel in this northern environment. Birchbark canoes were used in summer, and snowshoes were used in winter. They also invented the toboggan, a long sled that carried their belongings.

Why Did Other People Come?

In the last chapter, you read that French explorers and traders started settlements in the Great Lakes–St. Lawrence Lowlands. New settlers were interested in things that were unique to Canada. They were especially interested in animal furs. It is not surprising that French and English explorers such as Pierre de La Vérendrye and David Thompson started coming to the Shield in the 1600s and 1700s.

Merchants in England looked at maps and compared the latitudes of London and Hudson Bay. They assumed that the climate would be the same as England's climate: gentle and mild. So when the merchants sent men from England to the Shield region, they ordered the men to provide their own food by raising pigs and growing gardens. From what you know about the Shield, how easy do you think this was to do?

Eager to expand the fur trade, explorers and traders soon started making their way west, across the Canadian Shield. They travelled for hundreds of kilometres into what was for them an unknown wilderness. They encountered muskeg, dense forests, rivers with dangerous rapids and waterfalls, and many lakes. Insects were ferocious in summer, and in winter the cold and snow might stop travel entirely. It was only with the help of the First Nations that the French and English traders could survive their journeys across the land.

Hudson Bay is frozen for at least six months of the year. It is colder than the Arctic Ocean! How many months of the year are lakes and rivers frozen in your community?

What Were the First Jobs in the Shield?

Many people in Europe wore hats made from beaver fur. Why do you think this made the fur trade so valuable?

words matter!

Coureurs des bois is a French term meaning "runners of the woods."

When the coureurs des bois began working in the Shield region, they adapted to the environment. They learned how to survive on the land and changed their clothing to suit their new way of life.

As Europeans explored the region, they found it ideal for obtaining furs. Explorers like Samuel de Champlain had already traded for furs with First Nations people in the Atlantic region. In the Shield, the fur trade would become an important industry for the next 200 years, until the late 1800s.

The fur trade flourished in the Shield because

- abundant forests, rivers, and lakes were home to many fur-bearing animals
- cold winters meant animals grew thick fur coats
- beavers built dams and lived in one place, making them easy to catch
- waterways provided ways for trappers and traders to travel

Étienne Brûlé

Étienne Brûlé, a French explorer, came to New France with Champlain. In 1610, Champlain sent Brûlé to live with the Ouendat. He hoped that Brûlé would create a friendly relationship with them. Brûlé learned their language and became a translator.

By 1618, he was trading independently with First Nations people and had become the first **coureur des bois**. From the Ouendat, he learned how to survive on the land and use the waterways for travel.

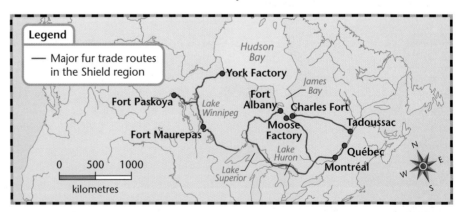

This map shows the main routes of the coureurs des bois in the Shield region. Compare the routes to the map on pages 96–97. Are there any present-day communities where the routes used to be? How does this map compare to the route Drew and Clare took?

Coureurs des Bois

Soon more men came to New France to work in the fur trade and they made their living as coureurs des bois. They became friends with the First Nations and explored on their own. They would load their canoes with goods from France, then travel north and west on the waterways. There, they met First Nations trappers and traded the items for furs. Once they returned to New France, they sold the furs and set out again.

What Was Life Like for Coureurs des Bois?

Coureurs des bois faced many challenges:
- sore muscles and severe muscle injuries from carrying heavy packs during portages
- bites from mosquitoes, black flies, and other insects
- intense heat and bitter cold, dangerous rapids
- no maps or compasses
- travelling through First Nations lands, sometimes without a guide and without permission

THEN AND NOW

Coureurs des bois paddled through rapids or portaged around them. Today, people can experience the same excitement. Whitewater rafting is a popular sport in the Canadian Shield.

The Hudson's Bay Company

Part of the Trans Canada Trail in Ontario is called the Voyageur Trail. It follows the northern shore of Lake Superior. Hikers enjoy the rugged beauty of the rocky shores.

In the mid-1600s, two coureurs des bois, Pierre Radisson and Médard Chouart des Groseilliers, went into the country north of Lake Superior. When they returned, they approached the governor of New France with their idea to explore the lands close to Hudson Bay. In response, the governor seized their furs and briefly jailed them. They had traded without permission, and the government wanted to keep control of the fur trade.

Angry at this treatment, Radisson and des Groseilliers approached the British. They proposed that British ships could carry fur traders into Hudson Bay, avoiding Montréal and going around the government of New France. The British agreed. In 1668, des Groseilliers sailed alone into Hudson Bay, after Radisson's ship was damaged in a storm. The British built Fort Rupert and claimed a vast territory they called Rupert's Land. In 1670, the Hudson's Bay Company (HBC) was created.

Rupert's Land

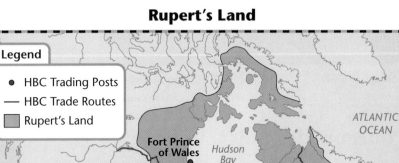

What geographic advantage did the HBC have over fur traders from Montréal?

The North West Company

words matter!

Voyageur is a French word meaning "traveller." Voyageurs travelled by canoe, working for fur-trading companies.

In the 1780s, a group of Scottish and Montréal businessmen created the North West Company (NWC). They wanted to compete with the HBC. They hired men called **voyageurs** to work for them. The voyageurs loaded supplies and trade goods into huge canoes and paddled from Montréal to Lake Superior. From there, traders in smaller canoes went out and traded with First Nations people. The goal was to get to these people before they took their furs to an HBC trading post. Soon there was an intense rivalry between the two companies.

The Voyageurs

The voyageurs were usually Canadien or **Métis**. Many First Nations people liked doing business with the Canadiens because they were willing to learn First Nations languages. They also respected the First Nations way of life.

Like the coureurs des bois, the voyageurs had a hard life. They portaged past waterfalls and rapids, camped outdoors, and paddled for hours. Unlike the coureurs des bois, these men worked in groups and were employees of the North West Company. They supported the traders who worked farther inland by delivering supplies. They also had special permits from the government of New France.

During this time, **Métis** were people who had one parent who was First Nations and one who was Canadien. Later, Métis also had Scottish and British ancestry.

This painting shows voyageurs travelling in the Canadian Shield. It was painted in 1869 by Frances Anne Hopkins, who came to the region with her husband and sketched what she saw. Find her in the painting. What other personal sources can be used to give us information about the past?

Voices of Canada

Voyageur Paddle Songs

To pass the time and to keep rhythm as they paddled, the voyageurs sang songs. Many of the songs were adapted from French songs they already knew. "V'là l'bon vent!," for example, has different versions in Acadia and France. Here is part of the song in English. How do you think the rhythm of the song would help the voyageurs paddle all day?

Here comes the wind, here comes the pretty wind,
Here comes the wind, my friend is calling,
Here comes the wind, here comes the pretty wind,
Here comes the wind, she waits for me.

The coureurs des bois and the voyageurs had the same job, but they were very different. For example, the voyageurs worked in groups, and the coureurs des bois worked alone. I think I'll use a diagram to help sort out what I'm learning about them.

Life in the Forts

Processing

A Venn diagram is another way to organize your information. It will help you compare things that are similar and different.

Both the Hudson's Bay Company and the North West Company built trading posts across the Canadian Shield. Many were built as forts. A fort was a group of buildings that was surrounded by high wooden walls. Some forts were also called "factories."

Warehouses and men's quarters

Administrators' quarters and guest house

Trading house and clerks' office

Carpenters' shed

Turret

Blacksmiths' shed

Ammunition storage

What can you learn about life in the forts by looking at this diagram? What do you think was important to the people who lived there? What languages did people speak in the forts?

Thinking It Through

- Have you ever visited a fort in Alberta? How do you think a fort in Alberta might compare to the one described here? Do some research to find out more.

words matter!

The **factor** was the HBC employee in charge of the trading post.

More About. . .

Jobs in the Hudson's Bay Company

In the HBC, labourers did work such as loading and unloading ships, portaging boats around rough water, cutting firewood, and shovelling snow. There were also craftsmen. These carpenters and blacksmiths built the forts and boats. Usually they were Francophones, or young men from Scotland. Why do you think so?

In charge were the administrators, chief traders, and the **factors**. These "gentlemen officers" were paid more. They had better places to live and more food. The highest official at a fort was the factor. He was usually an Englishman or a Scot.

Life Outside the Forts

Groups of Cree often camped outside company forts. The Cree would hunt and fish for the fort employees. In exchange, they received food and other goods. When the voyageurs arrived at the North West Company forts, they camped outside, too.

Skill Smart

- With a partner, research a community, such as Moose Factory, that began as a trading fort. Discuss how life in this community might have shaped life in other communities in the Shield.

Voices of Canada

Working for the HBC

Louis Bird tells of the First Nations people who worked for the HBC at York Factory.

[There were] local people, who were hired to do all the labour. To get the wood... and the food, to be able to feed the people who worked there in the summer.

Louis Bird, Cree First Nation, James Bay

Making a Difference

A Role Model from Moose Factory

Jonathan Cheechoo is a member of the Moose Cree First Nation, and he is also the first person from Moose Factory to play in the NHL. When Cheechoo's team plays in Canada, he makes sure to meet with any young Aboriginal people who want to talk with him. Cheechoo understands that he can be a good role model for them. "I set aside some time after our morning skates to talk with them. They're pretty excited when they meet me, and I take that as an honour. I must be doing something right if the kids are looking up to [me]."

In 2006, he met with more than 100 Cree young people from northern Québec who came to see him play in Ottawa. He told them, "Stay true to yourself and remember, if you work hard enough, you can do anything you put your mind to."

How Did the Fur Trade Affect the First Nations?

First Nations people relied on the land and their ingenuity for food, clothing, utensils, and weapons. Nothing was wasted. When French, English, and Scottish fur traders arrived at HBC forts, they brought copper kettles, knives, rifles, wool blankets, flour, and salted meat to trade with the Woodland Cree and Anishinabé for furs.

Voices of Canada

Trading with Europeans

When the fur trade began, the Hudson's Bay Company set up its headquarters at a place that became known as York Factory. It is in Manitoba. Abel Chapman, a Cree storyteller, grew up there. He heard this story from his grandparents.

This was a long time ago. There were [First Nations people] living here but there was no store... food came from the land... One day [the people] saw something way out in the bay... there was a boat coming closer to shore. A lot of the people ran and hid! The men pulled to shore and they had someone to interpret for them. The interpreter said that the [men were] looking for [First Nations people] to trade with. These men took all the fur... and unloaded a lot of trade items. That's when trading began in York Factory.

Abel Chapman

Thinking *It Through*

■ Why do you think Abel's grandparents wanted him to know this story? Why did some of the people run and hide?

Check the map on page 106 and find York Factory. Why do you think it was a good location for the HBC's headquarters?

Changing Ways of Life

The Cree and Anishinabé had been trading for generations before the European fur trade began. They knew what they needed and what they valued. They were used to working with others to get a fair trade. During the fur trade, the First Nations people knew that the French and English were competing for their furs. They often took their furs to different trading posts to see who would give them the most in return.

Look at the chart on this page. What does it tell you about the value of these items?

Item	Number of beaver pelts
1 kettle	1
1 pair of breeches	3
1 gun	12
12 fish hooks	1

Some of the favourite items from the trading posts were buttons, beads, and mirrors. Why do you think these items may have been so popular?

Voices of Canada

Value of the Beaver

This Innu chief talks about the value of the beaver to a Jesuit missionary.

The Beaver does everything perfectly well, it makes kettles, hatchets, swords, knives, bread... The English have no sense: they give us twenty knives... for one beaver skin.

Innu chief, recorded in the Jesuit Relations, 1610-1791

These are kettles from 1610 to 1620. Objects like these are found today in museums.

The HBC also traded wool blankets for furs. The black lines, called points, showed how large the blanket was. Is the HBC blanket still part of the Canadian identity today?

The Cree and Anishinabé also traded for guns. These made hunting easier, but they forced the hunters to rely on the trading posts for bullets. Another problem was that once the hunters started spending most of their time getting furs, they had less time to look for food for their families. As a result, the Cree and Anishinabé became dependent on the trading posts for much of their food. Many of them moved near the posts for this reason.

Who Are the Métis?

words matter!

Pemmican is dried meat, pounded to a paste and mixed with melted fat and berries.

Relationships between the First Nations and the French, English, Scottish, and Canadien fur traders often resulted in unions between the traders and First Nations women. Their children were the first Métis.

The Métis played an important role in the fur trade. They often worked as administrators or translators. Many were guides and voyageurs. Métis women played a key part in the fur trade, too. They removed the fur from the animals and made snowshoes and moccasins. They also made **pemmican**, an important source of food for the traders. These women helped their European husbands understand First Nations languages.

Métis culture started as a mix of First Nations and French cultures. Soon it became unique. The Métis have their own music and stories. They have a language called Michif, which combines French and Cree. When Métis children grew up, they often married other Métis. This was the beginning of the Métis Nation. You will learn more about the important role played by Métis in the exploration and development of Canada.

Métis Youth Paddle West

Thunder Bay—In 2006, six Métis youth will take part in the Métis Canoe Expedition. They will paddle an eight metre (26 foot) voyageur canoe from Thunder Bay, Ontario to Batoche, Saskatchewan. It will take eight weeks to paddle the same route that their ancestors took during the fur trade. Tony Belcourt, president of the Métis Nation of Ontario, said, "This expedition will provide our Métis youth with a unique, once-in-a-lifetime opportunity to follow in the shadow of our ancestors."

The Métis Canoe Expedition celebrates the role that the Métis had as voyageurs during the fur trade. How do you think it felt for these young Métis people to participate in this voyage?

How Did the Fur Trade Help Canada Develop?

Young children often play "leapfrog." It is a game in which you move forward by jumping over people crouching on the ground. The development of Canada during the time of the fur trade was kind of like a game of leapfrog.

In order to reach First Nations people before they brought furs to HBC trading posts, the NWC traders travelled farther west and north, to areas past the HBC posts. They built their own posts and forts in these new areas. The HBC soon realized that it had competition, so *their* employees began to build posts in areas past the NWC ones!

English, French, and Métis traders and voyageurs explored the country as they went farther west and north through the Shield. Their reports and maps helped settlers establish communities as far away as British Columbia and the Northwest Territories. These places might have become part of the United States if it were not for British and Canadien explorers like David Thompson and Pierre de La Vérendrye.

David Thompson

David Thompson came from England as a young man. First, he worked for the HBC, and then for the NWC. During his life, he and his Métis wife, Charlotte, explored and mapped almost 4 million square kilometres of North America!

Thompson drew a map of western Canada in 1814. It was so accurate that it was still used 100 years later by the government and the railways. Today, some people call him "the greatest land geographer who ever lived."

I'm going to use maps to see how the two companies moved across the country.

Skilled Guides

David Thompson thought the First Nations person was very skilled in being able to guide himself through the darkest pine forests to exactly the place he intended to go, his keen, constant attention on everything; the removal of the smallest stone, the bent or broken twig... all spoke plain language to him.

Olive Dickason, Métis historian

This stamp was issued in honour of David Thompson in 1957.

Pierre de La Vérendrye

This painting shows La Vérendrye at Lake of the Woods. Why might the artist have chosen to show La Vérendrye this way?

La Vérendrye was born in New France in 1685. He was the first Canadien to travel far into the West. Why did La Vérendrye and his sons journey from Québec as far as the Assiniboine River and beyond? While he was commanding a fur-trading post on Lake Nipigon, La Vérendrye heard about a huge western sea from First Nations people. La Vérendrye made many journeys to try to find a route to this sea (the Pacific Ocean).

On his journeys in the West, he set up six fur-trading posts for the French. As commander of the western posts, La Vérendrye opened this vast area to French trade. His sons, François and Louis-Joseph, were the first Europeans to reach the Rocky Mountains.

? Critical Inquiry TIP

Sharing

A map is one way to present information. Different maps share different information.

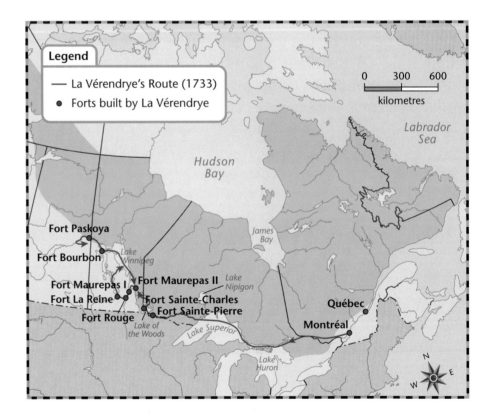

Legend

— La Vérendrye's Route (1733)

● Forts built by La Vérendrye

0   300   600
kilometres

Labrador Sea

Hudson Bay

James Bay

Fort Paskoya

Fort Bourbon

Lake Winnipeg

Fort Maurepas I

Fort Maurepas II

Lake Nipigon

Fort La Reine

Fort Sainte-Charles

Fort Rouge

Fort Sainte-Pierre

Lake of the Woods

Lake Superior

Québec

Montréal

Lake Huron

N E S W

Skill Smart

- Look closely at the map above and note the forts La Vérendrye built. In what ways do you think his journey westward influenced the development of Canada?

- Did you match any forts with cities of today?

What Jobs Do People Have in the Shield Today?

In the past, many jobs in the Canadian Shield were related to the fur trade. However, by the late 1800s, the fur trade was coming to an end. What did people do for work then?

There are many jobs in the Shield in medicine, tourism, government, and other industries. Still, many of the industries in the Shield depend on natural resources such as water, minerals, and forests.

Many people in my community have jobs that depend on natural resources. I wonder if it's the same in other communities in my region?

Mining

Forestry

Tourism

How do natural resources provide jobs?

Thinking *It Through*

■ When the availability of natural resources changes, what impact does it have on the community?

Where Do People Live in the Shield?

My Community: Opaskwayak First Nation

Thousands of years ago, Cree people from all around this area met here because two rivers come together. Today, about 4500 Cree people live in my community. Sometimes tourists come through Opaskwayak First Nation and hire people like my dad. He works as a hunting and fishing guide.

You already know that some communities are built near a source of water. First Nations communities in the Shield were no exception. Many were built on rivers or lakes. Others, such as Opaskwayak First Nation, were built where two rivers came together.

When the European fur traders started building trading posts, they built along rivers, too. Some of the trading posts and forts in the Shield grew into towns. Other communities in the Shield region were founded near natural resources. Some were settled by Francophone missionaries. Every community has different people living there and depends on many different resources. Read about some different communities in the Shield.

Trading Posts Built During the Fur Trade

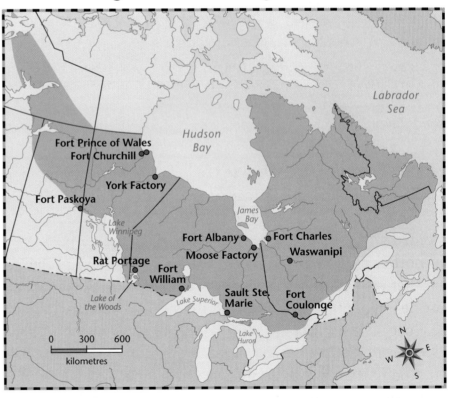

This map shows only some of the trading posts that were built in the Canadian Shield during the fur trade. Which ones are still communities today?

Chisasibi, Québec

Some First Nations communities in the Canadian Shield are in isolated areas. Like Chisasibi in Québec, many began as trading posts. In Chisasibi, the trading post became a permanent settlement for Cree people who stayed to trade with the English at Fort George. Many people still fish and hunt, while others work for Hydro-Québec, since the James Bay Hydroelectric Project is located nearby.

This is a view of Chisasibi from the air. About 4000 people live here. Look at the map on pages 96–97 and find Chisasibi, which is on the shore of James Bay.

Sault Ste. Marie, Ontario

Most of the early explorers, settlers, and missionaries in the Canadian Shield were Francophone. They started many communities in the region, and several other towns are named after them. Étienne Brûlé originally named a town in northern Ontario "Sault du Gaston," in honour of the brother of the King of France. It was renamed "Sault Ste. Marie" in 1669 by French Jesuit missionaries. Radisson, Québec, is named after Pierre Radisson, whom you read about on page 106.

Today, many communities in the Shield, such as Timmins, Sudbury, and North Bay in Ontario, have large Francophone populations and a strong Francophone presence. Collège Boréal is a Francophone college in Sudbury. Find other Francophone communities in the Canadian Shield region. Research the origin of the name of one of the communities you find.

More About. . .

The James Bay Project

The James Bay Project began in 1971. The government of Québec wanted to use the natural resources of the province to generate electricity. The Cree, Inuit, and Innu people who lived in the area were opposed to the project. The construction affected their traditional hunting areas, and the Québec government had acted without their approval. They sued the government and stopped construction of the dams. The government later agreed to set aside a protected area in northern Québec. They also relocated the James Bay Cree to new living areas.

Thinking It Through

■ What were the main concerns of each group in the James Bay Project?

Communities and Natural Resources

Mines and mills are built to take advantage of the minerals and forests of the Canadian Shield. At first, workers live in tents, trailers, and shacks in the wilderness. Soon families come to join the workers. Houses, schools, places of worship, and stores are built. Soon, a whole community has developed. These are called "resource communities" because the residents depend on the processing of a resource for their way of life.

Today, thousands of Canadians live and work in resource communities. Jobs in mills and mines are hard and dangerous, but workers and their families form close communities. What would happen to such a community if too many trees were cut down or a mineral started to run out? Look at the cycle below to find out.

The city of Sudbury, in Ontario, grew very quickly when nickel was discovered in the area. Nickel is used to make coins and stainless steel. What can you discover about Sudbury today?

The Natural Resources Cycle

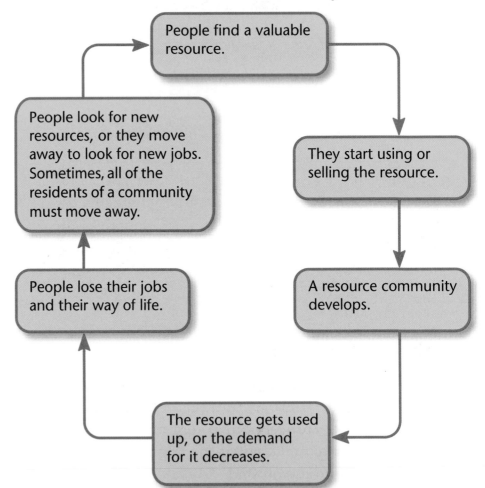

People find a valuable resource.

They start using or selling the resource.

A resource community develops.

The resource gets used up, or the demand for it decreases.

People lose their jobs and their way of life.

People look for new resources, or they move away to look for new jobs. Sometimes, all of the residents of a community must move away.

Elliot Lake: Living the Cycle

Elliot Lake is a great example of a resource community. It has gone through the natural resources cycle many times. Its location near Lake Huron in Ontario has made it popular for many different reasons over the years.

For centuries, the Anishinabé gathered in this area to hunt and fish. They started a village where Elliot Lake is today. In the late 1800s, European loggers and trappers moved there because of the forests and the animals. Then, in 1948, **uranium** was discovered in the area. By 1960, there were 11 mines near the town.

Over the next 35 years, the mines closed and reopened. As a result, the population dwindled and then rose. In 1996, the mines closed again and the population dropped. Residents decided that they needed a new, more dependable resource. The people of Elliot Lake looked around their town and realized it would make a great tourist destination.

Look at the photos and read the Voices of Canada on this page. What is life in Elliot Lake like today? Where would you place the town in the Natural Resources Cycle on page 118?

words matter!

Uranium is an element used to create both nuclear energy and X-rays.

This is Westview Park in Elliot Lake. How can a community work together to find new resources in their area?

Thinking *It Through*

■ Why do you think the residents of Elliot Lake thought that their community was a good destination for tourists? What makes your own community good for tourism?

Voices of Canada

Elliot Lake

My husband and I moved here two years ago, and we couldn't be happier. When we're not out hiking or fishing, we love sitting and watching the wildlife around the lake.

Sheila Jordan, retiree

What a wonderful vacation we had at Elliot Lake last summer! We enjoyed the exhibits at the arts college and all the water sports in the lake. And the town's people were so friendly!

Edward McLeod, tourist

Is It Good to Discover Natural Resources Near Your Home?

Today Elliot Lake, Ontario, is a city of about 12 000 people. When uranium was discovered, many people were excited about the opportunities it would provide. Not everyone felt the same way. Many people wonder if the search for natural resources beneath Earth's surface is worth the damage caused by mining and processing these resources. Cree Elder, John Petagumskum said, "The earth was created the way it was by the Creator, and changing it is unnatural and wrong. The land and the rivers where the Cree people hunt and fish are a garden, a gift from the Creator ... it has to be treated with love and respect to ensure that its spirit lives forever." Look at some of the other viewpoints on these pages.

Near Elliot Lake, a mining company built a plant at Serpent River First Nation. Bonnie Devine is an artist and a member of the Serpent River First Nation. This piece is about the damage caused by uranium mining and refining there.

Mining provided jobs for thousands of people like me. The town grew a lot. Many businesses came. This provided even more jobs. When the mine closed, I could not find work. I have remained unemployed ever since.

The waste at the mine sites will be poisonous for thousands of years. It has caused many health problems for people in the area. The mine has destroyed our community.

The world wanted uranium as a fuel, for X-rays, and to make nuclear weapons. Canadian mines helped supply the world with this important resource. I am proud to be a leader in this area.

Canada has so many forests, rivers, and lakes that it can spare some of these areas for developing mines. I think it is important to maintain the mining industry here.

Over to You

- Discuss the points of view on these pages, and the painting by Bonnie Devine. How do you think each opinion was formed?

- What natural resources have been developed in Alberta? Is there a community in Alberta like Elliot Lake?

Use Information from a Chart

Shield Community	Distance to Edmonton	Main Resource	Annual Snowfall
Moose Factory	2225 km	Tourism	226 cm
Sudbury	2426 km	Mining	268 cm
Thunder Bay	1781 km	Forestry	196 cm
Churchill	1323 km	Tourism	200 cm

- What information is being compared?
- Based on the chart, write down two ways the Shield communities are the same, and two ways they are different. For example, both Moose Factory and Sudbury are more than 2000 km away from Edmonton.

Research a Park

Find out more about a provincial or national park in the Canadian Shield.
- Why was the park established?
- How did it get its name?
- What does the park protect or conserve?

Create a report outline. Use headings and jot notes to share what you learn about the park. Include some interesting facts about the park.

Look at an Article

Find an article in the opinion section of a newspaper or magazine about the use of natural resources.
- What is the main argument in the article?
- What evidence does it give to support its argument?
- Do you agree with the writer? Why or why not?

Putting It All Together

I organized some of the information that my brother and I got from interviews on a fishbone chart.

Why do people live in the Canadian Shield today?

Ancestors have always lived here

Love of land, water, and animals

Mining or forestry jobs

To help provide services people need, like nursing

Review the inquiry questions for this chapter:
- What would Drew and Clare have to know about the geography and climate of this region in order to have a successful journey?
- List the factors that drew Europeans to explore this region.

Take Time to Reflect

Before you go on to the next chapter, think about what you learned in this one. During their journey across the Canadian Shield, Drew and Clare met with many people who helped them. Write a short description of what might have happened had Drew and Clare not received any help. You can use the journal entry on page 94 as the start of your story. Save your work for your Canada Collection.

Interior Plains
Land of Open Skies

I n the late 1700s, explorer and mapmaker David Thompson travelled west after exploring the Canadian Shield. He kept a journal as he travelled, and this is how he described the region that would be called the Interior Plains.

What I now relate is of the great body of dry land at the east foot of the mountains, the northern part of the forests, and the southern part of the plains, through which roll the Bow and Saskatchewan Rivers with their many branches. The Bow River flows through the most pleasant of the plains, and is the great resort of the bison and the red deer.

The snow of the glaciers of the mountains, which everywhere border the west side of these plains, furnish water to form many rivers. The rivers that roll through this immense unbroken body of land of plains and forests are beautifully distributed... The climate is good, the winters about five months, the summers are warm, and the autumn has many fine days. The soil is rich and deep... and agriculture will succeed...

Canada: Our Stories Continue

The Interior Plains is a large region that covers parts of Manitoba, Saskatchewan, and Alberta, as well as parts of the Northwest Territories and Yukon Territory. This region is fairly flat, with low hills. It has areas of grassland, wooded parkland, and large northern forests. First Nations, such as the Blackfoot, the Cree, and the Dene, have always lived here. As the fur trade expanded into the West, Francophone traders, Métis, and British explorers travelled throughout the region and built trading posts. Years later, people from different countries settled here. Communities and cities developed in the grasslands and parklands. Natural resources, such as coal, oil, gas, and forests led to the growth of communities throughout the region.

? Critical Inquiry TIP

Retrieving

Look at graphs, maps, tables, charts, and diagrams when you are doing research. They are all sources of information.

More About. . .

Prairies

Canadien explorers gave the name "prairie," meaning "meadow," to the vast grasslands that cover much of the region.

? Inquiring Minds

Here are some questions to guide your inquiry for this chapter:

- How did the physical geography of this region shape its history?
- How did settlers change the region?

Let's Explore the Interior

Hello! My name is Brianne Lysenko. I live on a farm in Saskatchewan's Qu'Appelle [kah-pell] Valley. My ancestors were farmers in Ukraine in Eastern Europe. They came to this region because they heard there was good farmland.

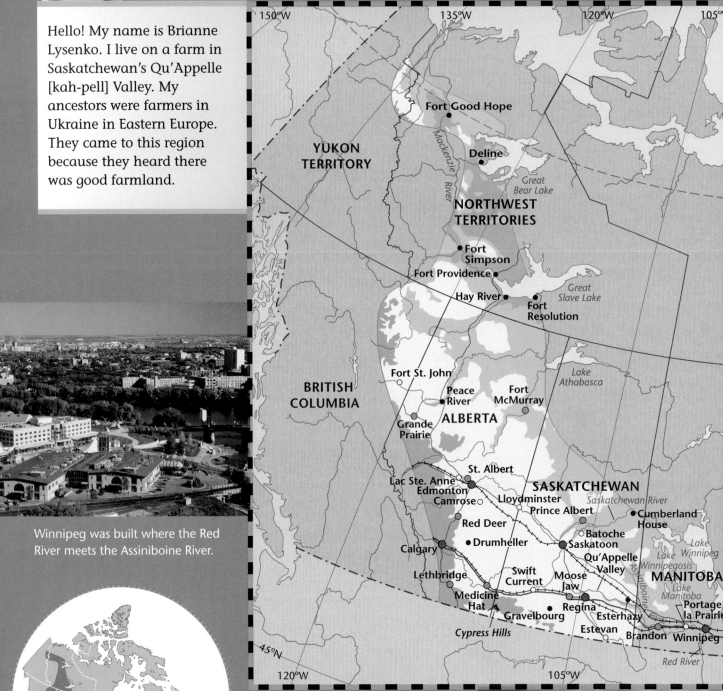

Winnipeg was built where the Red River meets the Assiniboine River.

The Cypress Hills area is unique because it is hilly. Why is it called a "prairie island"?

Plains!

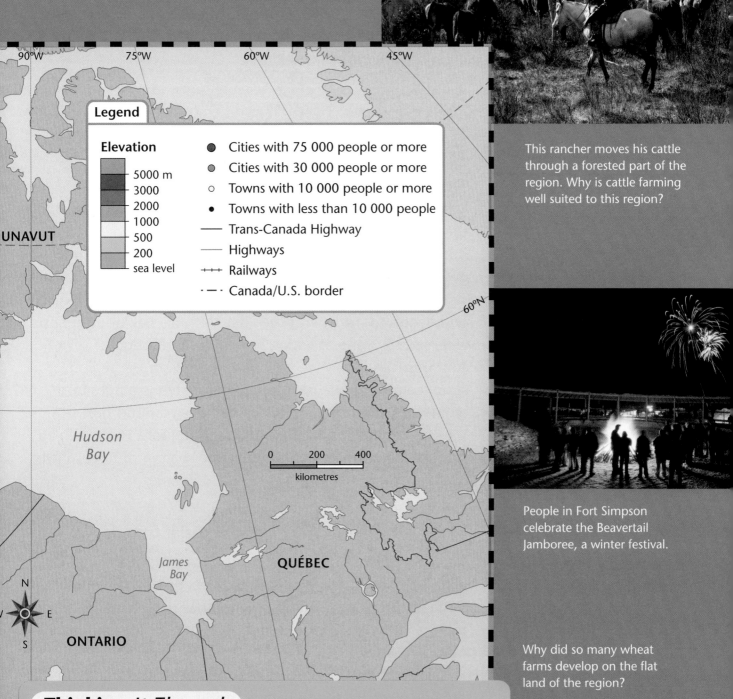

This rancher moves his cattle through a forested part of the region. Why is cattle farming well suited to this region?

People in Fort Simpson celebrate the Beavertail Jamboree, a winter festival.

Why did so many wheat farms develop on the flat land of the region?

Legend

Elevation

5000 m
3000
2000
1000
500
200
sea level

● Cities with 75 000 people or more
● Cities with 30 000 people or more
○ Towns with 10 000 people or more
• Towns with less than 10 000 people
— Trans-Canada Highway
— Highways
+++ Railways
·—· Canada/U.S. border

90°W   75°W   60°W   45°W

60°N

NUNAVUT

Hudson Bay

James Bay

QUÉBEC

ONTARIO

0   200   400
kilometres

Thinking *It Through*

■ Identify the major transportation routes shown on the map. Where are cities located in relation to those routes? Why do you think the cities are located there?

■ Reread David Thompson's journal entry on page 124. How do his descriptions compare to the map and the images on this page?

The Interior Plains

The Verreau family moved to Bon Accord, Alberta, in the 1890s.

The Interior Plains has many natural resources, such as oil, natural gas, coal, forests, and farmland. It often has severe weather—**droughts,** flooding, tornadoes, hail, dust storms, blizzards, and ice storms.

What Are the Roots of the Region?

The Saulteaux, Cree, Blackfoot (Siksika, Piikani, and Kainai), and Dene First Nations developed ways of life on the Interior Plains, depending on where they lived. They hunted caribou, moose, or **bison**, and travelled on the grasslands or through the forests.

In the 1700s, Francophones came to explore the region and began to trade with the First Nations. Fur trading posts were set up, some of which developed into larger communities. The Cree and Métis people in the region supplied food to the fur traders and acted as guides and scouts, allowing them to travel farther west and north.

The completion of the railway in the late 1800s helped bring many settlers, including farmers, from different parts of the world to the Plains.

Why People Live Here Today

The First Nations of the Interior Plains continue to live and work here, as do the descendants of people who came to settle in the region. Today, many other people continue to move to the region from other parts of Canada and from around the world.

Natural resources, such as coal, natural gas, and oil provide work for many people in this region. Thousands of people also work in industries related to farming. In towns and cities, people work in government, manufacturing, medicine, and education.

What Affects Quality of Life?

My older sister works at the university in Regina. When I visit, we shop and go to the museum and the parks. I'm glad that we have such a large, beautiful city close by.

Winter in Lethbridge can be hard, with lots of snow and cold winds! But that's life in the Interior Plains. The summer will bring warm temperatures and sunshine.

People working in the oil industry work long hours outdoors, sometimes in remote locations. The oil industry provides a variety of jobs.

Mountain biking is a popular pastime in the parkland areas of the region. Visitors often come to enjoy its natural beauty and bustling cities.

Thinking *It Through*

■ Look at each example. How do the land, resources, and climate affect ways of life for people in this region?

Brianne's Inquiry

Easter is my favourite time of year! My cousins, aunts, uncles, and grandparents get together. My favourite food is Easter bread. It's called **paska**. My family makes the best paska. We take it to church. The bread is blessed and then we take it home to enjoy.

I asked my Baba why everyone in my town does not make and eat paska. She told me that our family came from Ukraine, and making paska is our tradition. She said, "Our family has been farmers for many generations, and making special breads from our wheat shows how important that is to us."

People from other places had also settled in the Qu'Appelle Valley, some long before our family arrived. There are people coming to our community now, too! They have their own traditions.

I want to know more about the people in my community.

- Who lived here first?
- What are their stories?
- What was life like long ago?
- What is life like today?

I made a plan to find the answers. I will ask my family questions, and look in our old photo albums. I can ask students in my class why they live in our community. I will also go to the library, look on the Internet, and visit the Fort Qu'Appelle Museum.

? Critical Inquiry **TIP**

Processing

Look at old photos as you do your research. Look carefully at what the people are wearing or doing.

Thinking
It Through

■ Does your family have traditions and customs that come from your ancestors or your homeland? How are they part of your life today?

Skill Smart

■ Write down two questions you have about the people in the Interior Plains. Like Brianne, make a plan for how you will find the answers.

Understanding Photographs

When Brianne looked through her family's old photo albums, she saw lots of pictures from the past. She looked at the photos carefully. Photographs do not tell the whole story about the person, place, or event. Important details may be missing. Long ago, people had to sit very still to have their portrait taken. The cameras used in those days took 30 seconds to take a single photograph, so people in old photos often look very serious. Try smiling and staying perfectly still for 30 seconds! Today, people can use technology to change photos. They can add or delete whatever they choose.

Practise the Skill

Look at the photos on this page and on pages 126–127. What can you learn about Canada and its stories from these photos? Think about these questions:

Type of Information	Questions
Geographic	• What is the land like? What was the weather like when the photos were taken?
Historical	• What is in the photo? • What is the style of clothing, hair, or furniture? • What does this tell you about the times?
About People	• What are the people doing? • Where do you think they are? • How do you know?
Viewpoint	• Who took the picture? Why? How did the photographer make the photo look pleasing?

Who First Lived on the Interior Plains?

Rain and Caribou

Whenever it rains, the caribou feeds [well], and that's how it gets fat. Long ago, when it rained, people used to exclaim, "Haaaay, it's raining! That's great, for the caribou is going to be fat!"

William Sewi, Dene Elder

The Plains Cree, Siksika, Piikani, and Kainai who lived in the grasslands settled near sources of water and food. They also hunted bison for food, clothing, and other items. Bison roamed in large herds, eating prairie grasses. First Nations people who hunted the bison moved with the herds.

Just as important to the Dene were the caribou. These animals provided food and clothing. Like bison, caribou travel across vast distances looking for food. Many of the Dene travelled too, following the caribou across the north. What do the Voices of Canada on this page tell about traditional ways of life?

Deline is a Dene community on the shore of Great Bear Lake. Deline used to be called Fort Franklin. Suggest reasons why the name was changed.

What can sites such as this one at Dry Island Buffalo Jump Provincial Park, Alberta, tell us about the past?

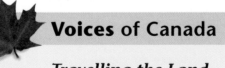

Voices of Canada

Travelling the Land

We knew every detail of this land. Our people travelled constantly throughout it, and their trails were well marked across the grassland.

Nitsitapiisinni: The Story of the Blackfoot People

What Are the Francophone Stories?

The majority of the coureurs des bois, explorers, and voyageurs who came to the region during the fur trade were Canadiens. French was the first European language spoken in the Interior Plains. In the 1720s, Pierre de La Vérendrye, with the help of his sons and his Cree guide, set up forts along the Saskatchewan River in Manitoba.

Laurent Leroux, a Canadien from Montréal, was a fur trader who set up Fort Resolution and Fort Providence on Great Slave Lake. The trading forts became centres for fur trade in each area. Most of the people who worked in them also spoke French.

La Vérendrye established Fort La Reine, which is now the city of Portage la Prairie. The fort was the headquarters for his explorations in the West.

More About. . .

The Qu'Appelle Valley

Pauline E. Johnson, a poet from the Six Nations of the Grand River, wrote a poem called "The Legend of the Qu'Appelle Valley." In the poem, she told of a young First Nations man who heard a ghostly voice calling his name. In response, he called "Kâ-têpwêt [KAA-tay-pwayt]?" When there was no response, he called in French, "Qui appelle [key ah-pell]?" Johnson based her poem on the local legend of the Qu'Appelle Valley. The Francophone traders who built the fur trading post in the valley knew the story and called their fort Fort Qu'Appelle. The valley has also been given the name, and the lakes in the area are sometimes called the "Calling Lakes." Find the Qu'Appelle Valley on the map on pages 126–127.

Voices of Canada

First People

The first people in Alberta, after the First Nations, were the French. Most of them were farmers. They first had to clear the forest before they could cultivate the land. So from a very early time you can see the contribution of the Francophones to Alberta's growth and development.

Edmond Levasseur, Edmonton

Father Albert Lacombe was a Roman Catholic missionary from Québec. Among many other accomplishments, he played an important role in creating schools in this region. What other contributions did Father Lacombe make?

How Did Some Francophone Communities Develop?

In the mid 1800s, as the population of Francophones grew in Western Canada, Roman Catholic priests and religious sisters came to Saint-Boniface and other settlements such as Fort Edmonton and St. Albert to establish missions that had churches, schools, and hospitals. Some of them were travelling missionaries, who ministered to the Francophone settlers who had established communities in the West.

In the late 1800s and early 1900s, Catholic clergy realized that many Canadiens in Québec were moving to the United States to look for work. They encouraged Francophone doctors, lawyers, and skilled tradesmen to settle in the Interior Plains.

Voices of Canada

Beaumont

These stories tell of life in the Francophone community of Beaumont, around the 1930s.

[My father] had heard of a place called Beaumont, a [Canadien] settlement. He went there and he liked what he saw. He found a quarter section [of land], which he bought.

Marcel Accarias, 1980

My parents worked very hard and taught me many things about working outdoors. I learned from [them] to love and care for animals, which helped me on our farm today.

Madeleine Demers, 1983

The town became an important centre of Francophone presence in Saskatchewan.

Gravelbourg

Gravelbourg was founded in 1906 by Father Louis-Pierre Gravel, a Catholic priest from Québec. He was given the title of "missionary-colonizer" by the Canadian government. He travelled throughout the United States and Eastern Canada telling Canadiens about the new town. Many families came to live in Gravelbourg as a result. Father Gravel also created a Francophone school.

What Are the Métis Stories?

The Métis were among the first to settle in the Interior Plains. One big settlement was along the Red River, where Winnipeg is today. It was an important meeting place for two reasons: the river and Lake Winnipeg led to fur trade routes in the Canadian Shield, and the Assiniboine River led farther west.

Métis often worked at Hudson's Bay Company and North West Company forts. They worked as trappers and as bison hunters, supplying food for the forts. The first Métis settlement in Saskatchewan was at Cumberland House, an HBC fort on the Saskatchewan River.

The Red River is called the Rivière Rouge in French. What are other French names in my region?

Voices of Canada

The Métis Nation

[The Métis] are a creation of the country, and our history, when Europeans joined with First Nations people... Métis are a very diverse people. Some lean more toward the First Nations way of life, and others lean more to a European way of life. I think, more than anything, Métis are good **ambassadors** of both cultures...

Mark McCallum, Alberta Métis

Many Métis settled in Saskatchewan. One town was named after a Métis trader and businessman named François Xavier Letendre, dit Batoche. Batoche is now an important historic site for the Métis. This painting shows what Batoche looked like in 1885. Find out two facts about Batoche that explain why the area is important to the Métis.

Métis Ways of Life

Traders and explorers from the Hudson's Bay Company and the North West Company relied on pemmican. These men were travelling great distances into the West and the North, and they needed preserved food like pemmican to survive. Pemmican became an important source of income for the Métis people.

Voices of Canada

Pemmican

Pemmican comes from a Cree word that means lard or grease-like. You make it by pounding dry meat (usually moose, buffalo, or elk). You can add dry berries... Then you mix the dry part half-and-half with

These Métis are drying moose meat to make pemmican at Île-à-la-Crosse, Saskatchewan.

rendered fat. This makes pemmican. It's very nutritious and easy to carry. You can eat it just like this, or you can put it in a soup or stew. One pound will last you three or four days.

Billy Joe Laboucan, Lubicon Lake Cree Nation, Alberta

Voices of Canada

The Red River Cart

The Red River cart was used by the Métis to transport goods and people across the plains. It could also float across rivers. Why would the cart be a good way to travel in this region?

Sometimes, we spent the whole day riding on the cart. The hardest part of our trip was listening to the wheels. When they turned, it sounded like thunder. My moshòm [grandfather] would play the fiddle, and we would sing. It helped take our minds off the noise!

Suzanne Cardinal

Skill Smart

■ List the titles, authors, and page numbers or Web sites for three sources of information about pemmican and Red River carts.

What Factors Shaped Ways of Life on the Interior Plains?

Life changed for First Nations people of the Interior Plains when trading posts were set up. Trapping animals for the fur trade became part of daily life. By the mid-1900s, many First Nations, such as the Dene, began to live in permanent homes near the trading posts.

The Horse

Would it surprise you to learn that horses have only lived in the Interior Plains for a few hundred years? For a long time, First Nations people such as the Siksika hunted bison on foot. They call this time period the "Dog Days" because dogs helped carry people's belongings across the Prairies. Horses arrived on the plains from the south. Spanish explorers had brought horses with them.

Moose Jaw, Saskatchewan, is one of the many cities Rick Hansen visited during his journey. The Trans Canada Trail in Moose Jaw is almost 10 km of wilderness trails, where people can hike, bike, ski, and horseback ride.

This is a cattle roundup in Marchwell, Saskatchewan. How are horses still part of life in this region today?

Horses could travel farther and faster and could carry a greater load than dogs. These Blackfoot men are using a horse and travois to carry goods and supplies.

Thinking It Through

- How did the horse change ways of life for people in the Interior Plains?

What Was the Red River Colony?

In 1811, the Hudson's Bay Company granted part of its vast territory, known as Rupert's Land, to an English nobleman, the Earl of Selkirk. Selkirk called it the "Territory of Assiniboia."

In Scotland, English landlords had forced many farmers off their land. Selkirk's plan was to bring these homeless farmers and their families from the Scottish **Highlands** and have them establish a new farming community in Assiniboia. These families became the settlers of the Red River Colony.

Territory of Assiniboia

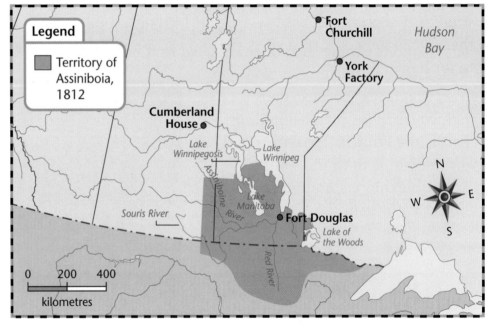

This map shows the Territory of Assiniboia. What does it tell you about the land where the settlers started their colony? Why do you think it was chosen?

Their journey to Red River in 1812 was not easy. Their ship landed at Fort Churchill on Hudson Bay. They then had to travel all the way to York Factory on foot. There, they waited out the winter.

When they finally arrived at Red River, they built a fort, called Fort Douglas. By then it was too late to plant crops. During the winter, the Scots were saved from starvation by the pemmican provided by the Métis who lived in the area. The next summer, they started to build houses and plant crops along the river. The Red River Colony had become the first farming settlement in the Interior Plains.

Thinking
It Through

■ Many Métis and fur traders in the Red River area were afraid that the new settlement would disrupt their way of life. Why do you think the introduction of an agricultural settlement might have an effect on these people?

How Did the North-West Mounted Police Help Shape the West?

Imagine that you are a settler in the Interior Plains in 1870. The Hudson's Bay Company has just given the new government of Canada control of Rupert's Land, creating the new North-West Territories. Lately there has been a lot of trouble in your small, isolated community. Is there someone you can turn to for help?

In 1873, Sir John A. Macdonald, first prime minister of Canada, wanted a police force to bring law and Canadian authority to the new Territories. The vast distances of the new Territories meant that a mounted police force, or a **cavalry**, would be best. So he created the North-West Mounted Police. They soon became known as the "Mounties."

The North-West Mounted Police force was modelled after the British cavalry. Why?

words matter!

A **cavalry** is a group of soldiers or police who use horses.

North-West Territories, 1876

Legend

\------- Territorial border

············ Undefined border

BRITISH COLUMBIA

NORTH-WEST TERRITORIES

NEWFOUNDLAND

MANITOBA

ONTARIO

QUÉBEC

PRINCE EDWARD ISLAND

NOVA SCOTIA

NEW BRUNSWICK

This map shows the North-West Territories as they were in 1876. Look at the maps on page 339 of the atlas section to see how the territories developed. Why was it necessary to have police presence in such a large area?

The March West

The new North-West Mounted Police (NWMP) trained in Fort Dufferin, Manitoba. Then, in 1874, a huge line (about 4 km long) of Mounties and their supplies trekked from Fort Dufferin to the Sweet Grass hills in what is now Alberta— a journey on horseback of about 1500 km.

These NWMP officers were photographed at Fort Walsh, Saskatchewan, during the 1870s. Fort Walsh became the headquarters for the NWMP in 1878.

Route of the NWMP, 1874

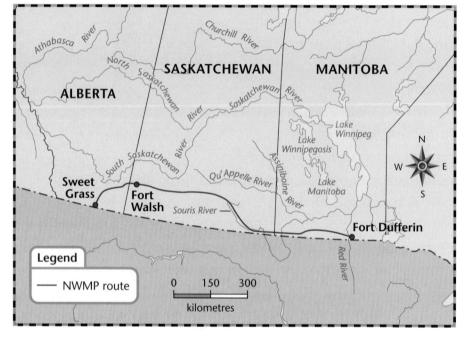

Some Mounties kept journals to record their travels. Why do these stories help us understand the NWMP?

Voices of Canada

October 22, 1874

...I pushed on with the horse teams and had the hardest trek that I have yet undertaken. The trail was worse than any we had encountered. It was knee-deep in black mud, sloughs crossed it every few hundred yards, and the wagons had to be unloaded and dragged through them by hand.

Sam Steele, RCMP Superintendent

Voices of Canada

Respect

Newspaper artist Henri Julien was sent to observe the march of the NWMP. This is what he wrote when the march was over.

Our mission was over. The force had accomplished its duty for which it had been sent out. I must express my respect for them as men and for the worthy manner in which they performed the arduous duties imposed on them by the government.

Henri Julien, October 1874

The presence of the NWMP on the Interior Plains meant that people felt safer. NWMP were stationed throughout the region, and also patrolled the isolated areas. More settlers were willing to come to create new communities.

The Mounties also enforced the new borders that were being developed with the United States. Soon the red-coated Mountie was seen as a symbol of Canadian presence in the West.

This RCMP officer is taking part in a ceremony in Victoria, British Columbia, in 2005.

The NWMP are known today as the Royal Canadian Mounted Police (RCMP). What was and is asked for in new members? Why do you think the name was changed?

Northwest Mounted Police.

Candidates must be active, able-bodied men of sound constitution and exemplary character. They should be able to ride well, and to read and write in either the English or the French language.

RCMP

ROYAL CANADIAN MOUNTED POLICE
GENDARMERIE ROYALE DU CANADA

Candidates must:
- be a Canadian citizen
- be of good character
- be proficient in English or French
- possess a valid driver's license
- be 19 years of age
- meet medical health standards
- be willing to relocate anywhere in Canada
- be physically fit

Thinking *It Through*

- The NWMP brought law and order to the Interior Plains. How do you think this would help in the settlement and development of the region?

141

How Were People of the Interior Plains Affected by the Railway?

I've read that the bison were also hunted during this time just for their hides. I think I'll find out more about how the loss of the bison affected quality of life for the First Nations who depended on them.

Building the Canadian Pacific Railway began in 1881. The railway helped bring many settlers to the Prairies and allowed the NWMP to move quickly in times of trouble. When the railway was completed, settlers were able to ship their produce by rail to both ends of the country.

The railway also changed ways of life for the First Nations and the Métis who lived in the Interior Plains. In order to make sure the bison stayed off the tracks, railway companies encouraged people to shoot them. During the late 1800s, hundreds of thousands of bison were killed. Eventually, they were almost wiped out. For the First Nations and Métis who depended on the bison for food, clothing, and shelter, this caused enormous hardship.

Why Were Treaties Made?

Treaty 8 negotiations, Lesser Slave Lake, Alberta, 1899. The treaty upheld sharing of resources and peaceful co-existence.

First Nations people had always lived on the land on which the railway was built. They were very concerned about how and where they would live now. Their leaders and government leaders met to discuss a compromise, which became a series of treaties.

? Critical Inquiry TIP

Processing

A two-column chart, like this one, is a way to organize your research. The chart can help you see what each group of people wanted.

Government of Canada Wanted	First Nations Wanted
• to build a railway and bring settlers in to farm the land	• peaceful co-existence with settlers
• to secure land for settlement	• to make sure the land they lived on was not taken over by settlers
• to take away the rights of First Nations people and assimilate them	• to make sure they would have a home and food, and to maintain their ways of life

Some First Nations people do not think signing the treaties was a good idea. They had always travelled freely throughout the region. With the treaties, they were allowed to live only on land provided by the government. Often the land was poor and difficult to farm. Sacred gatherings were forbidden, so they had to be held secretly. Despite these hardships, First Nations people continue to preserve their cultural heritage and traditions.

How Were the Métis Affected by the Railway?

The lives of Métis in the Interior Plains were also changing. Canada now controlled the land where the Métis had lived, including the Red River settlement. Many things made the Métis worry about their future:

- The fur trade had slowed down, and many Métis had lost their jobs with the trading companies.
- More settlers had arrived on the Prairies. They were creating communities where the Métis had once hunted, farmed, and camped.
- Bison were becoming scarce.

The Métis were given **scrip** at the same time that First Nations signed treaties with the government. Scrip was a coupon that could be exchanged for land or money. But the concept was not explained well to the Métis. Some people took advantage of them and persuaded them to sell their scrip for less than it was worth. Others forged Métis signatures and took their land. Many Métis were left with very little.

This photo shows Gabriel Dumont in Red River. Give two reasons why the First Nations and the Métis would want to preserve their traditional ways of life.

Thinking It Through

- Some people thought the treaties and scrip were a good idea. Others did not. Why do you think people might have different opinions about these issues?

- How do the offers of treaties and scrip compare to the offer given to the Acadians by the British?

How Did Settlers Shape Ways of Life in the Interior Plains?

Where can I learn more about settlers from Russia, Germany, Poland, and Ukraine?

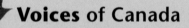

words matter!

A **homestead** is the land owned by a settler.

In the late 1800s, land and work were scarce for many people in Eastern Europe. Canada offered great opportunities for people from Russia, Ukraine, Germany, and Poland. Many settled in the Interior Plains, where the government gave each family its own **homestead**. They brought with them farming techniques and ways of life. They cleared land, built schools and churches, and created communities, many of which still exist today.

Read the Voices of Canada on these pages to discover what it was like for new settlers in this region.

Ukrainian Settlers

The first Ukrainian settlers were mostly farmers. Education was very important, and the children of Ukrainian settlers often became teachers. Today, the University of Manitoba and the University of Alberta both have centres for Ukrainian Studies.

Voices of Canada

Homesteading

My parents arrived in 1898. From the first day on the farm [near] Sifton we all worked hard. Though the soil was light it was not as poor a land as in the stony areas farther west.

Toma Demchuk, Ukrainian settler, Manitoba. He would later help found a credit union in Sifton.

After Ukrainian settlers built their homes, they built churches. Why were churches important to communities?

Russian Settlers

Many Russian settlers were Doukhobors, a religious group that believed in peace and hard work. They settled vast tracks of land in the region. Some varieties of wheat that are still grown in the region today were brought here by these farmers.

Voices of Canada

Hardship

The hardships of the first few months of our pioneer life are unforgettable. We all lived in canvas tents which provided poor shelter against the cold, incessant rains. The tents dripped and leaked, so that everything inside was soggy and cold.

Tanya Postnikoff, Russian Doukhobor settler, Saskatchewan. She wrote a book about her experiences.

Thinking
It Through

■ What can you see around you today that shows the contributions of these settlers? Think of community and street names, books, foods, organizations, or people.

German Settlers

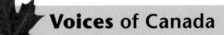

The Mennonites were the first group of German-speaking settlers to arrive in Canada. They were some of the most successful farmers in this region. In 1888, John Schultz, the child of German settlers, became Lt. Governor of Manitoba and played an important role in the development of the province.

The Klassen family lived in Hanna, Alberta

Voices of Canada

A New Home

Our destination was Herbert, Saskatchewan. We were taken to church right away, and were given food and a house to live in.

Elizabeth Boese, German Mennonite settler, Saskatchewan. She helped her husband with his ministry.

Polish Settlers

Polish settlers farmed in the Interior Plains, and also worked in mines and in the forest industry. These settlers created community groups and associations that helped other Polish settlers when they came to Canada. Today, Polish associations offer scholarships and support the community in many ways.

The Wawel Meat Market in Winnipeg specializes in Polish food. It is located in an culturally diverse neighbourhood.

Voices of Canada

Knowing a bit of the language and having some money, I decided to open a store. This was in 1903. As time went on my business was very extensive.

John Gilewich, Polish settler, Manitoba. He was the first postmaster of Elma.

Why Did British Settlers Come?

People from Britain were also encouraged to settle in the Interior Plains during the Great Migration. Many came because Britain was crowded, and jobs were hard to find. Owning their own land was something many families wanted. Although some did not have farming experience, people like James Clinkskill would find other ways to make a living in Canada.

Voices of Canada

Making a Living

My sojourn on the prairie convinced me that I was not cut out for farming operations. I decided it was no use to start learning. I determined to try some other way of making a living. I [met] a young man from Ontario, and we agreed to combine our money, and start a store.

James Clinkskill

What Was the Barr Colony?

In 1903, the Reverend Isaac Barr encouraged people from England to come and settle in a new colony in Saskatchewan. About 2000 people agreed to come, but when they arrived they found that many of Barr's promises could not be kept. He also charged them money for food and necessary equipment.

Soon the colonists voted on a new leader, a man named Reverend George Lloyd. With a new leader, the colony prospered. The main community in the colony was named Lloydminster. It became a city in 1958.

Voices of Canada

The Barr Colony

What could these changes have meant for the Barr Colony settlers?

In May 1903 at most one dozen tents were all that could be seen on the bare prairie and now [we have] stores of all kinds, a fine building for the bank, drugstore, a printing office... it is just marvellous.

Alice Rendell, Lloydminster, 1905

The Corbett family arrives in Saskatchewan in 1911 from Surrey, England.

Has Farming and Ranching Changed in the Interior Plains?

 David Thompson wrote that the Interior Plains would be a great place for agriculture. He was right!

Large areas of flat land and fertile soil meant that agriculture has been an important way of life in the Interior Plains. The first gardens in the region were at fur-trading forts. Settlers in all parts of the region, from the southern grasslands to the northern forests, raised animals and farmed the lands to support themselves.

At first, settlers farmed small areas of land. They used horses and plows, but the work was slow and hard. Many farms remained small because more land meant more work than one family could do. Ranches were often larger, since the animals needed a large area for grazing.

Farming Today

Technology has changed farming today. Where there is farmland but little rain, farmers use **irrigation** to water crops. Combines are used to harvest grain, and trucks transport the grain to buyers. Chemicals fertilize crops and prevent insect damage.

Chemicals that are used on farms can also harm crops or animals. Many people are concerned about chemicals getting into our food. Some farmers, like Marc Loiselle, have switched to **organic farming**. How might personal values affect how someone chooses to run a farm?

Areas in the northern parts of the Interior Plains are also good for agriculture. This is the Peace River Valley, in British Columbia.

Voices of Canada

Organic Farming

This farmer helps run an organization for organic farmers in Saskatchewan.

We started organic farming in 1985. The attraction to [organic] farming came from our desire to be better stewards of the land and resources, without the use of toxic substances.

Marc Loiselle, Vonda, Saskatchewan

Thinking *It Through*

■ Check the map of agricultural areas in the atlas section, on page 350. What are the main agricultural products in the Interior Plains? Discuss how and why agriculture within the Interior Plains region might vary.

words matter!

Irrigation is water supplied to dry land using pipes, ditches, or streams.

Organic farming uses no chemicals on plants or animals.

147

Ranching Today

The Interior Plains region has good conditions for raising cattle. The grasses, streams, and rivers provide food and water. In the past, sheep and cattle were raised for the settler's family. The railway made a difference, enabling larger ranches to sell their cattle and sheep to different parts of Canada.

Dangers faced by ranchers in this region were wildfires, drought, and severe storms. Disease among animals could destroy entire herds. Today, vaccinating animals helps prevent many diseases. Some ranchers are also raising different kinds of stock, such as ostriches, elk, and bison.

Why have these animals become part of ranching in this region?

What impact might a feedlot have on the environment?

Thinking
It Through

■ What are the advantages and disadvantages of new technologies being used in farming and ranching?

The Factory Farm

A "factory farm" is one where large numbers of only one type of animal, such as cattle or chickens, are raised. Such farms began because of the huge demand for the animal and its products. Technology on these farms makes it easy to raise large quantities very quickly.

However, some people think that factory farms are unhealthy and treat animals cruelly. The farms also cause pollution, especially from the large amounts of animal waste.

What Are the Effects of Drought?

Skill Smart

- Think of problems that farmers and ranchers in the Interior Plains face today. Make a Cause and Effect chart showing the source of the problem and the way it affects people.

The southern parts of the Interior Plains often have dry periods during the summer. But what if these dry periods last all year? What if there is little snow in winter? What if the spring rains do not come? This is what happened in 2002 in southern Alberta and southwestern Saskatchewan. The summer of 2001 was very dry, and over the next year, the earth continued to dry out.

Effects of Drought

Other people affected are business owners and farm workers.

Farmers lose their crops. There is no grass for cattle to eat. Farmers and ranchers lose money.

Some farmers choose to find other ways to farm, or try new crops. This can be hard to do.

Some farmers are forced to sell their farms. They must find new ways to make a living.

In 2002, farmers in Ontario and Québec organized Hay West, a plan to ship hay from their own farms to farmers and ranchers in the Interior Plains. What other ways could we help farmers in need?

Viewpoints

How Should People Farm on the Interior Plains?

Over time, farm equipment and farmland has become more expensive. Drought or flooding can ruin crops. The money farmers make from their crops can be barely enough to live on. People across Canada have started looking for other ways to farm. What are the advantages and disadvantages of different farming methods? Look back to pages 147–148 to review the information on factory farms and organic farming. Then read the points of view below.

We need large-scale production of livestock. We cannot satisfy the growing demand for meat from small farms alone.

New technology increases production, saves farmers money

Organic foods healthier and better for the environment

We are really worried about having so many factory farms. Some of these farms have more than 20 000 animals on them! The waste made by these animals is polluting rivers and lakes. It could make people very sick. We are afraid the animals are not well cared for.

My family owns an organic farm in Manitoba. Even though we sold some of our land, my parents said we make more money now than when we had a big farm and used chemicals. Many people will pay more for food they think is healthier. I am very happy digging in the rich soil and watching our crops grow!

Waste from factory farms could be used to generate electricity

Over to You

1. As a class, discuss the different points of view. How do the different ways of farming have an impact on the land? How do they affect the farmers' ways of life?

2. Find out about organic and factory farms in your area. How do they work? Hold a debate to discuss the pros and cons of each method.

How Do Natural Resources Shape Communities in the Interior Plains?

words **matter!**

Potash is a substance that is mainly used in fertilizer. It is rich in potassium, an important nutrient for plants.

Esterhazy is known as the "potash capital" of the world! How do you think the presence of such an important resource affects the people who live here?

Thinking *It Through*

■ How do you think the natural resources of the Interior Plains have shaped ways of life for the different groups of people who live there?

As you have seen in previous chapters, towns often develop around a place where there is a natural resource. The Interior Plains have many huge deposits of oil and gas underground. There are also large deposits of salt, gypsum, and **potash**. Other natural resources include forests, rivers, and rich soil.

Natural resources create jobs for thousands of people. As a result, communities of different sizes have developed across the Interior Plains. The map below shows mineral deposits and oil and gas sources. Compare the map below to the one on pages 126–127 to see where communities may have developed around these resources.

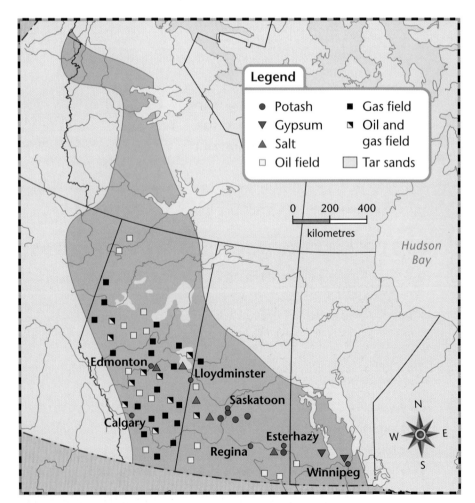

This map shows some natural resources of the Interior Plains. What resources are there?

152

Winnipeg, Gateway to the West

Railcars transport Canadian grain to Winnipeg.

Winnipeg, Manitoba, began as a fur-trading post founded by Pierre de La Vérendrye in 1738. In 1876, the community adopted the name Winnipeg. Railways coming from western farms transport grain and other natural resources through Winnipeg and into Eastern Canada.

Today, Winnipeg has a population of over 650 000 and the city is a centre for government, commerce, and the arts.

Making *a Difference*

Protecting Natural Resources

The land west of Great Slave Lake has always been a traditional hunting ground for the Dene First Nations. The rich natural resources of the area are still important to the people who live in the area. In 2002, an agreement between First Nations people and the government of the Northwest Territories was signed. With this agreement, the government promised not to allow development of oil or gas industries, mines, or other industries.

The area has many lakes and large patches of muskeg. It also has bird habitats and caribou. The Horn Plateau, part of the protected lands, is an International Biological Program Site because of the lichen that is found there. These unique natural resources will now be protected.

Understand Photographs

Using books or the Internet, find photographs of early settlements and present-day communities on the Interior Plains. Examine the photos using the Skill Power information headings on page 131. Answer the questions. How do the historic and present-day photos compare?

Plan an Interview

Find out more about someone in your community.
• Why do they live here?
• What country did their family originate from?
• What languages do they speak?
Add five more of your questions to the list. After the interview, share what you learned by creating a web.

Examine a Poster

The Canadian government advertised the Interior Plains as a good place to settle. They wanted to attract many people to come there. Look at the poster on this page. Think about how a person in Europe might see this poster. How would different people see the poster? What would they think about Canada from the poster?

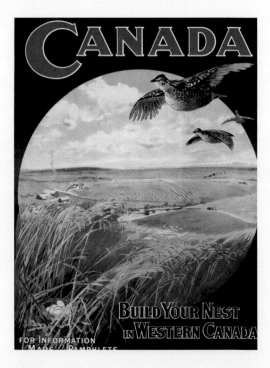

Putting It All Together

For part of her inquiry, Brianne used a KWL chart to record her findings about her family's history.

What I Think I Know	What I Want to Know	What I Learned
My family came from Ukraine.	When did they come?	They came in 1896.
They made temporary homes at first.	What were they called?	My Baba called these homes burdei.

Review the inquiry questions for this chapter:

- How did the physical geography of this region shape its history?
- How did settlers change the region?

Take Time to Reflect

Before you go on to the next chapter, think about what you learned in this one. Make a cartoon to show how the land and agriculture has shaped this region. What does it mean to the identity of the region? It could show a part of history, much like David Thompson's observations in the past, or it could show something from today. Save your work for your Canada Collection.

Cordillera Region
Life by the Mountains

What is your favourite animal? Simon Jackson would probably say bears. When he was 13 years old, Simon learned about the Kermode or "spirit" bear. This is a special kind of black bear that lives only on one small part of the coast of British Columbia. About one in ten Kermode bears is pure white.

People were arguing about whether logging should be allowed in the bears' habitat. Logging provided many jobs, but how would it change the forests where the bears live? Would spirit bears disappear forever?

Simon became an active citizen when he decided to take action to protect the bears. He organized a letter-writing campaign, and made speeches in public. He began the Spirit Bear Youth Coalition, and young people from around the world joined together to help save the spirit bear.

"In April of 2000, people really started listening. I was selected as one of *Time Magazine*'s Sixty Heroes for the Planet—one of only six young people chosen from around the world. It wasn't that I was a hero—I wasn't, but what this honour did was give credibility to the spirit bear campaign and it gave credibility to the youth movement that was working to give the spirit bear a voice. Overnight this issue went from a middle school letter writing campaign to a broad-based global issue."

Simon Jackson

Canada: Our Stories Continue

The forests that are home to the spirit bear are an important part of the Cordillera region. The Cordillera region has towering mountains, fast-flowing rivers, and large forests. There is a long coastline along the Pacific Ocean, where birds, fish, and whales can be found. This region includes the mountains of Alberta and the Northwest Territories, almost all of British Columbia, and most of the Yukon Territory. Here, people have relied on different resources for their food, transportation, and ways of life.

? Critical Inquiry TIP

Retrieving

Try organizing what you are learning with a concept map. Print the name of the region in the middle of a page. Add details about the people, land, water, other natural resources, and climate in boxes.

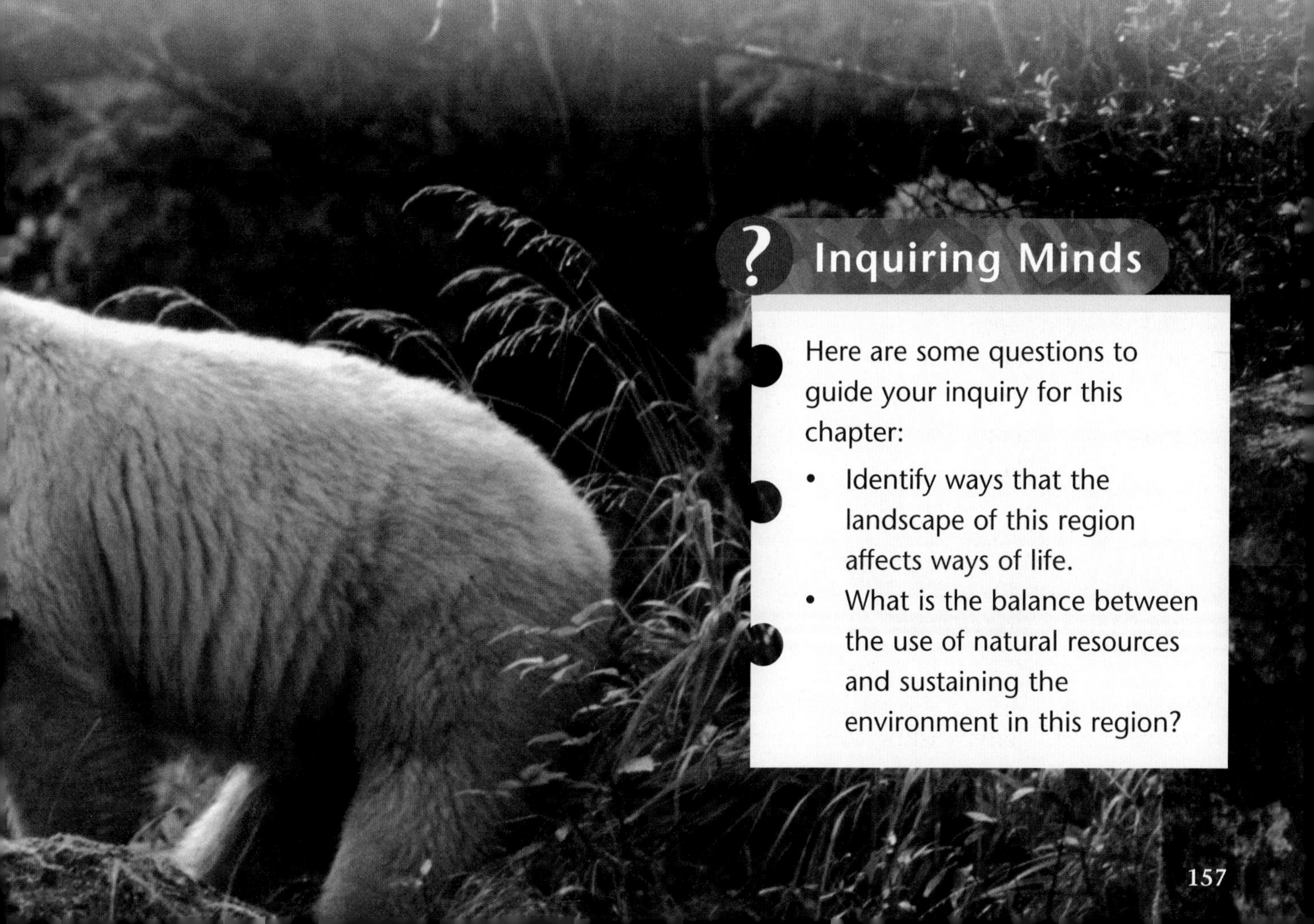

? Inquiring Minds

Here are some questions to guide your inquiry for this chapter:

- Identify ways that the landscape of this region affects ways of life.
- What is the balance between the use of natural resources and sustaining the environment in this region?

Let's Explore the Cordillera Region!

Hello! My name is Sunjeet Gill, but my friends call me Sunny. That's a good nickname because I live in Kamloops, one of the warmest cities in Canada. Kamloops is in a valley in the Cordillera region.

On the coast, people can look for whales.

Outdoor activities, such as camping, are very popular in this region. Here, a kayaker enjoys a park at Kluane Lake, in the Yukon.

The area around Kamloops is the northern end of a very dry area called the Sonoran desert. How does this area compare to other parts of the region?

The town of Smithers developed on a trade route that was used by First Nations and gold miners. What routes are close to Smithers today? Look on the map to find out.

Skill Smart

- Make a Venn diagram comparing the Cordillera region with another region in Canada. Use pictures and words. What does the diagram show about the two different regions of Canada?

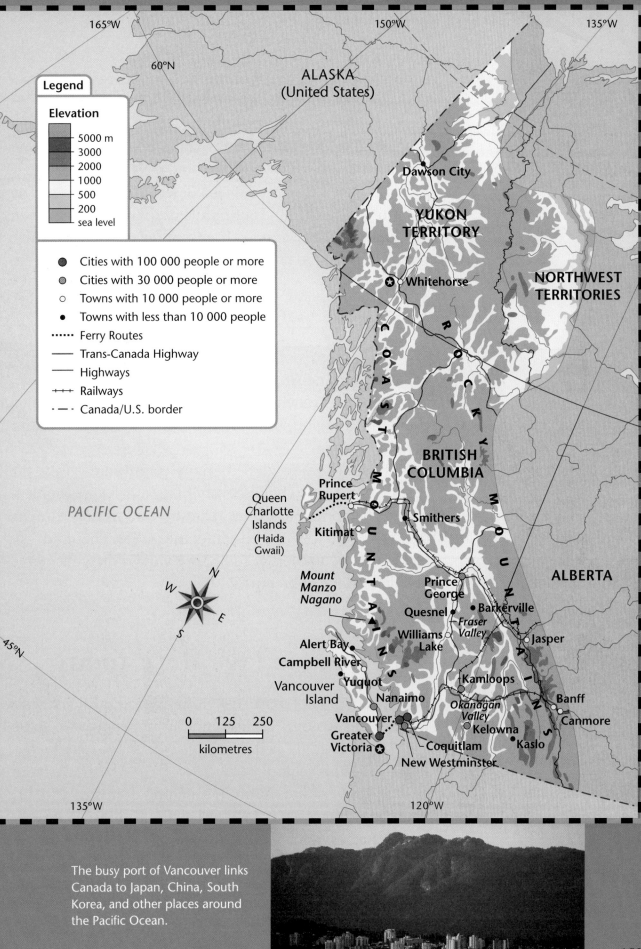

Legend

Elevation

	5000 m
	3000
	2000
	1000
	500
	200
	sea level

- ● Cities with 100 000 people or more
- ● Cities with 30 000 people or more
- ○ Towns with 10 000 people or more
- • Towns with less than 10 000 people
- ••••• Ferry Routes
- —— Trans-Canada Highway
- — Highways
- +++ Railways
- –·–·– Canada/U.S. border

165°W

150°W

135°W

60°N

ALASKA
(United States)

Dawson City

YUKON
TERRITORY

NORTHWEST
TERRITORIES

Whitehorse

C O A S T   M O U N T A I N S

R O C K Y   M O U N T A I N S

BRITISH
COLUMBIA

PACIFIC OCEAN

Prince
Rupert

Queen
Charlotte
Islands
(Haida
Gwaii)

Smithers

Kitimat

ALBERTA

Mount
Manzo
Nagano

Prince
George

Quesnel   • Barkerville

Williams   *Fraser*
Lake   *Valley*

Jasper

45°N

Alert Bay

Campbell River

Yuquot

Vancouver
Island

Nanaimo

Kamloops

Banff

0   125   250

kilometres

Vancouver

Okanagan
Valley

Canmore

Greater
Victoria

Kelowna

Coquitlam

Kaslo

New Westminster

135°W

120°W

The busy port of Vancouver links
Canada to Japan, China, South
Korea, and other places around
the Pacific Ocean.

The Cordillera Region

First Nations groups in this region have traditionally used cedar in their carvings. Today, artist Pawl Victor Auges carries on the tradition.

The Cordillera region has some of the most popular ski resorts in North America. What kinds of activities could people do in the mountains in summer?

A **cordillera** is a chain of mountains. There are many different chains of mountains in Canada's Cordillera region. In between the mountains, there are fertile valleys, lakes, and rolling hills. On the coast, there are deep harbours, sheltered waterways, and **deltas**. The region also includes very old forests, rivers, deserts, and beaches. There are more different kinds of plants and animals here than anywhere else in Canada. The weather varies throughout the region—rainy, hot and dry, or snowy.

Roots of the Region

The rich resources of the land and water provided for the needs of the First Nations who have always lived in this region. When French, British, and other European explorers came to the region, they used the waterways and oceans to travel.

As the region developed, many communities were built around resources. The discovery of gold brought people who wanted to work gold claims. Forestry and fishing camps also grew into towns, and sometimes cities. The mild temperatures and fertile soil of the valleys drew farmers and people to work in orchards.

Why People Live Here Today

More than 100 different First Nations groups have always lived in this region. The descendants of people who settled here in the past, as well as people who move here today, also live in this region.

Logging, fishing, mining, ranching, tourism, and oil and gas exploration helped build communities. Farmers grow peaches, herbs, and grapes in the valleys. Many people enjoy the mild climate and beautiful natural areas.

What Affects Quality of Life?

Here is how the land, water, other natural resources, and climate affect quality of life for some people in the Cordillera region.

People come to this region from all over the world to see the beaches and the rainforest. Surfing is a popular pastime.

Barkerville was once the largest town in Western Canada. Now, it is a historic site. Tourists can ride in the stagecoach and learn about life in Gold Rush times.

Each February, the city of Victoria has an official flower count. The mild climate on the south coast means that daffodils are blooming while some other Canadians are still shovelling snow. Many people retire in Victoria because of its pleasant climate.

Thinking *It Through*

- Many communities in this region are on islands. They can only be reached by plane or boat. How would this affect people and businesses? What do you think are the advantages and disadvantages of living on an island?

Sunjeet's Inquiry

About Me
Contact
My Web Page
Links

Archives

January
February
March
April
May
June

I'm writing this blog while I'm with my family in Vancouver. When I get home, I'm going to share my information with my class. Today, we took a bike ride around the seawall at Stanley Park. We saw ships from all over the word entering the harbour. You don't see ships that big in Kamloops!

We also watched the dragon boat races in False Creek, which is an inlet of the Pacific Ocean in Vancouver. I noticed that the people rowing the traditional Chinese boats were from many different cultures. There were also many languages being spoken in the crowd. I recognized some of them, but not all!

People have to work together to row the dragon boats in False Creek. What is the history behind this event?

I have some questions about the people living in Vancouver:

- Who lives here?
- What kind of jobs do they have? What do they do for fun?
- How do the people use the ocean, land, and mountains?

Skill Smart

■ As a class, brainstorm some questions you have about the Cordillera region. Record them on chart paper. Display the questions on a bulletin board so you can refer to them as you go through this chapter.

SKILL POWER Using Electronic Information

The Internet can be a great source of information, but how can you make sure that the information you find is true? When researching on the Internet, look for

- three or four sites that give the same information
- Web sites that have been recently updated
- addresses that contain *edu* or *gov*. This means they are educational or government Web sites
- Web sites that show where they got the information (they show sources)

Remember that Web sites set up by only one person are more likely to contain opinions rather than facts. Carefully comparing several Web sites that discuss the same topic is a good way to decide if the information is reliable.

Practise the Skill

Choose one of the questions you wrote down about this region to research on the Internet.

Step 1
Input two or three keywords to start your Internet search. Make a list of five Web sites your search engine turns up. List the Web sites that seem reliable by copying and pasting the Web sites onto a Word document.

Step 2
From the first site, select two pieces of information. Record these, making sure to show the address of the Web site. It might look like this:
http://vancouver.ca/aboutvan.htm
- Vancouver is Host City of the 2010 Olympic and Paralympic Winter Games.
- Vancouver's climate is one of the mildest in Canada.

Step 3
Compare these to the information you find on the other sites. Do the different sites say the same thing? If so, then your information is likely to be true. If not, then you need to do further research.

Who First Lived in the Cordillera Region?

I wonder why people speak so many different languages in this region in the past and today.

Although the Cordillera region is fairly small, more than 100 different First Nations live here. First Nations living in different parts of the region developed different languages and ways of life. Although there was some trade between groups, they did not live close together. Groups also developed ways of life that suited their environment. Life was different in the northern mountains, compared to life on the coast.

First Nations of the Coast

The First Nations of the coast are closely connected to the forests, rivers, and ocean. In the spring, summer, and fall, families travelled from one village or camp to another within their territories. Areas were chosen that were good for fishing, hunting, gathering berries, or growing plants. In the winter, people gathered in large winter villages.

Skill Smart

- Check the map on pages 336–337 of the atlas section. What First Nations live in this region? Where did each group live?

Thinking It Through

- The First Nations of this region also developed a way to harvest cedar planks without killing the tree. Why do you think it was important to not kill the tree?

Voices of Canada

Tree of Life

Look at me friend!
I come to ask for your dress,
For you to have pity on us;
For there is nothing for which you cannot be used…
For you are really willing to give us your dress,
I come to beg you for this,
Long-life maker
For I am going to make a basket for lily-roots out of you.

Prayer of Kwakwaka'wakw women before taking bark form cedar tree— from the Royal BC Museum

What else do you think the tree was used for? Why do you think the First Nations would call the cedar the "tree of life"?

The First Nations living on the coast have always had a strong relationship with the sea. It was a source of food and a way to travel. The Haida First Nation built canoes that could be taken onto the ocean, and often travelled long distances. Many kinds of fish, plants, and animals like seals were used for food.

Read "Haida Culture" on this page. What can you learn about Guujaaw's relationship with the land?

First Nations of the Inland Areas

First Nations groups living inland, away from the coast, developed their own ways of living. For example, the Secwepemc [shuh-kwep-im] people built pit-houses in winter. These sheltered them from the cold. They made summer homes from bulrushes or animal hides.

Voices of Canada

Hunting in the Interior

Deer had many uses. The meat was eaten fresh and smoke-dried. The brains were used when tanning deer hides to make buckskin. Root-digging sticks were made from the deer's antlers. Awls, made from the deer's shinbones, were used by the women when they were weaving baskets. The deer was our most important animal.

Sam Mitchell, Salish First Nations

More About. . .

Chinook Jargon

"Chinook Jargon" is the name given to a special language that was developed among the different First Nations groups of this region. It was a language that included words from many different groups, and it was easy to learn. This way, there was one common language for the groups to use if they met with each other. Later, as European traders came to the region, French and English words were added. Often, the traders would learn and use Chinook Jargon as well.

Voices of Canada

Haida Culture

Haida culture is not simply song and dance, graven images, stories, language or even blood. It is all of those things and then... waking up on Haida Gwaii anticipating the season when the herring spawns. It is a feeling you get when you bring a feed of cockles to the old people, and when you are fixing up fish for the smokehouse, or when walking on barnacles or moss.

Guujaaw, Haida artist

Scientists can tell from these petroglyphs that the Secwepemc First Nation lived in this area. What else can the petroglyphs tell us about the past?

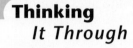
Thinking *It Through*

- Discuss the quotes on this page about the potlatch. Why do you think it was important for the ban to be fought?

Voices of Canada

The Potlatch

The Europeans didn't understand that [the potlatch] aimed towards giving to family and the community and against personal gain.

Kevin Cramner, Kwakwaka'wakw artist

Potlatches were still held in secret throughout the ban. This potlatch took place in Alert Bay, in 1900.

The Potlatch

A **potlatch** is an important event for some First Nations of the Cordillera region. It is a celebration that brings communities together to eat, sing, dance, and tell stories. Giving gifts at a potlatch ensured that the wealth of the community was shared. This was important in times of need. The potlatch is the centre of life.

European missionaries did not like the potlatch. They campaigned to have the potlatch banned. In 1884, the Canadian government passed a law that banned the potlatch.

First Nations fought against the law for many years. They believed that they had a right to observe their own laws. As one Kwakwaka'wakw chief said in 1896, "It is a strict law that bids us to distribute our property among our friends and neighbours. It is a good law." In 1951, the ban was lifted. The potlatch is once again an important part of life in many First Nations communities.

Making *a Difference*

The Commissioner's Potlatch

Judy Gingell was the first First Nations Commissioner for the Yukon Territory. In 1998, she and the Yukon Elder's Council held the first Commissioner's Potlatch in Whitehorse. It was a celebration, with dancers, singers, storytellers, and a feast. The event was open to  the public, and it was free. Judy Gingell has said that the potlatches were a common part of life for the First Nations in the Yukon, when people would get together and socialize. She knew that the potlatches were also events that passed on knowledge of First Nations ways of life, and that this made it important to share the potlatches with everyone. Today, the Commissioner's Potlatch is an annual event.

Who Were the First Europeans to Come to This Region?

In the late 1700s, British explorer James Cook came to the Cordillera region by ship. He was looking for a route between the Pacific and the Atlantic Oceans, and had sailed north along the coast. At Yuquot, on Nootka Island, he met with the Mowachaht/Muchalaht First Nations. Later, George Vancouver, one of Cook's officers, returned to further explore the region.

Europeans travelling across the land also came. Alexander Mackenzie was sent by the North West Company to find new sources of furs. Canoeing along rivers and travelling across the mountains in 1793, he became the first European to reach the Pacific Ocean by travelling across Canada.

Simon Fraser also explored this region for the North West Company. He built forts, such as Fort George, which would become the city of Prince George. In the early 1800s, he travelled farther west, down a river that would later be named after him. Eventually Fraser would follow that river to the Pacific Ocean.

Yuquot became known as "Friendly Cove." Why would it have gotten that name?

Voices of Canada

First Encounter

What was the reaction of the First Nations when Captain Cook arrived on Vancouver Island?

When Captain Cook first landed in Nootka Sound, the [people] didn't know what on earth [the ship] was. The Chief told them to try to understand what those people wanted and what they were after.
   Captain Cook must have told his crew to give the warriors some biscuits, and they started saying amongst themselves that they're friendly. Those people up there are friendly. We should be nice to them.

Winifred David, Mowachaht/Muchalaht First Nations

Routes of Mackenzie and Fraser

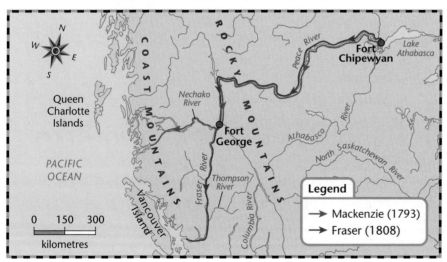

Fraser and Mackenzie both travelled by canoe, on rivers that were very dangerous. Why did one explorer follow a route north and the other south?

British Names

Many of the place names in this region reflect British influence. Some examples are British Columbia, Vancouver, Victoria, Prince Rupert, and the Queen Charlotte Islands.

Two New Colonies

British mapmaker David Thompson, who explored the Canadian Shield and the Interior Plains, also explored the Cordillera region for the North West Company. He mapped much of this region.

After joining the North West Company in 1821, the Hudson's Bay Company controlled most of what is now British Columbia. They set up trading posts, and in 1843 they built Fort Victoria. It is now the city of Victoria, on Vancouver Island.

Over time, two colonies developed under the direction of James Douglas, an HBC employee. One was on Vancouver Island, and was called the Colony of Vancouver Island. The other, on the mainland, was called New Caledonia.

THEN AND NOW

Fort Victoria, founded by the HBC, would be the capital of both the Colony of Vancouver Island and the colony of New Caledonia. The city of Victoria is now the capital of British Columbia. What can you tell about Victoria in the past and in the present from these two pictures?

? Critical Inquiry TIP

Retrieving

If you type *Simon Fraser* when searching on the Internet, you will find Web sites that include "Simon" or "Fraser." To find information about the explorer, put quotation marks around "Simon Fraser" and include the word *explorer* in your search.

Francophones in the Cordillera

The voyageurs were the first Francophones to come to this region. They travelled with explorer Alexander Mackenzie in the 1790s.

By the 1800s, Francophones made up more than half of the population of settlers in the region. The region's first newspaper, *The Victoria Gazette*, was followed by first French-language newspaper, *Le Courier de la Nouvelle Caledonie*, in the 1850s.

In 1889, a Francophone community called Maillardville developed near a sawmill on the Fraser River. Francophones from many parts of Canada moved to the community to work. Today, Maillardville is a part of Coquitlam, near Vancouver. There are streets named after Francophone settlers and bilingual signs.

Associations and organizations throughout the region work to bring together and support the Francophone community. There are French schools in Campbell River, Kelowna, and Prince George, to name a few. The British Columbia Family French Camp gives families with children of all ages the chance to camp and use French in a fun outdoor setting every summer.

Francophone Missionaries

In the mid-1800s, Roman Catholic missionaries started coming to this region to minister to people's spiritual, health, and education needs. In 1842, a Francophone priest, Father Demers, visited the interior of British Columbia, meeting many First Nations people. He later became the first Catholic bishop of Vancouver Island.

The Mercier Brothers

The Mercier brothers were born in Montréal. François-Xavier and Moïse Mercier left home at 18 to join the fur trade, and worked with the Hudson's Bay Company.

In 1869, François-Xavier built some of the first trading posts in the Yukon. Soon François-Xavier became known as the "King of the Fur Trade" in the North.

The Nanaimo **Bastion** was built in 1853 by the HBC, using French-Canadian construction methods. Léon Labine and Jean-Baptiste Fortier, both from Québec, designed the building. The main source of income at this fort was from coal, not furs. Find Nanaimo on the map on page 159 and discuss why.

words matter!

Bastion is a word that means "stronghold." Protection often is provided by a natural rock formation.

How do you think the Mercier brothers influenced the fur trade in the Yukon?

The Chinese and the CPR

In the late 1800s, the Canadian Pacific Railway was already being built in the Interior Plains region. The mountains of the Cordillera region were a challenge for the railway builders, and there were not enough workers. So the CPR hired thousands of workers from China.

Gold Mountain

The Chinese men who came to British Columbia called the province "Gold Mountain." Many came after hearing rumours of gold, which had already been discovered in the province. However, most of these men would work for the railway.

It was hard, dangerous work. Thousands of Chinese men worked on the railway, and hundreds died. The Chinese men were paid less than the European workers, and were expected to do some of the most dangerous work.

Read how Mary Chan describes what her grandfather told her about his life in the railway camps.

Skill Smart

- Find historic photos of the building of the railway. What do the photos tell you about the lives of the workers? Write a paragraph to share your thoughts.

Even though the work was dangerous and they were paid less, thousands of Chinese people still accepted jobs with the CPR. The wages were still better than what they earned in China. What does this say about their quality of life at that time?

Voices of Canada

Working on the Railway

Many people died during the construction of that railway. They lived in tents along the track and it was cold. Some people got arthritis. They were attacked by mosquitoes and black flies... And then, after it was finished, there was no more work.

Mary Chan

The Head Tax

Once the railway was finished, the Chinese were no longer welcomed in Canada. To stop more Chinese people from coming into Canada, the government required Chinese immigrants to pay what was called a "head tax." At first, each Chinese person entering Canada had to pay $50. This tax was later raised to $100 and then to $500. This was equal to the amount of money a Chinese immigrant could make in Canada after two years of work. How do you think this affected the Chinese people who wished to move to Canada?

The Chinese workers who stayed after the railway was built and those who came afterward worked in such jobs as forestry, fish canning, and coal mining. Other Chinese immigrants opened service businesses such as restaurants, stores, and laundries.

Examine this document carefully. How much did this man pay to enter Canada? Why would he still come?

The Chinese Community Today

Today, the Chinese community in the Cordillera region is one of the largest in Canada. New Chinese immigrants continue to arrive from places such as Hong Kong, Taiwan, and mainland China. About 70 percent of those newcomers settle in cities, such as Vancouver, Richmond, and Coquitlam.

People coming from China today include entrepreneurs, investors, and the self-employed. They create business in real estate, hotels, and advertising, making a large contribution to the region's economy. There are now three newspapers, two radio stations, and two television channels available in Chinese.

Voices of Canada

The Cheng Interchange

The Cheng Interchange in Kamloops honours Chinese workers who helped build the CPR.

Our grandfather was just one of many Chinese men who worked on this railway. These men accepted the risks involved and many perished; but most survived. Our family was fortunate that our grandfather not only survived, but also prospered after working for the CPR.

Kevan Jangze, Cheng Ging Butt's descendant

The Japanese Create Opportunities

The first Japanese settler in Canada was nineteen-year-old Manzo Nagano, who stowed away on a British ship in 1877. In 1977, the one hundredth anniversary of his arrival, the Canadian government celebrated the event by naming a mountain after Nagano. Mount Manzo Nagano is part of the Coast Mountains range.

Other Japanese immigrants followed. Some Japanese families settled along the Fraser River. They worked in canneries. This was hard work, but it allowed families to save enough money to invest in other businesses.

The Japanese Internment

During the Second World War (1939–1945), Japan was at war with the Allied countries, including Canada. Japanese people living in Canada were regarded as the enemy, even though many of them were Canadian citizens and had never been to Japan. In the Cordillera region, Japanese people were sent to internment camps in the interior of British Columbia. Their property, including their homes and businesses, was taken by the government.

When the war ended, the Japanese Canadians were released. Some moved to Japan. Others began their businesses again.

Japanese people, such as these shopkeepers in Victoria, often began their own businesses.

Thinking It Through

- How do you think experiences like the ones described here might shape the identity of Japanese Canadians?

Voices of Canada

Japanese-Canadian Family Memories

Aya Higashi was born in British Columbia. Here, she talks about her life before and after the internment.

My father was in charge of the fleet of fishing boats for the cannery. He fished only to take us out for the fun of fishing (we loved those outings) or to bring home salmon for the table.

[After the internment] everyone was scattered. You never knew where you were going and the people who were left behind didn't know if we would ever see each other again. There were heartbreaks.

Aya Higashi, Kaslo

The Sikhs Build Communities

In the early 1900s, several thousand Sikhs came to Vancouver from India. They had heard about the opportunities for work in Canada and wanted to make money for their families. Once in Canada, Sikhs took jobs in railway construction, forestry, and the lumber mills.

Despite poor treatment and poor pay, Sikhs stayed and built communities. In 1908, the first Sikh temple was built in Vancouver. This temple, and many others after it, would become the centre of Sikh communities. The temples were both places of worship and important social and community centres.

The Temple

Why would building the Vancouver Sikh Temple be a priority for the new community?

Our elders built this temple. There was a lot of bush and forest that had to be cleared first, big huge trees cut and cleared away by hand. It was a lot of work, but they built this temple with pride so that we would have a place of our own here.

Dhan Kaur Johal, 1908

Some Sikh men worked in sawmills in British Columbia. This photo was taken in the 1940s on the Queen Charlotte Islands.

The *Komagata Maru*

In 1908, the Canadian government passed a law called the Continuous Passage Act. This law stated that anyone who wished to emigrate from India to Canada could only do so if they came directly by ship, without stopping at any other port. Since no ships sailed directly from India to Canada, this law made sure that no more Indian people could come to Canada.

A man named Gurdit Singh thought this policy was wrong. In 1914, he arranged passage to Canada on a ship called the *Komagata Maru*. But when they reached Canada, they were still refused. After two months of waiting and arguing, the ship was sent away. Only 24 of the 400 passengers were allowed off the ship.

The *Komagata Maru*, 1914

How Are Natural Resources Used in the Cordillera Region?

How do natural resources affect where people live in this region?

Natural resources played an important role in the development of the Cordillera region. As you have seen, resources were important to the First Nations people. Natural resources also provided jobs and opportunities for other people who settled in the region.

Fishing

Do you like to eat salmon? The Pacific Ocean and the many rivers and lakes of the Cordillera region are a good source of fish, especially salmon. Most salmon are caught at the mouths of rivers, because they travel from the ocean and into the rivers to spawn, or deposit their eggs.

Fish are exported from this region to places all over the world. The fishing industry provides thousands of jobs for people here. However, because there is so much fishing, the number of some types of fish is decreasing.

Pacific salmon can be found in this region. What other kinds of fish can be caught here?

Hydroelectricity

The many rivers in this region are good sources for hydroelectric power. Factories that use electricity to operate have been built in the cities close to the hydroelectric plants. These factories, as well as the dams, provide people with jobs.

In order to supply hydroelectric power to the city of Kitimat, part of the Fraser River was dammed. The water was sent through a tunnel in the mountains. This blocked the salmon from spawning. This led to fewer salmon.

This is the hydroelectric dam on the Kootenay River. What other effects would a dam have on the environment?

Forestry

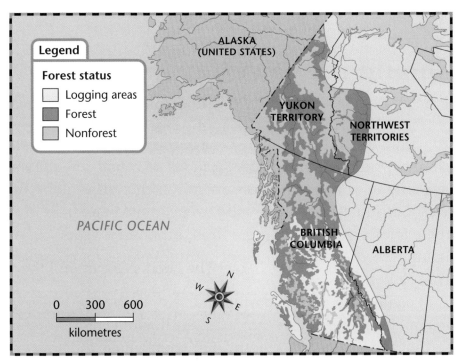

This map shows forestry areas in this region.

Legend

Forest status
- Logging areas
- Forest
- Nonforest

ALASKA
(UNITED STATES)

YUKON
TERRITORY

NORTHWEST
TERRITORIES

PACIFIC OCEAN

BRITISH
COLUMBIA

ALBERTA

0   300   600
kilometres

With much of the region covered in forests, the forestry industry has always been important. In the mid-1800s, lumber mills supplied wood for building the fast-growing towns. Now both wood and paper are exported to countries all around the Pacific Ocean. The Cordillera region helps make Canada the largest exporter of forest products in the world.

Skill Smart

- Research "clear-cutting" and "select cutting." Use a Cause and Effect chart to compare the two and determine your viewpoint.

Clear-cutting is the removal of all trees in an area. What are the advantages and disadvantages of this method?

A worker operates the conveyor belt to move boards in a Delta, B.C. sawmill. What are other jobs created by forestry?

175

Viewpoints

Should the Government Allow Clear-Cutting in Rainforests?

You read about the Kermode bear in the opening story of this chapter. Animals such as the Kermode bear and some plants live only in rainforests. These are forests that grow along the West Coast. Because of the mild, wet climate here, trees in these forests can live for more than a thousand years. Rainforests are often important spiritual places for coastal First Nations.

Logging is a very important industry in the Cordillera region. Everyone agrees that logging should be done carefully, so that the forests stay healthy. But people have different views on what this means. Clear-cutting is a method that many people debate.

Old-growth rainforests have never been logged before. They are home to many types of wildlife and have trees that do not grow anywhere else in Canada.

CLEAR-CUTTING QUESTIONED

Logging in Fraser Valley Provides Jobs

Stopping logging in the Fraser Valley would have huge effects on a large number of people.

Bruce Fraser, Forest Practices Board

Back in the old days, [people valued] timber, employment, and wealth—and that kind of forestry gave people what they wanted. Now society wants protection of nature, and that means forestry has to change.

Hamish Kimmins, ecologist

Forests should be left alone. We need to take a few cedars to make canoes and build longhouses. But the areas that have been logged don't always come back. Some logged areas have just gone dead.

Corbett George, Ahousaht First Nation Elder

The spotted owl is an old-growth dependent species. [We have] a special resource management area for the spotted owl, and the government has allowed logging in that area.

Gwen Barlee, Western Canada Wilderness Committee

Re-growing these sorts of [forests] isn't a problem. Most of the saplings that are growing on this site won't have been planted, they'll be regenerating naturally.

Andy Mackinnon, ecologist

Over to **You**

1. In a small group, identify the different points of view. What are some logging challenges? Do any of the points of view show bias? How?

2. What are some possible solutions to the challenges discussed? Use technology to keep a record of your suggestions.

Natural Disaster: Forest Fire

With all of the forests in the Cordillera region, a fire can cause a lot of damage. That is just what happened in the summer of 2003, when a bolt of lightning set fire to trees on a rocky slope above Okanagan Lake. Within minutes, 911 took the first calls from anxious cottagers across the lake. They had good reason to be concerned.

The southern Cordillera region was suffering the driest summer in almost 75 years. **Wildfires** were already burning in many areas.

By mid-afternoon, the fire was out of control. It was headed toward the city of Kelowna. By the time it had burned out almost three weeks later, the blaze had destroyed 256 square kilometres of forest land. It had forced 30 000 people out of their homes. It had destroyed 238 houses—223 of them in a single night!

It took thousands of firefighters, loggers, heavy equipment operators, and Canadian Forces personnel to put out the fires that burned for weeks around Kelowna.

Voices of Canada

Disaster

It was scary when we heard a couple of firefighters were trapped. We thought it was [my dad]—he was working in the same area.

Lucas Belgrove, 14 year old

Helping Out

People sure came together. It taught us that "love thy neighbour" really means something.

Alisa Brownlee, resident who lost her home

The Community Responds

More than 1000 volunteers worked together to help people who were affected by the fires. They donated food, clothing, shelter, and money. Kelowna's mayor, Walter Gray, said, "While tragedy struck and destroyed hundreds of our neighbours' homes, we still have so much to be thankful for. Most importantly, we lost no lives."

Mining

In the Cordillera region, there are more than 14 000 mineral deposits! This region is the largest producer of copper in Canada. The many mines and mineral quarries provide lots of jobs for people in this region. Quarries are open pits from which minerals or stones are dug.

Many of the mining towns in the Cordillera region have gone through the natural resources cycle. When much of the coal was used up in the early 1900s, some mines had to close. People had to find new jobs, so many moved away. Later, new methods were developed to obtain coal in other areas. This led to the growth of new towns.

The huge smelter-refinery at Trail processes ore from British Columbia, the Yukon, and the Northwest Territories.

Some Mining Areas in the Cordillera

Legend
- ○ Gold
- ▲ Silver
- ▲ Copper
- ■ Coal

ALASKA (UNITED STATES)

Dawson City

YUKON TERRITORY

NORTHWEST TERRITORIES

PACIFIC OCEAN

Stewart

BRITISH COLUMBIA

ALBERTA

Logan Lake

Trail

0   200   400
kilometres

Use an atlas to find out which towns have been built near these resources.

More About...

Quesnel

The Quesnel River, Quesnel Lake, and the town of Quesnel are named after Jules Maurice Quesnel, a Canadien who travelled with Simon Fraser when he was exploring the Fraser River in 1808.

words matter!

Prospectors are people who search for valuable minerals such as gold.

Skookum Jim Mason, a member of the Tagish First Nation, became very rich mining gold on Bonanza Creek. He would later leave money to support other First Nations people living in the Yukon.

The Cariboo Gold Rush

In 1861, gold was discovered in a creek near a town called Quesnel. This was the beginning of the "Cariboo Gold Rush." Several towns grew around this gold rush, such as Barkerville, which is now a heritage site. Getting the gold out of the area proved to be a big challenge. The Cariboo Wagon Road was created just for this. It was a project that took engineers and other workers years to finish.

The Trans-Canada Highway now follows much of the old route of the Cariboo Wagon Road through the Fraser Canyon.

The Yukon Gold Rush

On August 16, 1896, **prospectors** named George and Kate Carmack, and Kate's brother, "Skookum" Jim Mason, discovered gold in a creek that ran into the Klondike River in the Yukon. The creek would later be called Bonanza Creek. However, only George Carmack would receive credit for the discovery.

News of the gold discovery travelled fast. Within weeks, people came to "the Klondike" from many parts of North America, hoping to find gold and get rich. About 100 000 people came to the area within a few years! It is not surprising that this period is called the Gold Rush.

Some people became wealthy finding gold. More often, though, people lost everything because they had spent all of their money travelling to the isolated region. If they could not find gold, they had to find other ways to survive. Many left the region after the Gold Rush. In Dawson City, the population dropped from 40 000 to less than 5000 in just a few years.

THEN AND NOW

Dawson City was founded in 1896. Within six months there were already 500 houses.

Today, Dawson City has a population of about 2000 people. That number changes when 60 000 tourists come to see the city every year!

What's in a Name?

Dawson City was not the only town built for all the newcomers during the Gold Rush. Towns and some landforms got new names. Here are a few of the place names from that period:

Forty Mile   **Bonanza**   **Quesnel**

WOUNDED MOOSE   **GOLDBOTTOM**

Champagne

Skill Smart

- Choose one of the place names above. Then do some research to find out more about the place. Is it still there? Why was it given its name? Has it changed over time?

In 1999, the Klondike Snowmobile Association and the Territorial Government signed an agreement to make the Dempster Highway part of the Trans Canada Trail. That makes this part of the trail the only one to cross the Arctic Circle! It starts just east of Dawson City, and connects to the Arctic Ocean more than 500 km to the north. Find Dawson City on the map on page 159.

People of the Klondike

Many people came to the Yukon during the Gold Rush and made their homes there. People came from all over Canada and the United States. They also came from other countries, such as Britain.

Robert Service came to Canada from England when he was 21 years old. In Whitehorse, Service wrote poetry about the Yukon and the Gold Rush. Read part of his poem called *"The Spell of the Yukon."* How do you think he felt about the region?

Voices of Canada

A British Poet in the Yukon

There's gold, and it's haunting and haunting;
It's luring me on as of old;
Yet it isn't the gold that I'm wanting
So much as just finding the gold.
It's the great, big, broad land way up yonder,
It's the forests where silence has lease;
It's the beauty that thrills me with wonder,
It's the stillness that fills me with peace.

Skill Smart

■ Think about the resources and physical geography of the Yukon and the needs of people. Make a web showing jobs, other than mining, that might be available in the Yukon.

Émilie Tremblay was born in Québec. She and her husband came to the Yukon in 1894. They mined gold, and Émilie also owned a clothing store. Émilie was well known for her commitment to her community. She founded organizations, welcomed travellers and missionaries into her home, and knitted socks for soldiers during World War I. A Francophone school in Whitehorse is named after her. How else might Francophone settlers have affected life in the Yukon?

Why Were the North-West Mounted Police Sent to the Yukon?

Towns grew quickly during the Gold Rush. There was no police force. A missionary in the Yukon wrote in 1893: "Oh, for some police or anyone to keep order!"

In 1894, the North-West Mounted Police were sent to the Yukon to bring order during the Gold Rush. New offices were built in every major mining area of the Yukon. The North-West Mounted Police dealt with thousands of people, settling disputes and maintaining order.

I think that the North-West Mounted Police helped make the Yukon a good place for people to live. What might have happened if they didn't come?

What does the need for the presence of the North-West Mounted Police in the Yukon tell about life in that area, at that time?

Voices of Canada

Lack of Law

Neither law nor order prevailed; honest persons had no protection from the gang of rascals...
Might was right; murder, robbery, and petty theft were common occurrences.

Sir Sam Steele, RCMP Superintendent

Skill Smart

- How might different people, such as traders, business owners, or miners, have reacted to the arrival of the NWMP? Create a chart to record your thoughts.

What Are Ways of Life in the Cordillera Region Today?

Ways of life in the Cordillera region can be very different, depending on where people live.

Life Inland

Only a tiny part of the Cordillera region is good for farming. However, this region produces five percent of Canada's fruit and vegetables!

Have you ever bitten into a juicy peach? Perhaps it came from British Columbia's Okanagan Valley! The fertile soil in this valley is good for growing fruit, so there are many orchards and vineyards. There is not much rain in this part of the region, though. Water from the many lakes in the valley is used to irrigate the land.

Some Fruits Grown in the Cordillera Region

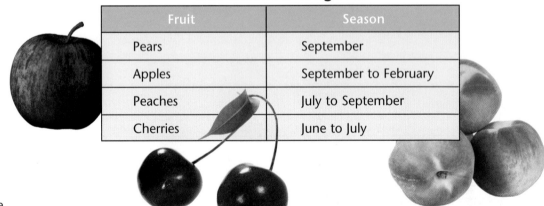

Fruit	Season
Pears	September
Apples	September to February
Peaches	July to September
Cherries	June to July

Cranberries are one of the many crops grown in the fertile Fraser Valley.

Farming

Many people farm in the Fraser Valley. The mild temperatures, good rainfall, and fertile soil make this area perfect for growing cranberries, strawberries, corn, and other crops.

The area around Kamloops gets very little rain, but the large, open areas with rolling hills are perfect for cattle to graze. Many people work on big cattle ranches.

Voices of Canada

Ranching

I work at Duck Ranch, a cattle ranch in the central interior of British Columbia. There are upwards of 300 cows down here. It's spring, so we could have maybe 10 or 20 newborns this morning. This big hayfield in the bottom of the valley is a good place for the cows to give birth. It's out of the wind, and we can keep an eye on them.

When the snow is gone, I'll help herd these cattle onto forested land. I will spend most of the summer making hay, mending fences, and doing other chores that keep a ranch running. In the fall, I'll go back into the hills to bring the herd home. I'll spend the winter feeding them in some sheltered corner of the valley.

A cowboy's job can be hard and often dangerous. But I love it. Sometimes I find a sick calf. I doctor it, and a few days later it's going strong. There's a lot of satisfaction in that. It's more than a job. This is a whole way of life. We get to live in this beautiful place. I couldn't stand to live in the city.

Alan Walsh, rancher

Cowboy Alan Walsh loves the peacefulness of working on a ranch in the mountains.

How is ranch life in the Cordillera region different from my way of life in Kamloops?

Skill Smart

- Using a Venn diagram, look at the similarities and differences between ranch life in the Cordillera and your own life in your region.

? Critical Inquiry TIP

Evaluating

Learning what others felt about the information you have shared can help you learn more about your inquiry. You could conduct a short survey to find out what others are thinking.

Life in Port Cities

Imagine living in a place with the ocean on one side and mountains on the other. Vancouver is such a place. You can even see people snowboarding and sailing on the same winter day!

Because it is an ice-free port, many ships come to Vancouver from places all around the Pacific Ocean. That is why the stores here have goods from many countries. The harbour is a great place to boat, swim, or fish. Since it is beside the ocean, Vancouver has mild temperatures and a lot of rain. But the people here do not let the rain stop them from doing things.

Vancouver is also the endpoint of the transcontinental railway, so a lot of businesses have been drawn here. With all the people in this city, there is a lot of traffic, especially on the bridges. These bridges connect the different parts of Vancouver, which is surrounded by water on three sides.

Another city with an ice-free port is Victoria. It is on Vancouver Island, so people come here from the mainland by ferry or by air. The very mild and wet climate allows the people to enjoy beautiful gardens year round.

Butchart Gardens is just one of the many beautiful gardens in the area around Victoria, also known as the "City of Gardens."

Vancouver is one of the most culturally diverse cities in the world. People come from many different backgrounds and have different cultures. What languages are spoken in your community or school?

Life on the Islands

Like those who live in cities on the coast, people who live on the islands also experience mild weather. There are small farms on some of the Gulf Islands and Vancouver Island. Many tourists come to the small communities and parks on these islands to enjoy the natural beauty and animals of this part of the region.

I'm going to check an atlas to learn more about the islands off the coast of the Cordillera region.

On the west side of Vancouver Island, the ocean can be quite rough. The West Coast Trail was made a long time ago so that shipwrecked sailors could find their way to safety. This trail is now part of Pacific Rim National Park and is used by hikers today.

Voices of Canada

Robert Davidson, a Haida artist, grew up on Haida Gwaii. He talked about his connection to the land during an interview.

[The Haida people] have a strong belief in the hundreds of supernatural beings. Our art illustrates this movement between humans, other beings, and landforms. This movement connects us to the land.

I reconnect with the land every time I go home. For example, I can eat fresh seafood right from the water beside me. In the modern world, I think, there is too much separation from the land.

Robert Davidson, Haida artist

This is a painting by Robert Davidson, called *Eagles*.

Thinking *It Through*

■ How do you think Robert Davidson's painting "Eagles" shows his connection to the natural environment? Find out more about Davidson and the work of other West Coast artists.

Use the Internet

In a small group, use the Internet to find out how schools in British Columbia are working to protect the salmon. Use the steps in the Skill Power on page 163 to help with your research. Brainstorm and record some ways your class could help. Pick an idea, and take action. Afterwards, send an e-mail or write a letter to a school in British Columbia and describe what you did.

Research British Settlements

Find out more about the early British settlements in the Cordillera region. Why were they started? What did they become? Who lived in the area first? Who lives there now?

Read the Newspaper

Look in your local newspaper, community newsletter, or on the Internet. Find articles about what people in your region are doing to protect the land, water, and forests. Come up with a plan that you can implement with your classmates that would contribute to the protection of the environment in your region. With the help of your teachers and parents, take the steps to put the plan into action.

Putting It All Together

While I was researching the different people who live in Vancouver, I found out more about how many people speak different languages there. I found the numbers on a government Web site and kept the information on a chart. I wonder how the numbers will change as more people move to the city.

Language	Percentage of People Who Speak That Language
English	49
Chinese	26
Punjabi	2.7
Tagalog	2.4
Vietnamese	2.2
French	1.7
Others	16

Review the inquiry questions for this chapter:
- Identify ways that the landscape of this region affects ways of life.
- What is the balance between the use of natural resources and sustaining the environment in this region?

Take Time to Reflect

Before you go on to the next chapter, think about what you learned in this one. What are the areas in this region that may need protection? How do human activities, such as forestry, affect the region? Using Simon Jackson's experience as an example, write a short plan of action to show how you could be a leader in the protection of the environment. Save your work for your Canada Collection.

Arctic Region

Life in the North

What would it be like to live on another planet? Samson Ootoovak knows what it might be like to live on Mars! Samson is an Inuk, and grew up in the Arctic region. He knows about living in extreme environments. When he was an engineering student, Samson joined the Haughton-Mars Project.

With a group of scientists from around the world, Samson lived in a research station on Devon Island, an island in Nunavut. They tested technology that was being developed for use on Mars. They studied the island's landscape and climate. They saw the sun cast shadows over the land. They felt bone-chilling winds whip in from the Arctic Ocean, and they watched sea ice float away from the coast.

The landscape and climate of Canada's Far North has more in common with Mars than with any other place on Earth. Scientists believe that by studying places such as Devon Island, we can learn how to live on Mars and in other extreme places!

Samson has said he would like to be the first Inuk astronaut!

Canada: Our Stories Continue

Canada's Arctic region is sometimes called the land of the midnight sun. The Inuit who live in Nunavut, the main territory in the region, call the area "our land." The region has rocky valleys, high sea cliffs, thick ice, huge snowdrifts, and frozen lakes. People who live in this region have to be prepared for extreme cold; long, dark winters; and endless sunshine in summer!

? Critical Inquiry TIP

Creating

Electronic files, journals, and photos are some different ways you might use technology to record information.

? Inquiring Minds

Here are some questions to guide your inquiry for this chapter:

- Explain how different communities have adapted to the climate and geography of the region.
- Has change always been good for people in the Arctic? Explain.

Let's Explore the Arctic

Hello! My name is Katie Tikivik. I am Inuk, and I live in Arviat, in Nunavut. Arviat is on the coast of Hudson Bay.

The aurora borealis, or northern lights, provide a colourful display in the northern night sky for much of the year.

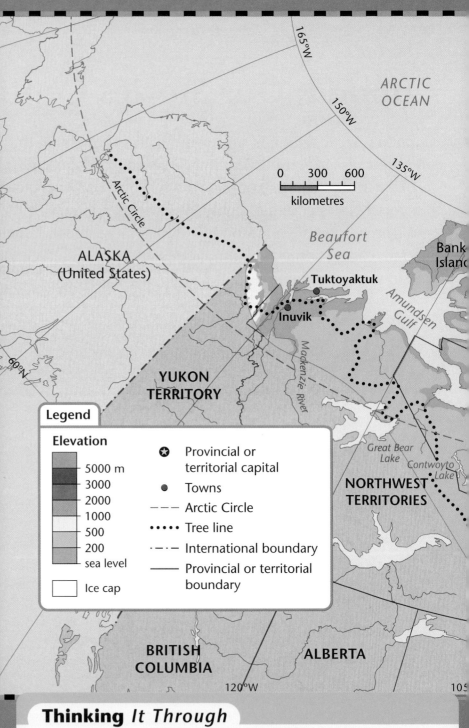

ARCTIC OCEAN

Arctic Circle

ALASKA (United States)

165°W

150°W

135°W

0   300   600
kilometres

Beaufort Sea

Bank Island

Tuktoyaktuk

Inuvik

Amundsen Gulf

60°N

YUKON TERRITORY

Mackenzie River

Great Bear Lake

Contwoyto Lake

NORTHWEST TERRITORIES

Legend

Elevation

5000 m
3000
2000
1000
500
200
sea level

Ice cap

⭐ Provincial or territorial capital

● Towns

— — Arctic Circle

•••• Tree line

—·—·— International boundary

——— Provincial or territorial boundary

BRITISH COLUMBIA

ALBERTA

120°W

105

Thinking *It Through*

■ Look at the map and the photos of this region. What challenges does the geography of the Arctic region present to the people who live here?

Region!

Map labels:

Alert

Ellesmere Island

Nares Strait

Queen Elizabeth Islands

Grise Fiord

Parry Islands

105°W

90°W

Devon Island

75°W

60°W

45°W

75°N

Baffin Bay

Davis Strait

Victoria Island

Baffin Island

NUNAVUT

Iglulik

Pangnirtung

Cumberland Sound

Ellice River

Foxe Basin

Back River

Thelon River

Baker Lake

Southampton Island

Cape Dorset

Iqaluit

Frobisher Bay

Hudson Strait

60°N

Arviat

Hudson Bay

QUÉBEC

N E S W

MANITOBA

90°W

75°W

Inuit whalers search for beluga whales in the Mackenzie Delta. In Canada today, some First Nations are the only groups legally allowed to hunt whales. In the Arctic, the hunt is managed by the Inuit and the government.

Long distances between communities in this region mean that most goods arrive by airplane. How might this affect ways of life in this region?

Iqaluit is the capital of Nunavut.

Skill Smart

- Make a chart to record the latitude and longitude of Iqaluit, Inuvik, Alert, and Katie's community, Arviat. What do you notice about the latitude readings?

The Arctic Region

Some of the islands in my region are the largest in the world! I wonder what the other big islands in Canada are.

The Arctic region includes a thin band of land along the coasts of the Yukon and the Northwest Territories, as well as all of Nunavut. There are desolate areas such as Devon Island, but other parts of the region have tundra, mountains, rivers, and lakes. Muskox, wolves, caribou, fox, and polar bears are found in this region. Whales, seals, and many kinds of fish are found in the rivers, lakes, and ocean. These animals have always provided the Inuit with what they need to survive.

Roots of the Region

The Inuit have always lived in this region. The traditional land of the Inuit has always been in what is now Nunavut, and in the many islands of the region. Inuit also live in the coastal areas of the Northwest Territories and the Yukon.

Europeans were first drawn to the North by the promise of a sea route to the Pacific. This route would later be called the Northwest Passage. Whaling stations were established along the coast, but were only used in summer, when ships could sail in the ice-free water. The possibility that the region might be rich in copper and gold encouraged Europeans to explore the interior.

The Arctic region has short summers, but the Arctic poppy can still grow there. What other plants grow in this region?

Why People Live Here Today

The Inuit continue to live in the region, as do the descendants of some of the Europeans who came to the region long ago. Other people come from the southern parts of Canada to work in the Arctic region.

The region has many natural resources such as copper, gold, zinc, and oil. Mining for diamonds is beginning in Nunavut. People work in service industries, or for the government. The natural beauty of the region and outdoor activities are enjoyed by many residents.

Voices of Canada

A Sea Poem

The great sea
Has sent me adrift;
It moves me
Like a reed in a great
    river.

Uvavnuk, an Iglulik woman, recorded by Knud Rasmussen in the 1800s

What Affects Quality of Life in the Arctic Region?

Here is how the land, water, other natural resources, and climate affect quality of life for some people in the Arctic region.

Tourists visit the region and buy jewellery, carvings, and paintings made by local people. A lot of Inuit art tells about the land, water, and animals that can be found in the Arctic region. Shops help the community and support the artists.

Tourists who come to Ellesmere Island National Park arrive by helicopter. Here they can see glaciers, muskox, and Arctic fox—on Canada's most northerly island. Parks in this region protect rare plants and endangered wildlife.

The long distances between communities and camps in the Arctic region mean that people need to use different technologies to find their way as they travel. People sometimes travel overland or on the water, and there are not many roads. Global Positioning System (GPS) technology can help travellers find their way home.

Thinking *It Through*

■ How might the land, water, other natural resources, and climate affect the type of work people do in Canada's Arctic region?

Katie's Inquiry

? **Critical Inquiry TIP**

Retrieving

Postcards, brochures, and guidebooks may provide information about the land, people, and history of an area.

My dad works for the Government of Canada. He goes on trips to different parks in the Arctic region. He works with local people to set up visitor centres, write guidebooks, or design Web sites about the land, animals, trees, and plants in the park. He also finds out stories about the people who have lived there in the past, and people who still live there today.

My dad just sent me a postcard from Qaummaarviit [how-mar-veet] Territorial Historic Park. It is on Baffin Island, near Iqaluit. How our ancestors lived long ago is shown by evidence found in the park.

The postcards make me want to ask:
- Why did people choose to live there?
- How can I learn more about them?
- Is life different in the area today? How?

I'm going to ask my dad if he can take some photographs, too. Until he gets back, I'm going to visit the library and look for answers to my questions. I'll also e-mail my cousins in Iqaluit to see if they can help. Then I'll create a presentation to show what I have learned.

Qaummaarviit Territorial Historic Park

There are remains of sod houses and rock rings. You can see whale bones that were used to make the roof.

Qaummaarviit Territorial Historic Park

Skill Smart

■ Brainstorm two questions you have about the Arctic region with a partner. Record your questions on the computer. Save your work so you can go back to this file when you have information to add.

SKILL POWER

Sharing Information with Others

When Katie prepared her presentation, she thought about the best way to share information. There are a few things to think about when making a presentation or a display.

Why?	Who?	What?
Why are you sharing your information?	**Who are the people you will be presenting to?**	**What will you use to present your information?**
Are you trying to • persuade? • inform? • entertain? • examine?	• classmates? • family members? • friends? • strangers? • Elders? • teachers?	• an essay? • an oral presentation? • a song? • a poem? • a dance? • a PowerPoint® or multimedia presentation?

Practise the Skill

1. Plan a presentation about a park or historical site in the Arctic region. Consider your purpose, your audience, and a creative way to present your information to your audience.

Where Do People Live in the Arctic Region?

I am Inuk, and my ancestors have always lived in Canada's Arctic region. I wonder why other groups of people have come here.

Many of the people who live in the Arctic region are Inuit. The Inuit have always lived along the coastal areas and deep inlets of this region. People traditionally lived where they could find the resources they needed to survive. Today, many Inuit are working hard to preserve traditional ways of life, such as hunting and fishing, culture, and language.

Most settlements in the Arctic region are along the coast. There are very few settlements inland. Why do you think there are so few Inuit settlements inland? What does this tell you about the traditional ways of life of the Inuit?

Voices of Canada

Arviat

This student at Nunavut Arctic College has watched her community grow.

I've been living in Arviat since I was born. As I grow up, everything changes very slowly and we see new people. The population is getting bigger, but they still have their culture.

Albina Aggark, Arviat, 1989

More About. . .

The Population of the North

- The Arctic region makes up more than 20 percent of Canada's land area, but less than 22 000 people live in the region. That is less than one tenth of one percent!
- The Inuit make up more than 85 percent of the population of Nunavut.

Cape Dorset is located on Baffin Island. What are the advantages of the location of Cape Dorset? Why would this be a good place for a settlement?

Inuit Communities

For the Inuit, the birds, animals, sea, mountains, tundra, and ice were part of everyday life. From their environment, the Inuit obtained everything they needed to live. They developed ways of dealing with extreme cold and frozen land. They lived with the environment, understanding and respecting the animals, weather, seasons, land, sea, and ice.

The bison were an important resource for the First Nations of the plains. Just as important to the Inuit are seals, walrus, fish, and caribou. These animals provided food, clothing, cooking oil, and other items. The Inuit travelled along the coast, hunting and fishing. They used tents in the summer and igluit (iglus) in the winter for shelter. What do the Voices of Canada on this page tell about Inuit ways of life?

Voices of Canada

Sheila Watt-Cloutier travelled by dogsled when she was a child.

My earliest memories are being connected to the rhythms and cycles of nature through the traditional way of travelling on the dogteam through this vast, majestic, wonderful arctic land.

Sheila Watt-Cloutier, 2006

How might new and larger communities affect the caribou herds and the people who depend on them?

Voices of Canada

Inuit Families

Each family spent much of the year travelling, setting up camps wherever food was available. Extended families were very important and would gather with others when the seasons and availability of food permitted. These were times of great joy and feasting—times for stories, singing, drumming, eating, playing, and chatting.

Rachel Attituq Qitsualik, Pond Inlet, 1999

Many Inuit continue with traditional ways, but also use modern technology. How might this be reflected in their communities?

Pangnirtung is beside a deep fjord on Baffin Island. It began as a whaling station.

Inuit Communities in the Past

Inuit lands have always stretched across what is now Greenland, Russia, Alaska, and Canada. The Inuit lived and worked together with their families. Elders and other adults taught young children the ways of the land, animals, and how to survive in the Arctic. Groups followed and hunted caribou, and travelled to other areas to fish, depending on the season.

Parents and grandparents had many ways to teach their children how to survive in the North. Games, songs, dances, art, and storytelling were some of the ways. During summer, families would teach their children how to make tools out of parts of seal, walrus, whale, and other animals. Children gathered eggs from the nests of wild birds on the tundra. Summer homes were tents made of seal or caribou skins. In winter, several families would camp together and make their igluit.

The arrival of Europeans in the 1800s brought changes to this way of life. New products such as guns, pots, and cloth made Inuit life easier. Many Inuit gave up their traditional lifestyle and set up permanent settlements near European whaling stations. They began working for Europeans so they could get the goods they wanted.

Making *a Difference*

Tracking Wildlife in Nunavut

The Nunavut Wildlife Management Board (NWMB) works to keep track of the wildlife in Nunavut. The project relies on youth, Elders, and scientists to ensure the protection and wise use of wildlife and the environment in Nunavut. The Elders contribute their wisdom about animals, and scientists add their scientific knowledge. This Board enables the Inuit to be involved in decision making about preserving the land and animals. They also have a say in the future development of Nunavut.

The muskox is one of the animals that the NWMB studies and manages. Every year, the board rules on how many muskoxen can be hunted.

Some projects the NWMB have paid for include determining the range of caribou, the number of polar bears in a certain area, and identifying the types of whales found in the north. The NWMB provides materials to schools and a Web site for children to help them understand the importance of wildlife in the North.

The NWMB consults Inuit hunters about wildlife in Nunavut. The hunters tell them what kinds of animals and birds they see, and where they see them.

Scientists also go out on the land to study wildlife for the NWMB.

Thinking *It Through*

- Why do you think it is important that organizations like the NWMB involve the Inuit in decision making?
- What role can Inuit Elders play in the work of the NWMB?

Inuit Communities Today

Inuit people live a contemporary and traditional lifestyle that includes living in modern homes, and driving snowmobiles and vehicles. Inuit people use the Internet, watch satellite TV and commonly use cellphones. Traditional ways continue to be an important part of life, and in the spring and summer, whole communities might return to the land for hunting and fishing.

Iqaluit has seen a lot of changes in the past few years. New roads, buildings, schools, and a skateboard park have been built. Here is what some Iqaluit residents think of the changes.

Thinking It Through

- What do the Voices of Canada on this page tell about life in Iqaluit? How do you think Inuit communities in the region have changed over time?

Voices of Canada

Iqaluit Today

I feel that Iqaluit has changed positively, like how the city is paving roads.

Elissa McKinnon

I think Iqaluit is becoming a very prosperous city.

Scott Flieger

There are a lot more things to do, and friendly people.

Anne Mullin

Skill Smart

- Find out more about Inuit inventions. How did these inventions affect quality of life?

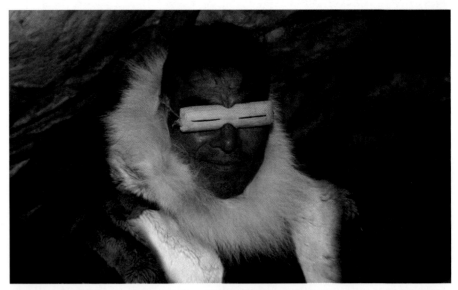

The Inuit invented sunglasses. Why do you think sunglasses are a necessary item in the North?

Iqaluit: A Government Town

Nunavut is Canada's only territory where the government follows mainly Inuit traditions. Iqaluit is the capital city of Nunavut. With a population of nearly 4000, it is the largest settlement in the Arctic region. Iqaluit is the centre for government. Many of the people who live here work for the government. People who do business with the government also live in Iqaluit. Often these people only live in Iqaluit for a few years, then move back to southern Canada.

Government workers in the North might speak one of the many **official languages** in Nunavut. **Inuktitut**, English, and French are all recognized as official languages by the Nunavut territorial government.

The government in Nunavut has restored cultural traditions by working with Inuit Elders. It works on a consensus model to reach agreements, and all members work together to resolve issues.

Many Francophones work for the government in Iqaluit and live throughout the Arctic region, from Inuvik in the west, to Iqaluit in the east. Francophones living in the North come from all parts of Canada, but most are from Québec. They have a newsletter called *Le Nunavoix*. A Francophone school, the École de Trois-Soleils, serves the community in Iqaluit.

words matter!

Inuktitut is the language of the Inuit. It is used in homes, schools, on the radio and on TV, and by the government of Nunavut. Language and culture are very important in Nunavut, which is why Inuktitut is recognized there as an official language.

Official Languages are ones that have equal status in the government. Canada has two official languages—English and French.

The Nunavut legislative building in Iqaluit was designed for a cold environment. How do you think this design is beneficial?

Inuit musician Susan Aglukark writes songs that show her ties to the land and to the past. She also sings songs that have been passed down through generations. How does this reflect her identity?

Radio, television, and newspapers are important ways for people to hear about their communities. The Aboriginal Peoples Television Network (APTN) and CBC North provide radio and television news and entertainment to people in the Arctic region. Local shows in Inuktitut are produced by CBC North in Iqaluit and Rankin Inlet. These shows cover local current events. The program *Sinnaksautit* features traditional Inuit storytelling. CBC North has a daily evening television newscast in Inuktitut called *Igalaaq*. It covers local, national, and international news. Nunavut newspapers, such as the *Nunatsiaq News* and the *Kivalliq News*, are published in Inuktitut and English. They are also available on the Internet.

More About. . .

Iqaluit Today

- 60 percent of the population of Iqaluit is Inuit.
- On January 1, 1987, the community changed its name from Frobisher Bay to Iqaluit, the name the Inuit have always used.
- For thousands of years, the site has been a camping and fishing spot. The name Iqaluit means "place of fish."
- At the end of April, Iqaluit celebrates the coming of spring with the Toonik Tyme festival, featuring games, dogsled races, iglu-building contests, and entertainment.

Iqaluit is a fast-growing city. It is also the most northerly capital city in Canada.

Thinking *It Through*

■ What challenges do communities in the North face? Think about how people work, travel, and communicate. What do you think might help solve these challenges?

Why Did the First Explorers Come to the Arctic Region?

Beginning in the 1500s, explorers from Europe began sailing into the waters of the Arctic region. They hoped to find a way to sail from the Atlantic Ocean to the Pacific Ocean. Their explorations into this region would lead to new discoveries and close contact with the Inuit.

The Northwest Passage

Between 1576 and 1578, Martin Frobisher, an explorer from England, made three voyages into the Arctic Ocean. Although he did not discover the Northwest Passage, Frobisher Bay is named after him.

Alexander Mackenzie learned from First Nations people about river routes to the northern sea. In the late 1700s, he explored what would become the Mackenzie River, following it to the Arctic Ocean. Although he did not find the Northwest Passage, Mackenzie became the first European to cross the continent by land, from east to west.

In the 1800s, explorers were able to map the many islands in the Arctic region. Often their ships were trapped in the ice when winter set in. Some expeditions were trapped for years, and often the sailors would rely on the local Inuit for help. Some were not so lucky. The voyage headed by Sir John Franklin, also an English explorer, would end in the deaths of himself and his crew.

 Tuktoyaktuk is the Arctic trailhead of the Trans Canada Trail. This community is close to the Mackenzie Delta, which is where the Mackenzie River enters the Arctic Ocean.

Thinking *It Through*

- Look at the map of the Arctic region on pages 192–193. Why might it have been difficult to find a route from the Atlantic Ocean to the Pacific Ocean?

Wooden ships that were used in Arctic explorations were reinforced with iron. What kinds of ships sail in the Arctic Ocean today?

The houses built in Qaummaarviit Territorial Historic Park were built with whale bones. This shows that people in the Arctic were hunting whales a long time ago.

More About. . .

Disease in the North

In the 1600s, only 87 diseases were known to the First Nations. There were about 30 000 diseases known to the Europeans. When the Europeans became ill, they often spread the diseases to the First Nations, who had no immunity because the sicknesses were new to them. The chicken pox and the flu often killed whole families of Inuit. How would this impact Inuit communities?

The Whalers

Before petroleum oil was used to make perfumes and fuel, whale oil was used to make these things. As early as the 1500s, whalers from Europe knew that many whales lived in the Arctic Ocean.

By the 1600s, European whalers were coming every year to the Arctic region. They began to trade with the Inuit, who were already experienced whalers. The Inuit had always used whales for food and fuel, and they now traded this skill for new things from across the ocean. They traded for tools, cloth, metal goods, and food such as biscuits.

The Inuit were also hired to be pilots, hunters, and seamstresses by the whalers. Their knowledge of the land, the water, and the many islands would be very important to the whalers.

The most important location for whaling in the Arctic region became Cumberland Sound. There, whalers established the first permanent whaling stations, and lived there year round.

Over time, the Inuit and the Hudson's Bay Company also began a fur trade. Fur from Arctic animals, such as Arctic fox, caribou, and seals, were traded for European goods.

Find Cumberland Sound and the community of Pangnirtung on the map on pages 192–193. Why do you think this location would be a good spot for a whaling community?

Living in Canada's North Today

People think of the Arctic as a very icy, snowy place. However, more snow could fall in another region of Canada than in the Arctic region! The snow that does fall stays on the ground for a long time, because the air is so cold. Some areas in the Arctic do not seem to be like Earth at all, which is why projects like the Haughton-Mars Project come to this region.

What does this photo show about summer in the Arctic region?

Effects of Dry and Cold Arctic Climate

Housing	Homes must be very well insulated.
Clothing	When people go outdoors in winter, they must wear warm clothing from head to toe.
Farming	Almost no farming is done in the Arctic. Things like flour and vegetables must be brought in by truck or plane. That can make some foods very expensive.
Travel	People use snowmobiles, planes, trucks, and boats. There are very long distances to travel in the Arctic region!

Thinking *It Through*

- How else could the environment in the North affect daily life? Think of what you do every day. How would a student do the same things in the North? Could they do the same things? Might they do others?

Lena Sikasluk fishes for Arctic char near her home in Pond Inlet. Ice fishing is a traditional way to fish in the Arctic region, because the water is frozen for much of the year.

Homes like these are raised off the ground to prevent warm air from melting the permafrost. Melting permafrost could make the house sink.

Permafrost

Most buildings in the Arctic region do not have basements. That is because much of the ground is always frozen. **Permafrost** is soil that stays frozen all year. In summer, only the top layer of soil thaws. Permafrost has many effects on the Arctic region:

- Without deep soil, there is no farming.
- Trees will not grow in permafrost, so forestry is not a major industry here.
- In the **tundra**, rare and fragile grasses and plants have adapted to grow in the thin soil.
- Frozen ground makes road construction difficult. Airstrips and roads are built on a bed of gravel above the permafrost to prevent melting. Melting causes potholes and uneven roads.

Pollution

In southern Canada, most garbage is buried, but permafrost prevents that in the North. In the past, waste was dumped onto the frozen ground or into lakes and wetlands. In some places, sewage polluted the water. This made people and animals sick.

Today, the government has rules to help prevent this problem. Companies have to find out what effect their work will have on the environment. If it will harm the environment, it will not be approved. The use of land must be agreed on by Inuit communities and the government before companies can begin operations. Communities have recycling programs to help reduce waste.

These Inuit students in Iglulik are recycling cans. What challenges might recycling programs face in the North? Why would recycling be important in the region today?

Thinking *It Through*

- What to do with garbage is a challenge for all communities. What are ways that improper disposal of waste can affect quality of life? What can people and governments do to help protect the environment?

Long Days, Long Nights

Imagine living in a place where in the summer, nighttime is only a few hours long, and in the winter, the daytime is just as short! The Arctic region is such a place because of its latitude. With very few hours of darkness in the summer, people can enjoy daytime activities, such as playing softball, long into the night.

In winter, it is often too cold and dark for many outdoor activities, but there are lots of indoor activities. People drive or walk to shopping malls, restaurants, and movie theatres. Children often play indoor games, or visit the library. Because of 20 hours of darkness during the winter months, students go to school in the dark!

Every year, people in the North celebrate the Festival of the Midnight Sun. This festival is held around the longest day of the year, in the summer. Why do you think people might celebrate this event?

Outdoor activities are usually enjoyed all year long by these children in Iglulik. How might the length of daylight hours affect what you do every day?

Climate Change

A few years ago, a robin appeared in the Arctic region. There is no word for robin in Inuktitut because no Inuk had ever seen one. The reason the robin appeared so far north is that temperatures are slowly getting warmer.

The Inuit also saw other things that told them the climate was changing. They noticed that wetlands were drying up. They saw insects, such as mosquitoes and beetles, which they had never seen before.

Climate change has also had a direct affect on Inuit ways of life. Melting ice meant more accidents, since people were used to travelling on thick, solid ice. Permafrost began to melt underneath homes. Storms have become more frequent. The Inuit have begun to voice their concerns. Recently, Inuit hunters and observers have worked with research organizations to track the changes. Workshops and community meetings are taking place. The information gathered is then shared with Canada and the rest of the world. The government of Nunavut is also developing a Climate Change Centre, a place where the information can be collected and organized.

We cannot pass on our traditional knowledge, because it is no longer reliable. Before, I could look at cloud patterns, or the wind or even what stars are twinkling, and predict the weather. Now, everything is changed.

Enosik Nashalik, Pangnirtung

This Inuit family in the Northwest Territories wears double-layer parkas, traditional clothing in the Arctic region. How might climate change affect how people dress in this region?

Thinking *It Through*

■ Read the Voices of Canada on this page. Why do you think traditional knowledge is challenged by climate change? How might climate change affect the speakers' quality of life?

Voices of Canada

Climate Change Affects the Inuit

How can the traditional knowledge and experience of the Inuit help us study climate change in the Arctic region?

Years ago, we used to travel by dog team in the middle of July over the ice, but now, by July, people are boating.

Kugluktuk, Nunavut, 1999

The weather pattern has changed so much from my childhood. We have more accidents because the ice conditions change.

David Audlakiak, Iqaluit, 2002

An Uncertain Future

Climate change has very serious effects on the lives of people and animals in the Arctic. The example of the polar bear can show how important it is to think about the ways we act in our world. Pollution in places as far away as South America and Alberta contribute to changes in the Arctic.

The big problem for the polar bears in the Arctic is that the ice they need to hunt on is melting and growing thin. This means that they cannot get to areas to hunt seals, their main source of food. One theory is that global warming is melting the ice. Gases released by burning things such as coal and gas are warming up the atmosphere. This increase in temperature is a part of the climate change being observed in the Arctic.

How do you think the loss of the polar bear might affect the people living in the Arctic region?

A Legendary Animal

The polar bear is central to the image of the Arctic. It's a legendary animal in our lives. It's spoken of with reverence. Life without it is unfathomable.

Duane Smith, Nunavut

Polar bears spend most of their lives on the ice. What other animals in the Arctic region might be affected by climate change?

The artist who made this sculpture is Ohito Ashoona. He says that the polar bear is the "king of the ice." What does that tell about his respect for the polar bear?

Thinking *It Through*

■ If the Arctic can be affected by what happens in the south, what can we do to stop the changes? In small groups, talk about this problem and make suggestions about the things you can do to help the people and animals of the Arctic.

Diamonds in the Arctic Region

More About...

Diamonds

Canada is the third-largest producer of diamonds in the world. Many of the workers at the mines are local people who are learning to mine diamonds. More than 2000 people in the North work directly with the diamond mines.

The people of Nunavut have discovered that their land has gold and other minerals, like zinc and copper. It also has diamonds. Already, diamond mines are providing jobs and opportunities to the people of the North. Companies are searching the waters of the Arctic Ocean for deposits of oil and gas. These too will provide work for the people of Nunavut.

While wealth does grow from mines and minerals, what problems might occur as the mining develops? What can companies do to make their mines safer for the environment in the North? Form small groups to discuss this important issue. Share your findings with the class.

This is the Jericho Diamond Mine, at Contwoyto Lake, in Nunavut. How do you think mines like this one might impact the local environment and the people who live nearby? Are there advantages? Disadvantages?

Thinking It Through

- What are the uses for diamonds today? Why might the discovery of diamonds mean so much to people who live in Nunavut?

What Makes Canada's Arctic Unique?

People who live in the Arctic region have combined traditional ways with contemporary ways. Many Inuit in the region still go out to live on the land, but they may use present-day equipment. In Nunavut, the government has a council of Elders to give advice about traditional ways.

Another combination of old and new ways of life is the Arctic Winter Games. Modelled after the Olympic Games, these games are held every two years. Athletes from northern nations such as Russia, Sweden, Norway, and Canada compete in games of skill.

Voices of Canada

Why I Am Proud to Be Inuk

I am proud to be Inuk because we can go caribou hunting and fishing. I'm happy because we can speak Inuktitut. We can go camping on other islands and we can go dogsledding. Other people down south can't do any kind of stuff like this.

Roberta Dion, Grade 6 student, Coral Harbour

Voices of Canada

Our Language

Within Inuktitut there are many dialects. When people are not exposed to a dialect, it can be harder to understand. But I think Inuktitut is becoming easier. When people were more isolated and had fewer contacts, it was harder to understand each other. But now with more contacts through travel, the media, and in larger communities, it is less confusing.

Nunia Qanatsiaq, Arviat

These young women are competing in the Arctic Winter Games. What other sports in the Games are connected to traditional skills?

Thinking *It Through*

- What do the Voices of Canada in this chapter tell you about life in the Arctic region? How is it different from other regions in Canada? Choose one of the other regions in Canada to create a comparison. Explain how communities in all regions might work together to preserve their languages and ways of life.

Viewpoints

Are the Benefits of Drilling for Oil and Gas Worth the Risk to the Environment?

On the map on pages 192–193, find the place where the Mackenzie River flows into the Beaufort Sea. Sediment flowing from the river has created the Mackenzie River Delta. This area is the largest delta in Canada, and it is made up of small islands, estuaries, and marshes. It is an important area for birds, as well as other animals. Thousands of birds migrate to the Delta every year to nest. Beluga whales come to the Delta to calve. Grizzly bears live in the area as well.

Several large deposits of natural gas and oil have been found here. These energy sources are valuable. But in order for the oil and gas to be used, they must be found and drilling platforms built. Roads and pipelines must also be built so that workers can get to the oil platforms, and the oil and gas can be moved farther south, where most people live. This will have an impact on the environment and wildlife of the Mackenzie River Delta.

The rich land of the Delta supports many kinds of plants and animals. It is also the location of rich deposits of oil and gas.

How will the gas fields affect the North?

Oil and gas development could harm wildlife

Mackenzie Oil Project to create thousands of jobs

These Arctic swans are among the bird species that might be harmed by the oil development.

The oil companies are committed to doing their best to protect the environment. I think we can develop this resource, give people jobs, and still protect the land and the animals.

The bird sanctuary in the Mackenzie River Delta is important. How can we risk an area that is the only place in North America where some species of birds nest and raise their young? Drilling, roads, and more people will disrupt this special place forever.

I'm going to work as a wildlife monitor when I leave school. That means that I will go out on the land and tell the government if any animals or birds are being harmed by the oil drilling. I think that's a good way to help take care of the Delta.

Over to You

1. Discuss the different points of view. Should drilling oil and gas be encouraged? Which issues are most important to the people of the communities affected? Which issues are important to the businesses? Make a chart to share your ideas.

2. What do you think the oil companies, communities, and governments should do to preserve the environment? What might this mean to further generations?

Make a Presentation

Climate change is a growing concern in the Arctic region. Research how the climate has changed in your community over the last 100 years. Look on the Internet or conduct interviews. Then share the information in a presentation. Look back to the Skill Power on page 197 to help plan your presentation.

Research a Current Event

Find out more about oil drilling or diamond mining in the Arctic region today. What types of discoveries are being made? What are companies doing to preserve the environment? Look on the Internet or use the library to conduct your research. Then write a newspaper article to share your facts.

Look at News Reports

Find two news reports about climate or environmental concerns in the Arctic region. Do the reports have similar opinions? Do they use interviews to support their arguments? Who wrote them? Why do you think they were written?

Putting It All Together

Once Katie had finished her research into Qaummaarviit Territorial Historic Park, she used her family's computer to create a PowerPoint® display. She chose to make this presentation because it would be a good way to include photos and maps. Here is what part of her presentation looked like.

Qaummaarviit Territorial Historic Park

The Place That Shines

- Qaummaarviit Territorial Historic Park is on Baffin Island. It is also called "The Place That Shines."
- People called the Thule once lived there. The park protects what is left of their houses.

Review the inquiry questions for this chapter:
- Explain how different communities have adapted to the climate and geography in the region.
- Has change always been good for people in the Arctic? Explain.

Take Time to Reflect

CANADA COLLECTION

Before you go on to the next chapter, think about what you learned in this one. If someone from the Arctic region came to visit you, how would you help them learn about your community? What would you show them? Prepare a bulleted list. Save your work for your Canada Collection.

Looking Back on Unit 1
Living with the Land

In this unit, you have explored the vastness of Canada and its diversity of land and people. You have learned about the six major regions in Canada and how climate, landforms, and natural resources affect the things people do in a particular region.

You have read about Canada's diverse people. Consider how the knowledge and understanding you have gained contributes to

- a sense of identity as a member of a community in Canada
- respect for the land and people of Canada

For each region, consider its land, people, and places. Decide on four factors that make each unique and tell why. These spiders are one way to organize your work.

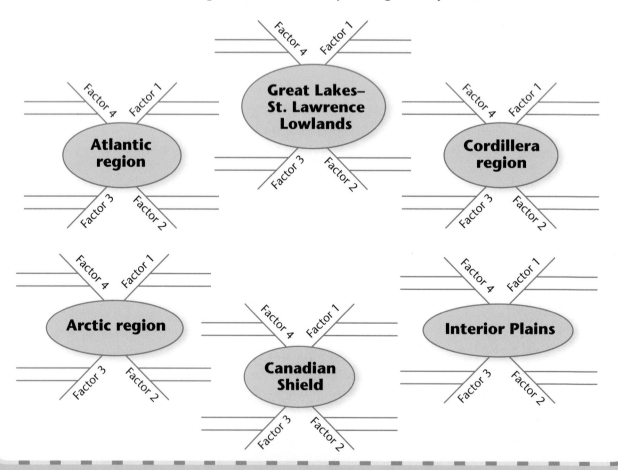

Share What You Have Learned

A game is a great way to share information and see what you have learned. Think of games you like to play—board games, card games, computer games. What are the rules of the game? How many can play? What do you need to play?

With a partner or on your own, create a game to share the players' knowledge about what they have learned in Unit 1. The key factors you chose on page 218 will be helpful in designing your game.

You can ask questions that cover the whole unit or focus on areas such as the following:

- maps and mapping skills
- unique physical features of regions
- natural resources—their use and effect on quality of life
- individuals or groups who have made a difference
- people of the regions—their heritage, ways of life, jobs
- words from Words Matter, sidebar information, Voices of Canada, captions

Tips

- Write several types of questions—ones that ask for facts, opinions, ideas, critical thinking, and comparisons.
- Provide the answers on an answer sheet or the back of cards.
- When creating your game, check it for organization, quality of the questions, neatness and appeal, creativity, and fun.

Canada, Our Country

As Canadians, we all have a unique story—where we come from, our family traditions and values, the languages we speak, and the things we like to do. Each of us is important, but we also recognize the importance of everyone else. The diversity of our stories, histories, languages, and experiences helps make us who we are and contributes to our identity and citizenship. Together, everyone makes up this country we call Canada.

On se souvient Lest we forget.

IN THIS UNIT

This unit helps you explore these questions.

- How does the diversity of Canadians and their stories contribute to Canada's identity?

- What key events have shaped ways of life in Canada?

- How do acts of citizenship add to Canadians' quality of life?

221

Building Canada

Every year on July 1, Canada celebrates its birthday. On Parliament Hill in Ottawa, there is a concert and a huge fireworks display. Why July 1? On that day in 1867, the country of Canada was created. Cannons were fired, bands played, and fireworks exploded.

On June 28, 1886, there was another day of excitement in the new country. The first passenger train, the Pacific Express, arrived in Vancouver from Montréal after travelling across the country. The train was amazing to people who had never travelled faster than the speed of a horse.

Today, people still travel by train. Each year, Canadians have a chance to tour a train if the CPR Holiday Express comes to their town. Visitors can bring a donation of money or canned food. The donations are given to people in need. This spirit of sharing was one reason that colonists long ago joined together to form a country.

Canada: Our Stories Continue

The CPR has existed for more than a hundred years. So has the country we call Canada. It officially became a country at the time of **Confederation** in 1867. Before then, several colonies made up what was known as British North America. Before 1867, the word "Canada" officially meant only the colony in the Great Lakes–St. Lawrence Lowlands region. Today that colony is part of Québec and Ontario. Colonies in the Atlantic region were Newfoundland, Nova Scotia, New Brunswick, and Prince Edward Island. Along the Pacific Coast was the colony of British Columbia. Each one had its own identity.

? Inquiring Minds

Here are some questions to guide your inquiry for this chapter:

- If you were creating a country from a diverse group of colonies, how would you overcome the challenges?
- Why does Canada have two official languages?

Canada's birthday is celebrated across the country on July 1. These people are celebrating on Parliament Hill in Ottawa.

Alistair's Inquiry

July 14, 8:00 a.m.

We are finally pulling into the train terminal in Vancouver. Dad and I have come from Halifax to visit

Grandma and Grandpa. It took five days to cross Canada by train! I saw forests and small towns in the Atlantic provinces. There was a long run along the St. Lawrence River from Québec City to Montréal and then Toronto. I saw huge rocks and vast columns of pine trees in the Shield for more than a day. Then we reached the Prairies. There was so much open space—fields and fields of yellow canola. It was like looking out over the ocean at home.

Then we got to the mountains. They're gigantic!

Taking the train is a comfortable way to travel. Rick Hansen must have had a long trip in a wheelchair, though! I can't imagine trying to get through some parts of Canada that way.

- Why does Canada have a railway from coast to coast?
- How did people build a railway through the mountains and the Shield?

As we travelled, my dad asked me to imagine that all the different provinces were different *countries*. In the past, each had its own money, laws, and ways of doing things.

- Why did all the colonies become one country?
- How did so many people from such different places agree on things like money and laws for the new country?

Skill Smart

■ Make a list of three things you would like to know about building the railway. Look for answers in this chapter. Use jot notes to record what you find.

SKILL POWER

Working Together to Make Decisions

Forming a new country and building a railway required a lot of cooperation. People had different ideas and spoke different languages. They faced many challenges trying to decide the best places to build a railway. But they found ways to agree and make decisions.

Working with others to make decisions is important for you, too. It is not always easy, but there are steps you can take to help the process along.

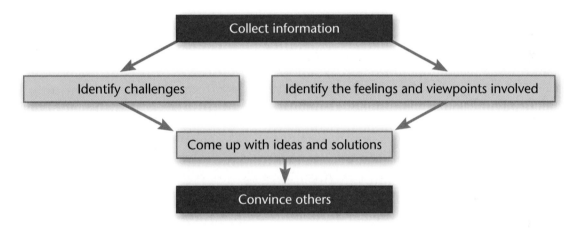

Practise the Skill

Step 1
Work in a group of five students and go through the many decisions needed to build a railway through the Canadian Shield or Cordillera region. Where would you build the railway? How would you decide?

Step 2
Each of the five students should "walk in the shoes" of a person from the region. Review what you have already learned about the region when you state your position. Take turns listening to one another's viewpoints.

Step 3
After you have agreed on a route, discuss other issues that would have to be solved. How will you convince others to follow your plan?

How Did Confederation Happen?

My dad told me that the story of how Canada came to be one country starts with John A. Macdonald, our first prime minister. I wonder why my dad thinks he is so important?

This is a caricature of John A. Macdonald. Caricatures often exaggerate a person's features. Compare this caricature with the portrait beside it. What features do you think have been exaggerated? Why was this done?

John Alexander Macdonald came to the colony of Canada with his family from Scotland in 1820. He was only five years old. His father became a shopkeeper and miller around what is now Kingston, Ontario. The family had no way of knowing that John would grow up to be a "father" of a new country. How did this happen?

John A. Macdonald became a lawyer. He was chosen by the voters to represent them in the government of the colony. There were many challenges. Schools, roads, and canals needed to be built and paid for. But nothing was getting done because people could not agree. Farmers and townspeople, for example, had different ideas about transportation and taxes.

Another challenge was that people in the colony spoke different languages and had different beliefs and values. The colony of Canada really had two parts: Anglophones lived mainly in "Canada West," and Francophones lived mainly in "Canada East." Sometimes they did not see things the same way. Macdonald had to find a way to get them to work together.

Parliament building under construction in 1863

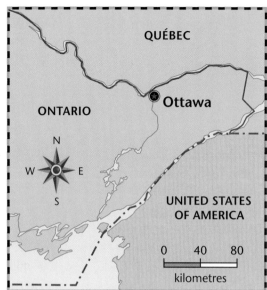

The colonies in the Atlantic region, as well as the colony of Canada, faced other serious challenges. They all needed to earn more money from the sale of resource products from their farms, oceans, mines, and forests. But it was difficult to trade with each other when each colony had different money and rules, and even weighed and measured things differently. Also, people were worried about being taken over by the United States. How could the small colonies defend themselves with no troops or transportation?

Canada East wanted Montréal or Québec City to be the capital of the colony of Canada. Canada West wanted Toronto or Kingston. Queen Victoria ended the disagreement by choosing Ottawa. Why do you think she made this choice?

Solutions for the Colonies

Macdonald and other leaders tried to find a solution. What if all or most of the British colonies joined together and formed one country? Together they would be stronger and richer. They would be better able to defend themselves. Most importantly, together the colonies might be able to afford to build a railway joining them together. This would allow the colonies to

- move troops in times of war;
- move trade goods between the colonies;
- take settlers to the Interior Plains and to British Columbia. These regions might then join the new country.

The leaders now had to convince others that Confederation, or the joining of the colonies, was a good idea.

If the colonies joined and built a railway, trains could carry goods between the Canadas and Halifax in winter for shipping across the Atlantic Ocean. Why couldn't Ontario and Québec use the St. Lawrence River to send ships to the Atlantic during winter?

But wait, all of the other colonies were English-speaking. Wouldn't the Canadiens be worried about losing their French language and their culture?

Convincing Québec

Macdonald made a friend and **ally** with George-Étienne Cartier. Cartier was a Francophone leader in Canada East. Both he and Macdonald had dreams for this new land. Cartier dreamed of a country that spread west into the lands first opened by Francophone explorers and voyageurs. There, Francophones could start new communities. But he also wanted them to have new opportunities and jobs in the cities of Canada. Above all, he wanted to protect his people's language, religion, culture, and identity.

The Canadiens were proud of their way of life, their traditions, their Roman Catholic faith, and their contributions to the development of the colony. What would happen if they joined with the other colonies, in which most people spoke English? If they did not join, would the small number of Anglophones in Canada East lose *their* identity?

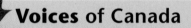

Voices of Canada

Cartier's Dream

The two Canadas stretching far out to the West will bring to Confederation a huge part of the Western territories.

George-Étienne Cartier

The Canadiens were not willing to lose their language, culture, and identity. They wondered if the union of colonies was a way of forcing them to give up their identity. Francophones would be a **minority** in the new country. But Cartier told the Canadiens that their identity would not be lost. He promised that the French language would be protected by Confederation.

Speaker 1: The number of Canadiens is not growing very quickly. No one from France has moved here for more than one hundred years. Our Francophone population only increases because families are large.

Speaker 1: With so many English-speaking colonies and all the new English immigrants, it will be much easier for the English to outvote us in the government!

Speaker 2: At the same time, many people are coming here from Great Britain. They all speak English!

Speaker 2: Will we have a way to make sure that the law protects our schools and our language?

Choosing Bilingualism

Cartier wanted Francophones and Anglophones to be equal partners. He, Macdonald, and their followers agreed that the new country should have both French and English as its official languages. This would mean that either language could be used in the Parliament of Canada and in the federal courts. Records of speeches and debates would also be kept in both official languages.

In the new province of Québec, Canadiens would be the **majority.** Their provincial government could control schools, religion, and the court system. Québec also chose to protect the Anglophone minority in its province. English was made an official language in the Québec government, and Anglophones had their own schools and hospitals. Later, Francophone minorities in other provinces were disappointed that they were not treated in the same way.

words matter!

A **majority** is the largest in number of two or more groups.

Skill Smart

■ What were some of the benefits and challenges of Québec joining the other colonies? Make a two-column chart to show your work.

Should We Join Confederation?

Each of the colonies had its own identity. Each also had its own challenges and concerns. Because of this, each colony had different reasons for wanting or not wanting to join with the others. Look at the information on these two pages. See if you can predict which colonies will join together to make the new country of Canada.

With Confederation, as we shall be in the great minority in the general Parliament... we shall have to carry on a constant contest for the defence and preservation of our political rights and our liberty.

Joseph-Xavier Perreault, Canadien, 1865

The stories of my Métis ancestors tell how our homelands on the Plains came to be part of Canada. Our lands were sold by the Hudson['s] Bay Company to Canada in 1869. No one even bothered to ask us, or even to tell us.

Jordan Brown, Winnipeg

The Morning Chronicle (St. John's)　September 28, 1869, p.1

NO CONFEDERATION!

Reduced (not Increased) Taxation!
Let us keep our Fisheries to Ourselves! – Let us keep our Lands, Mines and Minerals to Ourselves! – Let us keep our Revenue to Ourselves!
Newfoundland for the Newfoundlanders

What do you think the Newfoundlanders were worried about if they joined Confederation? Think about what you have already learned about Newfoundland.

 As we crossed our huge country, I wondered how people in each region felt about joining Canada. I know the people in the Atlantic region are proud of their communities and their way of life. I can just imagine some of the conversations.

In New Brunswick, we have great forests and ports, and the best sailing-ship builders in the world! We are doing just fine. We have no need for a railroad. We have no need to join the Canadian colonies.

I read that steel steamships are starting to replace wooden sailing ships. Maybe we should think about the future. And I think a railway would help with trade and defence. I think New Brunswick's future is to be part of the new country of Canada.

We have just a short railway in Nova Scotia. Wouldn't it be better if we could take a train to Montréal or Toronto? We could trade with the other colonies and learn new things. Together we would be stronger than we would be as separate colonies. Wouldn't it be exciting to be part of a larger and stronger country?

We have learned that the new nation of Canada dreams of stretching from the Atlantic to the Pacific. We here in the colony of British Columbia would like to be part of this dream. But not unless we could be joined by road or railway to the East. George-Étienne Cartier has promised to build one. Is this even possible?

Over to **You**

1. Why is it important to hear and understand all sides in a debate?

2. What do you think the First Nations people would say about joining Confederation?

3. Do you think of yourself as an Albertan, a Canadian, both, or neither? Why?

Last year I had to do a project with a new student. First, we talked and got to know each other better. We found out we had a lot in common. It made working together easier.

No women were part of the Confederation conferences. But in the evenings in Charlottetown and Québec City, the wives and daughters of the "Fathers" joined the men for dinners and dances, such as the one shown in this painting called *Ball at Legislature* by Dusan Kadlec. They helped the men get to know one another better. Why did this help the men agree on important decisions?

Thinking It Through

- Why was it important for the Fathers of Confederation to see different parts of the country?

Convincing the Atlantic Colonies

Before Confederation could happen, Cartier, Macdonald, and Member of Parliament George Brown needed to meet the Atlantic colonists so they could convince them of the advantages of joining together. They travelled by boat to Charlottetown, PEI, in the summer of 1864. There, they held a conference with leaders from the Atlantic colonies.

The Canadians and Canadiens visited Halifax, Saint John, and Fredericton. Politicians from the Atlantic colonies and their families were invited to a conference in Québec City. The representatives at these conferences became known as the "Fathers of Confederation." At the conferences, the Fathers decided upon the rules for sharing power in their new country.

Choosing to Unite

Macdonald and Cartier identified the colonies' challenges. They examined facts and listened to colonists' views. They decided that Confederation was the best solution to make a better life for citizens. On July 1, 1867, three colonies—New Brunswick, Nova Scotia, and Canada (East and West)— joined together to form the Dominion of Canada. The colony of Canada was divided into the provinces of Ontario and Québec. New Brunswick and Nova Scotia became provinces, too. Each province's government would be in charge of its schools, hospitals, and communities.

Canada's central government in Ottawa controlled defence and trade. It would also make decisions about a national railway. The Fathers of Confederation were excited to create a new country without fighting a war. They hoped people across the land would proudly call themselves citizens of Canada.

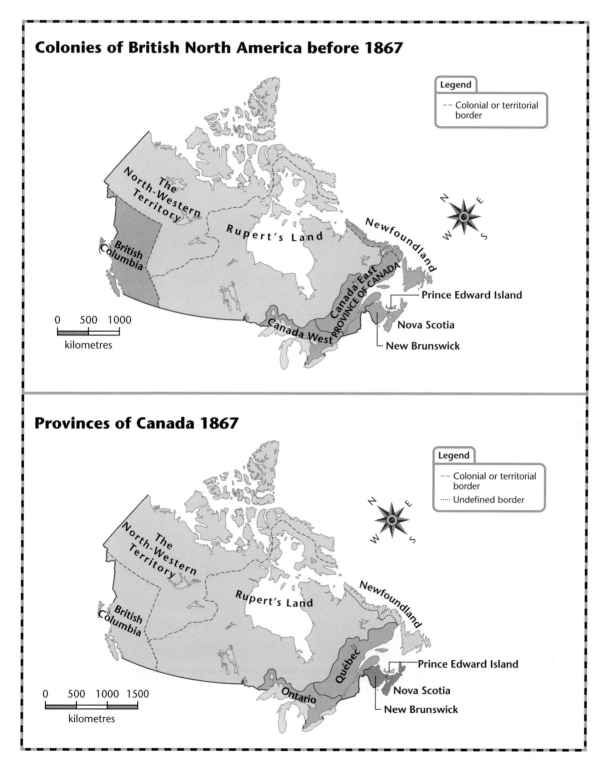

Colonies of British North America before 1867

Legend
-- Colonial or territorial border

The North-Western Territory

Rupert's Land

British Columbia

Newfoundland

Canada East
PROVINCE OF CANADA

Canada West

Prince Edward Island

Nova Scotia

New Brunswick

0   500   1000
kilometres

Provinces of Canada 1867

Legend
-- Colonial or territorial border
···· Undefined border

The North-Western Territory

Rupert's Land

British Columbia

Newfoundland

Québec

Ontario

Prince Edward Island

Nova Scotia

New Brunswick

0   500   1000   1500
kilometres

Compare these two maps. Which colonies did *not* join Confederation in 1867?

Who Was Left Out of Confederation?

Why weren't any First Nations invited to these meetings and conferences?

In earlier times, First Nations and Europeans worked closely together, especially during the fur trade. Fur traders and settlers across the land depended on the skills and knowledge of First Nations people. So why didn't First Nations have a say about the future of the land? The main reason was that the fur trade was not very important in the colonies by the 1860s. This meant that many colonists did not think First Nations people were very important. The colonists also did not agree with First Nations people about land ownership. The Europeans believed that land could be owned, but First Nations people disagreed.

Voices of Canada

First Nations leaders in the years before Confederation realized that they were no longer being treated as allies and friends. Little Pine, chief of the Garden River Ojibwa near Sault Ste. Marie, wrote a letter to the governor of Canada in 1849.

When your White children first came into this country they... told us they came as friends.... Time wore on and you have become a great people... You have hunted us from every place... you have swept away all our pleasant land. [You] tell us "willing or unwilling, you must now go from amid these rocks... I want them now! I want them to make rich my White children..."

? Critical Inquiry TIP

Retrieving

Sometimes it can be difficult to find information about an event that happened long ago. Good researchers know where to find information. Make a list of places you would go. Ask a librarian about letters, diaries, newspapers, and other sources.

Effects of Confederation

The Fathers of Confederation did not think of First Nations as citizens of the new country of Canada. How do we know? After Confederation, a special government department was created to decide how First Nations should live. Many First Nations were forced to live on reserves. These people were not allowed to vote. If they wanted to vote, they had to leave their reserves and begin living like the colonists did. This meant they had to farm or move to a city.

First Nations Take Action

By the 1950s, First Nations representatives had started working together to improve the lives of their people. Their group would later be known as the Assembly of First Nations. First Nations finally won the right to vote in federal and provincial elections in 1960.

Canada made more changes to its government in the 1980s. This time, the Assembly of First Nations made certain its people were included.

Making *a Difference*

Harold Cardinal

Harold Cardinal was a Woodland Cree chief from Alberta. In 1969, the Canadian government announced that they wanted to end all treaties made with First Nations. The government wanted to treat First Nations people the same way it treated other minority groups. They did not want First Nations to have their own land or special rights.

Harold Cardinal, at a meeting of First Nations in Calgary, April 1975

Cardinal and other chiefs knew that something had to be done. Cardinal wrote a book called *The Unjust Society*. In it, he said that First Nations were a founding people of Canada. They had a unique history that could never be taken away. Cardinal said, "*The Unjust Society* was written… to bring to the attention of the Canadian public, perhaps for the first time, a voice that was ours, a voice that reflected First Nation thoughts and reactions to the situation facing us."

The book helped people to understand the feelings and beliefs of First Nations. Many protesters came together, and eventually, the Canadian government changed its mind.

Thinking *It Through*

- How might Canada be different if First Nations had been included in the Charlottetown conferences?

- How do you think First Nations people felt about John A. Macdonald being called the father of a new country?

What Were the Challenges to Building a Railway?

When I look at the mountains near Kamloops, I wonder how people ever built a railway through them.

A railway across Canada started as a dream. John A. Macdonald wanted the new country to stretch from the Atlantic Ocean to the Pacific Ocean. For his dream to come true, though, people would have to build 5000 km of railway tracks across the muskeg of the Shield and through steep mountains. No one had ever built such a railway in Canada or anywhere else in the world. Many people thought it was an impossible dream. But once again, Canadians worked together to identify the challenges and discuss possible solutions.

Collecting Information

People called surveyors collected information so they could suggest the best path for the railway. They travelled across the country measuring, thinking, and testing ideas. Many times, they discovered even more challenges. The surveyors had to be very tough. Their work was hard and lonely. They faced dangers like wild animals, sunstroke, and bone-chilling winds. They had to raft rivers, climb mountains, wade through swamps, and camp out in the wilderness.

British Columbia would not join Confederation unless the railway stretched all the way to the West Coast. Finding passes through the mountains was difficult, though. These surveyors collected information in the Cordillera region.

Think about clearing a path through this forest for railway tracks. What would have to be done? Remember, there were no trucks or bulldozers in the 1800s.

Deciding on a Route

Besides wondering *how* to build a railway, people wondered *where* to build it:

- Would it take the shortest and the cheapest route? Or would it run through the best farmland and resources?
- Which towns should the railway run through? What would happen to towns that it did not run through?
- Should it run close to, or far away from, the United States border? Should it run through the United States itself?

Skill Smart

- In a small group, plan the development of a road or rapid transit to improve travel in your community. Discuss its affect on different groups of people.

Even if you could build tracks through the Rocky Mountains, could a train go up and down them safely?

How would you get through the rock in the Canadian Shield?

What would happen if you tried to build railway tracks over muskeg?

During the mid-1800s, huge herds of bison still roamed the Prairies. What problems might they cause for the railway?

Solving Challenges

The story of the railway was a story of great determination. People such as William Van Horne, Andrew Onderdonk, and Major A.B. Rogers wanted to make Sir John A. Macdonald's dream come true. William Van Horne was the chief engineer for the railway.

Andrew Onderdonk was in charge of the British Columbia section of the railway.

Major A.B. Rogers was a surveyor who would not quit until he found a way, or a pass, through the Rocky Mountains. Each of these men believed the impossible could be done. They imagined what the country of Canada might look like. They saw factories, mines, and mills, and more cities and towns.

Some people said that Van Horne did not know the meaning of the word "cannot." It was also said that he seemed to never need sleep, and assumed that nobody else did, either!

Skill Smart

- William Van Horne, Andrew Onderdonk, and Major A.B. Rogers were all very interesting people who solved huge challenges in building the railway. Find three interesting points about one of these men.

This is a whirlpool at Hell's Gate Canyon on the Fraser River in British Columbia. The surveyors had to find a way around it!

The Workers

A few people made the decision to build the railway, but others did the physical work. Railway workers risked accidents, disease, malnutrition, and death. In the mountains, Chinese workers had to build bridges across flooded rivers and canyons. They built tunnels. They twisted track around glaciers. Their dynamite set off avalanches and rockslides that sometimes buried construction camps.

Through the Canadian Shield there are countless kilometres of muskeg. How could tracks be built across this swampy land? One area of muskeg swallowed six sets of tracks and three locomotives. Workers tried to fill the muskeg with gravel and soil. But these tracks sank too. Eventually, workers drained the water from the area, then filled the holes and drilled down 30 m to the rock below.

Workers from Sweden and Italy also had to put up with mosquitoes, black flies, and extreme temperatures—all for very little pay.

 Part of the Trail includes the Kettle Valley Railway. It is a 600-km route on an abandoned railway bed that winds through south-central British Columbia between Midway and Hope. The Trail has many tunnels here. Some of them hang on the sides of the Myra Canyon. This route is for hardy travellers.

Along Lake Superior there are hard granite cliffs. Granite is one of the toughest materials in the world. Dynamiting it is very dangerous. In an 80-km stretch through the Canadian Shield, 30 workers died in explosive accidents.

The railway was completed in November 1885. Donald A. Smith drove in the last spike, joining the sections of railway through the mountains of British Columbia. Lord Smith was one of the owners of the CPR. Why do you think he put in the last spike, and not one of the railway workers?

Thinking *It Through*

- Nominate two people who should be remembered for their significant contribution to the railway.
- How has transportation changed since the building of the railway?

How Did the Railway Affect People?

June 28, 1886, was a day of great excitement. The Pacific Express, a train that had left Montréal, arrived in the station at Port Moody, British Columbia. The railway changed the face of the whole country, especially the West. What changes did the railway bring to ways of life in Canada?

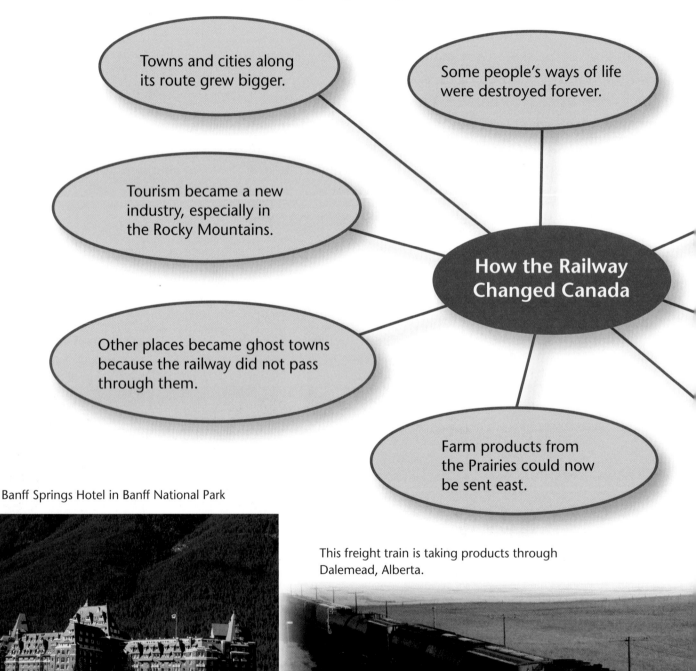

Towns and cities along its route grew bigger.

Some people's ways of life were destroyed forever.

Tourism became a new industry, especially in the Rocky Mountains.

How the Railway Changed Canada

Other places became ghost towns because the railway did not pass through them.

Farm products from the Prairies could now be sent east.

Banff Springs Hotel in Banff National Park

This freight train is taking products through Dalemead, Alberta.

The CPR started to provide sleeping cars in 1884. Although basic, they made the trip westward much easier for settlers. This photo was taken between 1885 and 1890.

It opened the Prairies and British Columbia to new immigrants from all over the world.

The Prairies and British Columbia were now linked to the rest of Canada (people did not have to go through the United States to travel west anymore).

The bison on the Prairies were nearly all killed.

Before there were telephones or the Internet, people sent messages by telegraph. Telegraph lines were put up at the same time as the railway, alongside the tracks. These workers put up lines in the Rocky Mountains around 1888. The telegraph was another way to join Canadians together. How will we communicate in the future? Will the Internet someday seem old-fashioned?

First Nations and the Métis People

Building the railway drastically changed the ways of life of the First Nations and the Métis of the Interior Plains. It destroyed the bison herds on which the Plains First Nations and Métis depended. The railway also brought farmers and settlers whose way of life was very different. Let's take a closer look at what happened during this time.

How do you think the way of life of Crowfoot's family would change because of the railway?

Voices of Canada

First Nations and the Railway

Chief Crowfoot led the Blackfoot First Nation at the time the railway was built.

The government has promised this land will be ours forever. We signed a treaty because we believed your government. Now you try to drive the railway across our land without even asking us. We will not allow it.

Chief Crowfoot

Voices of Canada

Change

Father Albert Lacombe was a Catholic missionary who worked among the Blackfoot First Nation. He convinced the government and railway officials to respect and help the First Nations of the Plains as the railway was being built. He helped the Cree and the Blackfoot adjust to their changed way of life after the railway was built.

I would look in silence at the [railway] coming on... cutting its way through the prairies; opening up the great country... changing the face of the whole country.

Father Lacombe

EFFECTS OF BUILDING THE RAILWAY

Cause

- One main purpose of the railway was to bring settlers to farm the plains and to build towns and cities.

- Farmers did not want bison damaging their crops. They sectioned off the land with barbed wire fences.

- Herds of bison travelling across the tracks could prevent trains from running on time.
- An animal with a hoof caught in a track could cause an accident.

- Trains caused damage.
- Horses were often hit by trains.
- Sparks came off the steam locomotives.

How would you feel if someone wanted to build a highway through your neighbourhood without your permission or without paying you? How would this be the same as building a railway through the Prairies? How would it be different?

ACROSS THE PRAIRIES

Effect

- The railway company or the Canadian government sold land to the new settlers. The farmers and settlers believed that they owned the land. But the First Nations and Métis had lived on the land for a long time. Now the First Nations had to live on reserves. They lost their independence.

- Bison could no longer roam freely. Without the bison, the way of life of First Nations and Métis was destroyed.

- Railway builders encouraged the killing of bison herds on the plains. As a result, the people of the Plains lost their main food supply. They eventually faced starvation.

- Horses were important to the lifestyle of the Plains People.
- Prairie fires were started by sparks. Fires destroyed grasslands and homes.

Voices of Canada

Ne-can-nete's Words

With the destruction of the [bison] herds, many First Nations had a choice: move to reserves and get food from the government or starve. Ne-can-nete, known as Foremost Man, was a Plains Cree chief at the time the railway was built. He loved the Cypress Hills where he lived. He and his people refused to move to a reserve unless it was near the hills. Ne-can-nete said, "Let them send the [bison] back, and take their own people to the reserve where they came from. Give us back the prairie again... But it is too late. The iron road has frightened the game away... It is too late: it is too late."

Ne-can-nete

243

Work Together to Solve a Problem

In a small group, look in the newspaper to find out more about an issue in your community. What is the problem? What are some different viewpoints about the issue? Brainstorm some solutions and create a plan to solve the challenges. Write a letter to the editor to convince other people of your idea.

Research the Railway

Research the impact of the railway on your town. Was your town formed because of a railway? Is there a railway station in your town? Is it still used as a station? If your town is not close to the railway, how does that affect your community? Present your research by making a poster.

Create a Cause and Effect Chart

Interview an adult in your family or community. Ask about the biggest change he or she has seen. Create a cause and effect chart to illustrate the impact of this change.

Draw a Cartoon

This cartoon shows John A. Macdonald's head. In it, you can see things like Love of Canada, Memory, and Hope. Draw a similar cartoon showing the thoughts and feelings that you have established about Canada's past.

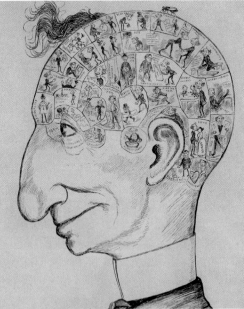

Putting It All Together

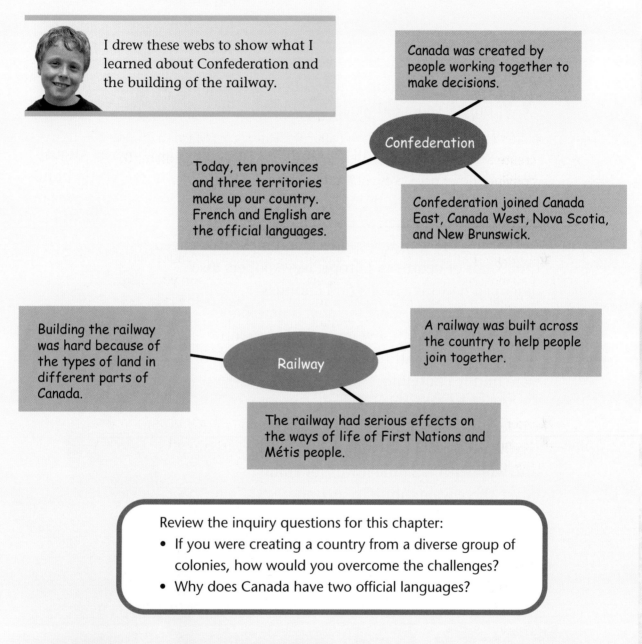

I drew these webs to show what I learned about Confederation and the building of the railway.

Canada was created by people working together to make decisions.

Confederation

Today, ten provinces and three territories make up our country. French and English are the official languages.

Confederation joined Canada East, Canada West, Nova Scotia, and New Brunswick.

Building the railway was hard because of the types of land in different parts of Canada.

Railway

A railway was built across the country to help people join together.

The railway had serious effects on the ways of life of First Nations and Métis people.

Review the inquiry questions for this chapter:
- If you were creating a country from a diverse group of colonies, how would you overcome the challenges?
- Why does Canada have two official languages?

Take Time to Reflect

Think about what you have learned in this chapter. How did decision-making skills help with Confederation and the railway?

Think of a decision you made with family members. Make a flow chart to show the steps you took. Use the flow chart on page 225 to help you. Save your work for your Canada Collection.

Changing Ways of Life

When do you think you will get your first job? Jimmie Gray was only 8 years old when he started selling newspapers on a Winnipeg street corner.

"Extra! Extra! Read all about it!" shouted the newsboys in August 1914. World War I had been declared in Europe. Soon marching bands were parading through the streets of every town. Their purpose was to encourage young men to become soldiers and to go overseas to fight.

During the war, newspaper headlines announced thousands of deaths in Europe. Newspapers also described new inventions and changes happening in Canada. One day, a newspaper headline declared that women had just won the right to vote. Attitudes toward women were finally changing.

When he was older, Jimmie Gray wrote a book about his childhood. He recalled: "What a marvellous, exciting, and wonder-filled time it was for small boys! There were things to do and places to go, and discoveries to make with automobiles, motion pictures, airplanes, and radio."

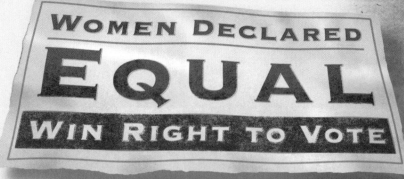

WOMEN DECLARED

EQUAL

WIN RIGHT TO VOTE

Canada: Our Stories Continue

Before 1900, most Canadians made their living from the resources around them. Many people lived on farms or in small villages. After 1900, some people moved to urban areas to look for work. Here, ways of life were very different. There were new kinds of jobs in factories, shops, and offices. People used the new products that were made in factories—everything from cars to breakfast cereals. In this chapter, you will explore how ways of life changed during and after **World War I**.

Some of the biggest changes affected women. During this time, they got paying jobs, new rights, and new responsibilities.

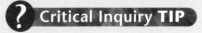
words matter!

World War I (1914–1918) was fought mainly in Europe and involved many countries, including Canada. It is also called the Great War. More than 60 000 Canadians died fighting in World War I.

The newspapers that Jimmie Gray sold had photos of soldiers marching, like this one. It was taken in 1915 and shows a troop from Saskatoon.

? Inquiring Minds

Here are some questions to guide your inquiry for this chapter:

- In what ways did World War I begin to change Canadians' identity?
- How would life be different if the Famous Five had not succeeded?

? Critical Inquiry TIP

Retrieving

As you read this chapter, jot down any information that might help you answer the Inquiring Minds questions.

Claire's Inquiry

When I look at pictures of myself from a few years ago, I cannot believe how much I have changed. Photos are a good way to remember what life was like in the past. Our teacher showed us how to browse through online collections of old photographs. I saw photos of people living in Canada around 100 years ago! I thought these two pictures were really interesting.

The photo on the left was taken in the small town of Didsbury, Alberta, in 1911. The one below was taken in Edmonton in 1918.

Compare the ways of life of the women in these two photos.

SKILL
POWER

Making Meaning of Historical Photographs

Pictures can tell us a lot about the past and about how people lived. Some of the photos Claire saw online had captions, or sentences that give more information, such as when and where the photo was taken.

Sometimes a caption tells us what the photo means. Remember, though, that this is just what the caption writer thinks. Other people may think the photo means something different. This is because everyone has a unique point of view.

Look at the photo at the bottom of page 248. Then read these two captions:

1. Times were good for the factories of Canada.
2. Women workers are overworked and underpaid.

What different points of view do these two captions show? Who might have written them?

Practise the Skill

1. Look at the photo on this page. Why do you think the photographer took this picture?

2. Write a caption that might accompany this photograph.

How Did World War I Change Life in Canada?

When people moved from the country to the city around the time of World War I, many of them missed the open and natural spaces. Today, people in cities still want to walk in peaceful, natural surroundings. That is why parts of the Trans Canada Trail pass through cities. In Edmonton, for example, 32 kilometres of the trail wind through wooded areas along the river and ravines.

At the beginning of the 1900s, many people moved to cities to look for better-paying jobs. Men worked in factories, or as carpenters, bricklayers, or painters. Some women worked as cooks and maids. Others worked in sewing factories.

When World War I began, some Canadian factories began making supplies and equipment for the soldiers. Because of the fighting in Europe, much of the best farmland there was destroyed. Europeans needed Canada to send them grain and meat. Canadian meat-packing plants started canning meat and sending it overseas.

The war kept Canada's farmers and factory workers very busy, and for a short time some made money. Unfortunately, there were not always enough jobs for everyone. Some jobs did not pay much.

Voices of Canada

Families with Low Incomes

I visited some truly needy families. It was a tearful sight to see those six, seven, or eight children, almost naked in a frigid home, heated by a stove filled with old papers, those beds without mattresses, a single flannel blanket on the springs... Mothers... were exhausted, hungry...

Toussaint Stephen Langevin, a Montréal doctor

This photo was taken in 1915. What challenges might this family face?

Factory owners, businessmen, and government officials became very wealthy during the war. Jimmie Gray was amazed when he got a paper route in the wealthy part of Winnipeg.

The people who lived in houses such as this one may have owned factories or stores. They often built summer cottages on lakes away from the city.

Voices of Canada

Families with High Incomes

There were no houses. There were only castles, huge castles three full storeys in height... all, certainly with dozens of rooms. *Sometimes, a maid allowed Gray into the front hallway at collection time. He remembers,* There were richly carpeted staircases, living rooms full of upholstered chairs. I wondered what it would be like to slide down such shiny banisters.

Jimmie Gray

Thinking *It Through*

During this time, many Francophones in Québec left their farms to find work in the city factories. Because most of the factory owners were Anglophones, Francophones often had to learn English to get a job or to be promoted. But in their homes, churches, and schools, they kept their French culture and identity alive.

■ What do you think the hardest thing would be about learning a new language? What would be the best thing?

■ How important do you think it is to keep your culture, language, and traditions? What can people do to achieve this?

More **About. . .**

Cars

Many city people started buying cars. New laws were made. Cars driving after dark needed headlights and speeding was forbidden. For many years, cars shared the same streets and roads as horse-drawn carts and buggies. What problems do you think this caused?

There were very few paved roads. Cars, such as this one near Milo, Alberta, often got stuck in the mud.

New Jobs for Women

Factory Work

I had a very hard job. It was interesting work, but very hard on your nerves. There was a machine [that] went on fire. This friend was on the machine that blew up and I ran to her and we had to go down on our hands and knees and crawl out of the place. So we have a little experience of what it was like to be right in a war.

A female factory worker

When the war started, thousands of men signed up. Jimmie's father could not because he had lost an arm in an accident. But Jimmie's uncle went to fight in France against the German army. His aunt and young cousins could not survive on the small amount of money the government provided. So Jimmie's aunt got a job in a store.

Before the war, married women were discouraged from working in stores. But because many men were away, some women were hired to work outside the home. Some even got jobs in factories. They made guns, ammunition, and airplanes for the war. This was dangerous work.

Some women from cities went to help farm women bring in the harvest because there were not enough men.

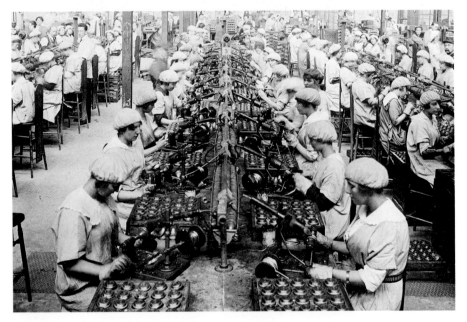

About 35 000 women worked in factories such as the one in this photograph. What can you tell about the factories by looking at the picture? How might a worker in this factory describe her day?

Patriotism

World War I changed how some Canadians felt about their country. They were proud of their soldiers, and they were proud that Canada was fighting for freedom. During the war, many Canadians showed their **patriotism** by doing things such as turning empty public spaces into gardens. Classrooms competed to see which one could grow the most food in their Victory Gardens. These were vegetable gardens planted on playing fields or empty lots. The food was then canned and sent to Canadian soldiers overseas.

words matter!

Patriotism means showing support or loyalty toward a country.

Voices of Canada

Knitting for Soldiers

Like so many women during the war, Jimmie's mother knit socks and mittens for the soldiers overseas. Schoolchildren were expected to help out, too. Great rolls of wool were sent to schools. The boys separated the large rolls into smaller balls, and the girls did the knitting. Jimmie remembers:

The beginners were started on scarves and every now and then a little Grade 3 girl would become so fouled up in her scarf-knitting that she would start everybody around to giggling. Then her work would all be unravelled and she'd start over again.

Thinking It Through

■ Why do you think women were not allowed to have certain jobs before the war? Are there some jobs that women today are not allowed to have? Why do you think this is so?

■ Today, women fight in wars, too. What attitudes do you think had to change for this happen?

Schoolchildren in Barons, Alberta, show their patriotism on "Flag Raising Day" in 1919. They practised songs such as "The Maple Leaf Forever," "Rule Britannia," and "God Save the King." They sang these last two songs because Canada was part of the British Empire during and after World War I.

Viewpoints

My grandfather told me that his grandfather fought in World War I. He wanted to show his patriotism. But I wonder— did everyone support the war?

This photo shows Cree soldiers from The Pas. About 4000 Aboriginal people volunteered to serve in the Great War. The Tyendinaga Mohawk First Nation allowed its land to be used for a flying school. The Blood Tribe of Alberta gave generously to the Red Cross war effort.

How Did Canadians Feel About the War?

The Great War caused many citizens of our country to ask: "Who are we? What do we believe in? What are we fighting for?" Many people of British descent supported Britain during the war. They eagerly volunteered to fight, at least at the beginning of the war. The *Toronto Globe* newspaper described the scene when a crowd was told in August, 1914, that war had been declared:

"For a moment the thousands stood still. Then a cheer broke. It was not for the war, but for the King, Britain, and... victory. Toronto is British. Heads were bowed and the crowd began to sing 'God Save the King. '[Then the] citizens joined... in that old song, 'Rule Britannia.'"

This photo was taken in front of City Hall in Toronto. What does it tell you about how these people were responding to the war?

Some of my classmates saw a TV show about Talbot Papineau, an important Québécois who died fighting in World War I. Talbot believed that the war was for a good cause. But not everyone in Québec agreed with him—especially his cousin, the newspaper editor, Henri Bourassa.

Many decisions in Canada affected how Francophones viewed the war: We were asked to fight in Europe for the British Empire's ideas of justice and freedom. But I agree with Henri Bourassa. We Francophones were having to fight for our own freedoms and rights here in Canada. Ontario was closing down French-language schools!

The Vandoos were brave, successful Francophone volunteer soldiers from Québec. But the Canadian government would not let Francophone soldiers fight together. They were put under English-speaking commanders. They did not have Catholic priests to be with them when they were injured or dying in battle. Do you think these decisions affected whether Québec supported the war?

The name Vandoos comes from the word "vingt-deux," French for "22." The men formed the 22nd regiment.

In 1917, the Canadian government introduced conscription. This law forced men to go to Europe to fight. Québec did not believe this was right. I say "NON" to conscription. It is always wrong to be forced to go to war. I agree with our former Prime Minister Wilfrid Laurier. He says that conscription is against the spirit of cooperation that we had at the time of Confederation.

Over to **You**

1. Should the government force people to enlist when there are not many volunteers to be soldiers? If so, should there be exceptions if some types of workers, such as farmers, are needed at home?

2. Can a citizen disagree with a war that his or her country is involved in and still be considered patriotic? Explain your answer.

What Challenges Did Canadians Face During This Time?

When my ancestors moved to Montréal from their farms around 1910, they were worried about stories they had heard about pollution, diseases, and unsafe working conditions in factories.

Conditions in Cities

Life in Canada's cities brought new challenges to the thousands of people who moved there in search of work. Factories polluted the air. Some parts of some cities had no electricity or running water.

Fire was another big problem in cities. Many buildings were made of wood and were built close together, so fire spread quickly. This photo was taken in Montréal.

In the crowded and often unclean conditions in cities, diseases spread easily. After the war, some soldiers brought a new and deadly disease back from Europe with them. It was called the Spanish influenza, or the flu. It spread quickly, and millions of people in the world died from it. In fact, more people died during the spread of the Spanish flu than during the war itself.

THEN AND NOW

The photo on the left was taken in 1918. Many people, such as these men, wore face masks so they would not catch the Spanish flu. Some provinces made everyone wear a mask. Today, there are still diseases, such as SARS, that spread easily and quickly. Why does our modern world make it even easier for these diseases to travel?

Conditions in Factories

Not all children went to school during this time. Many never got to play, either. They had to work. Even though child labour was against the law in most provinces by the time of the Great War, greedy employers and desperately poor parents found it easy to break the law. Often, children were sent to work under terrible conditions for very little pay.

Some children, like these young miners, worked underground in the dark for long hours. They had small lamps and bottles to carry their drinking water.

Voices of Canada

A Child Worker

This interview was done between a government official and Joseph Larkins, a child worker. "Q" means the official's question. "A" means Joseph's answer.

Q. How old are you?

A. I am 11 years.

Q. What is the matter with your hand?

A. I got hurt in the machinery.

Q. How?

A. It got caught in the rollers... of a cracker machine —a biscuit machine.

Q. How much wages did they give you?

A. A dollar a week at first, and then $1.25.

Q. What were you doing at the machinery?

A. I was brushing the dough off as it came through.

Q. Did you lose any fingers?

A. I lost one.

Q. Did you lose any of the joints of the others?

A. I think I will lose a second finger.

There is no further information about Joseph or about what was done to help him.

The working conditions in factories were terrible for women as well as for children. One day a woman named Nellie McClung led the premier of Manitoba into a dirty, noisy basement sewing factory. Here, immigrant women worked ten hours a day, six days a week, for very little pay. "Let me out of here. I'm choking," he gasped. *Then why didn't he outlaw such working conditions?* Nellie wondered.

Thinking It Through

■ Joseph was 11 when he worked at the factory. Jimmie was 8 when he got a paper route. At what age can children legally work in Alberta? Do you agree that this is a good age? Why or why not?

■ Many women who had worked during the war now had to give up their jobs to the returning men. Do you think this would happen today? Explain.

I think it would have been awful to work in a factory back then. I wonder if Nellie McClung was able to do anything to change the working conditions.

Attitudes Toward Women

It was not easy for women like Nellie McClung to make changes in society. Part of the reason was because women did not have much power. The first thing that had to change was the attitudes many men had toward women.

Women's Roles

How would you feel if you were not allowed to play your favourite sport just because you were a girl? Growing up in the late 1800s, Nellie McClung was not allowed to play sports as her brothers did.

Nellie learned that there were many things she was not allowed to do because she was a girl. For example, girls were discouraged from attending university.

Voices of Canada

Nellie McClung

At 16, Nellie became a schoolteacher. She bought a football and organized noon-hour games. She wanted the children to work off their energy and learn to play as a team. Nellie played with them. Nellie remembered:

One day, one of the girls came to me almost in tears, and told me that her mother... and [other women] had said that I should not play football: it wasn't a ladies' game...

Nellie explained her reasons for letting the children play the game. She found out that she had a special skill. She could convince people to change their minds.

Nellie became determined that girls and women have new opportunities. She wanted to change attitudes and laws to make life better for mothers and their children.

Skill Smart

- Imagine you are in Nellie McClung's class. Write a persuasive letter to your parents to convince them to let boys and girls play football together.

Women's Identities

At the beginning of World War I, women were not considered citizens of Canada. In fact, women were not even allowed to vote. Married women could not own property or money. The law said that homes, farms, and even children belonged only to the husband. Even though they could not own property, married women worked hard for their families.

Voices of Canada

Farm Women

There is no harder worked woman than the woman on the farm. Not only must she perform her duties as housewife, not only must she nurse and care for her children, but she... usually is the general servant of the farm itself. Her working day is the length of time she can manage to stand upon her legs.

The Western Producer, Oct. 23, 1924

Have you ever heard a story of something unfair happening to someone? Did it make you want to take action? An Albertan named Emily Murphy had this experience. She met a woman whose husband had left her and their children. He sold their farm, but the law did not force him to share the money with his wife. She and her children now had no money.

Murphy was determined that this law must be changed. With Nellie McClung, she tried to change people's attitudes. They worked to convince people that women should be allowed to participate in government. That way, women could help change unfair laws. They could also pass new laws that would improve the lives of families on farms and in cities.

Skill Smart

■ Look back at the inquiry questions on page 247. Check which ones you have found answers to. Take time to jot down your answers, along with notes for sources of information.

How Did Women Help Change Canada?

I know that I can become anything I want—a lawyer, doctor, soldier, athlete—I can even become prime minister. But I also know that 100 years ago, women were not allowed to do these things.

Have you ever heard someone say "Many doors are open to you"? An "open door" means an opportunity. Today, Canadians have many more opportunities than they did 100 years ago. How did this change?

Murphy, McClung, and many other brave women in Canada began fighting for change by trying to win the right to vote for women. The struggle took great courage and determination. Many people were afraid that allowing women to vote was too big a change. Some people made fun of the **suffragists.** They even accused the women of neglecting their children. But McClung, Murphy, and others believed that women should have a voice in government. They could then make the future better for their children.

These suffragists are protesting in front of the House of Commons in London, England, in 1924. Women in Canada were not alone in their fight to win the right to vote. What does this tell you about the importance of this struggle?

These women were gas-station attendants during World War I. How do you think the new jobs and responsibilities that women had at that time helped change people's attitudes?

Voices of Canada

Nellie McClung

Disturbers are never popular—nobody ever really loved an alarm clock in action—no matter how grateful they may have been afterwards for its kind services.

Nellie McClung

What do you think Nellie McClung meant when she said this?

The Right to Vote

By 1916, women in the Prairie provinces were celebrating their victory. They had won the right to vote! By the end of the war in 1918, women across Canada were allowed to vote for the governments in Ottawa and in most provinces.

Around the same time as they won the vote, women were allowed to take on new jobs and responsibilities. For example, a few women were allowed to train as doctors. Emily Murphy became a judge. But she was soon to discover that not all doors were open yet for the women of Canada.

More About. . .

The Vote

Not all women were allowed to vote by 1918. Neither were all men. For example, the laws of Canada did not permit Aboriginal people or people from Asia to vote. But over the years, attitudes changed, people fought hard, and new laws were passed.

1940: Québec women get the right to vote in provincial elections.

1947: East Indian and Chinese Canadians get the right to vote.

1949: Japanese Canadians get the right to vote.

1960: First Nations get the right to vote.

1971: Young people between 18 and 20 get the right to vote.

Voices of Canada

The Importance of Voting

Getting the right to vote allows people to participate as citizens in their country. It makes people feel like they belong. "When I voted I felt like I could finally join the human race."

Japanese resident of British Columbia, 1949

Marie Lacoste Gérin-Lajoie (1867–1945)
Marie Lacoste Gérin-Lajoie once led 400 women to ask the premier of Québec for the right to vote. She opposed the old laws that said married women could not own property or be their children's legal guardians. In 1940, women in Québec became full citizens with the right to vote.

Dr. Emily Jennings Stowe (1831-1903)
In 1867, Emily Jennings Stowe, an Ontario woman, graduated from an American medical school. She had not been permitted to study medicine in Canada because she was a woman. When she returned to Canada, Stowe became active in organizations that fought for women's rights, especially the right to vote.

The Persons Case

After she became a judge, Emily Murphy heard things like "You are not even a person. You have no right to hold office." A law at the time said that certain important government jobs could only be held by "qualified persons." Most people thought this meant that only men could hold these jobs. But some Albertans thought that Emily should become a senator in Ottawa. Was this possible? Were women qualified persons? Murphy decided to find out what the law really meant. She asked Nellie McClung and three other women—Henrietta Edwards, Irene Parlby, and Louise McKinney—to help her. Here is a part of her letter to them:

> "For the several years past the women of Canada, owing to what appeared to be a hopeless situation, took... little interest in this matter of the interpretation of the word 'Persons.' Our action in appealing to the Supreme Court of Canada... (gives to) women of all parties a renewed hope... Nothing can prevent our winning."

THEN AND NOW

At the time of World War I, all Governors-General were British men. At left is Prince Arthur, Duke of Connaught. He was a son of Queen Victoria and served as Governor-General from 1911 to 1916. At right is Michaëlle Jean. She was born in Haiti and is the first Black person to be Governor-General. She is also the third woman to hold the position. She was appointed in 2005. What does her appointment tell you about Canada's changing identity?

In 1927 the Supreme Court of Canada answered the five women. It said that the Fathers of Confederation had not meant the word "persons" to include women.

The Famous Five, as the group was now called, was disappointed. But these women did not give up. They asked the highest court in the British Empire to decide. On October 18, 1929, the decision was announced: "[T]heir lordships have come to the conclusion that the word 'person' includes... male and female... " The Famous Five had helped to bring about change for Canadian women.

The Famous Five

I know what Nellie McClung and Emily Murphy did to fight for women's rights. My classmates and I wondered what work the other three women in the Famous Five did. Our teacher gave us this list of questions to help us do some research.

1. Which member of the Famous Five are you most interested in researching? Why?

2. What was her childhood like?

3. Why do you think she became interested in women's rights?

4. What jobs did she do in her life?

5. Did she become part of the government? In what position?

6. List changes that she helped to make. Include any organizations she started.

7. Does she deserve to be famous? By herself or as part of the Famous Five?

Emily Murphy—helped change property laws in Alberta to protect women and their children; first woman in the British Empire to become a judge in a police court

Nellie McClung—famous author and speaker who helped women get the right to vote in Manitoba and Alberta

Henrietta Muir Edwards

Irene Parlby

Louise McKinney

Thinking *It Through*

■ Do you think the suffragists succeeded in making the future better for their children? Explain.

■ Think of a situation today which shows that women are still treated differently than men are. Why do you think these situations still exist?

What About Other Citizens and Their Rights?

After the Famous Five victory, were all Canadians treated fairly and equally?

The work of the Famous Five was an important step in making Canada a fair or just country. These women proved that old laws and old attitudes could be changed. But women still struggled for equal and fair treatment. So did many other groups in Canada.

Lieutenant Frederick Loft

When First Nations soldiers returned from World War I, they were frustrated that they could not vote. Aboriginal people were awarded more than fifty medals for bravery and heroism during the war. They became known as some of the best snipers and scouts because of their traditional knowledge and skills. Lieutenant Frederick Loft of the Mohawk First Nation said, " ... in the... war we have performed dutiful service to our country and we have the right to claim and demand justice and fair play." Loft helped organize a national Aboriginal group to fight for the right to vote and to control reserve lands.

Thérèse Casgrain

Although Casgrain came from a rich Québecois family and married a wealthy man, she worked hard to get more rights for women and people with low incomes. She was inspired by stories of Québec women helping others in the past. She said, "The charitable activity of our women was particularly necessary during the frequent epidemics that ravished Québec."

Casgrain remembers her mother making fancy gift baskets for the poor every Christmas. "[My family] never dreamed, however, of trying to find out why these people were in need." Casgrain spent her life trying to discover and change the causes of poverty.

Mary Two-Axe Earley

In 1979, Mary Two-Axe Earley, a Mohawk, won the Governor General's Award in Commemoration of the Persons Case. Mary was honoured for her long struggle to make life better for First Nations women. Before 1985, when an Aboriginal woman married a non-Aboriginal man, the law said she lost the right to live on the reserve. But Aboriginal men who married non-Aboriginal women did not lose their rights. Mary married a non-Aboriginal man and had to leave her home on the Kahnawake reserve. For 25 years, she wrote letters and made presentations to the government. Finally, the law was changed. In 1985 Mary became the first woman in Canada to regain her Aboriginal rights. When she died, she was buried on her home reserve.

People can work together to make life better for themselves and others. In 1926, two student nurses in Calgary cut their hair short. It was more comfortable and practical, but they were fired for doing it. Then, thirty other nurses cut their hair. Their vacation was cancelled until their hair grew back. The thirty nurses quit. Sixty more nurses cut their hair. Finally the rule was changed.

Are voting and making laws the only ways to bring about changes?

Making *a Difference*

The Victorian Order of Nurses

In Canadian cities in the early 1900s, overcrowding and polluted water and air often made babies and children unhealthy. There were very few doctors and nurses in the rapidly growing cities. Not many people could afford to get medical care. Where could mothers turn for help? Women like Henrietta Muir Edwards of the Famous Five helped start the Victorian Order of Nurses, or the VON. In cities, these nurses gave advice and helped mothers keep their children healthy. They also travelled to small communities to bring health care to families.

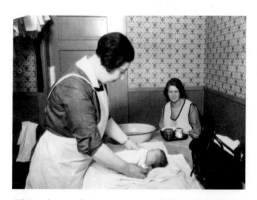

This photo shows a nurse visiting a mother at home in Calgary. The nurses often made home visits to teach mothers how to care for their babies. The Victorian Order of Nurses were among the first women in Calgary to drive.

Build Your Skills!

Make Meaning of Historical Photographs

This photograph was taken around 1914, or near the beginning of World War I. What can you tell from the photograph? How do you think the man is feeling? How do you think the child is feeling? Write two different captions for this picture and explain the points of view that each caption shows.

Honour Five Canadians

In 1999, a group of Albertans had a monument built to remember and honour the Famous Five. Other famous Canadians are honoured by having schools or streets named after them. Brainstorm a list of five Canadians who deserve to be remembered. Explain each person's contribution and why he or she deserves to be honoured. What would be an appropriate way to honour each of these Canadians? Which of the five do you think is the *most* honourable?

Imagine the Past

Imagine that you were born 100 years ago. Write a letter to a friend describing what you do every day, what you want to be when you grow up, and what the future probably holds for you.

Research Ways of Life

Choose one aspect of the Canadian way of life between 1900 and 1920. It could be entertainment, recreation, fashion, food, work, or school. Use the Internet or library to research your topic. Share your findings by creating a collage. You could also use a paint-and-draw program.

Putting It All Together

When I looked at old photographs, I saw that life in Canada changed a lot around the time of World War I. I made a Positive/Negative Chart to show some of the changes that happened.

Positive	Negative
• World War I made some people feel proud of their country.	• During the war, 60 000 Canadian soldiers died, and many were wounded.
• There were more jobs and cities grew. Factories, electricity, running water, and cars made life easier for some people.	• Many people were forced to work in terrible conditions in factories.
• People such as the Famous Five helped to make lives better, especially for women. Women finally won the right to vote. Later, other groups won the right to vote, too.	• Crowded cities made diseases spread easily.

Review the inquiry questions for this chapter:
* In what ways did World War I begin to change Canadians' identity?
* How would life be different if the Famous Five had not succeeded?

Take Time to Reflect

In this chapter, you learned that certain events can change the way people think or live. Think of an event or idea that caused you to change. Did you move to a new place? Did you read a book that gave you new information? Draw two pictures, one before and one after the change. Write captions to explain the pictures. Add the pictures and captions to your Canada Collection.

What helps people get through bad times? Talking to family and friends and focusing on positive things can help. Finding creative ways to solve problems is another solution.

Canadians are extremely creative during hard times. The 1930s were difficult years here and in other parts of the world. There were few jobs, and thousands of people could not afford food or proper housing. Here is one girl's story about growing up during this time.

Her family had very little money, and often only had potatoes to eat. She remembers how cleverly her mother dealt with this challenge: "At supper, we'd each get a big potato on the plate. Mother would cut off one end and say, 'Now, this is your soup. Isn't it good?' We'd eat that. Then she'd slice off another piece and say, 'Here's your meat.' Then she'd pick up the last piece and say, 'And here's your chocolate pudding.' It got so we'd almost believe her."

By the time this girl became a mother herself, conditions in Canada were better. In the 1950s, there were more jobs and families had more money. New inventions, such as the television, were changing the way people spent their free time.

These children lived in Québec in the 1930s.

These children are part of a fashion show in Calgary in 1953.

Canada: Our Stories Continue

Life in Canada changed a lot between the 1920s and the 1960s. After Canada recovered from the disruption of World War I, there were jobs in factories and on farms. By the 1920s, most Canadian families had enough money to buy food and clothing.

But then trade between countries slowed down, and factories had to close. Workers lost their jobs. Years of drought across the Prairies made growing crops very difficult. Many people across the country—especially farmers—did not have enough money for food or clothes. We call this time **The Great Depression.** Even during these bad times, though, Canadians found ways to help themselves and one another.

These hard times were replaced by another great hardship—World War II. Although it was a terrible world event, the war provided many people with jobs. After the war, good times returned for many Canadians and especially for children and young people.

words matter!

The **Great Depression** occurred between 1929 and 1939. Thousands of Canadians lost their jobs and could not find new ones. Most people had little money. Their quality of life changed for the worse.

? Inquiring Minds

Here are some questions to guide your inquiry for this chapter:

- Why was everyone affected by the Great Depression, even people with jobs?
- Consider the ways that life changed for most Canadians after World War II. Decide if all these changes improved their ways of life.

Brianne's Inquiry

My parents always tell me how good my life is, compared to when they were growing up. Their parents told them that, too. And guess what? So did their parents! But for those like my great-great aunt Mary, who remembers the 1930s, it really is true. Times were very, very tough back then.

During spring break, I went to Saskatoon with my parents and grandparents to visit my great-great aunt who lives in a seniors' residence. While we were there, we went to the Western Development Museum. The galleries about the Great Depression and the one on the years since 1940 got everyone talking. My grandparents do not remember the Great Depression, but they do remember the excitement of new things in the 1950s, like their first TV and a toy called the Hula Hoop. I began to wonder:

- How have people's ways of life changed since my great-great aunt was young? Why were times so hard then?
- How do people help each other in hard times? What about when times are good?
- What did people do for fun, both during hard times and good times?

I am going to find out by reading, researching, and talking to people.

This young girl is playing with a Hula Hoop. The photo was taken in 1958.

270

Helping Others

Every day in your community, there are people helping others. In fact, there are even people helping you, such as volunteers at the museum and library, sports coaches, and firefighters. Use the following steps to find things that you can do to help others:

Find out what groups in your community need help. Is the food bank looking for donations? Does the seniors' residence need volunteers? Choose one group and learn as much as you can about it. Find out exactly what it needs.

Make a list of ways you could help. Will you be doing or giving? Raking lawns is an example of doing. Raising money is an example of giving.

Make a plan. List the things that need to be done and who would be best to do each one. Decide when you want each task to be accomplished.

Decide if the plan is right for you. Make sure that you have the time and the skills you need to make it a success.

Put your plan into action! You will find that you can have a lot of fun and feel good about yourself, too.

Practise the Skill

1. Work with your classmates to help people in your community. First, place someone in charge of keeping your group's discussions on track. Have someone take notes. Remember to listen respectfully to others in your group.

2. Then, follow the steps in the flow chart above. Identify a group of people in your community who are living through a hard time. For example, are there people who do not have enough money to buy food or clothing? Would it be best to collect money for them, or to collect food and clothing?

3. Make a plan, make sure you are ready to commit to it, and then follow through with it.

How Did the Great Depression Affect Canadians?

During the Great Depression, the government did not provide any medical care or child support. People were left to take care of themselves. But without jobs or crops to sell, people could no longer afford basic things like food and clothing. Many Canadians wrote letters to the prime minister of the time, Richard B. Bennett. The letter writers expressed their frustrations and asked the prime minister for help.

? Critical Inquiry TIP

Retrieving

One way to learn about Canada's stories is to read historical letters. Before the Internet, writing letters was the main way people communicated over long distances. Letters provide information about ways of life and important events.

Voices of Canada

Letters to Bennett

Haven't any milk for three months. Never have any vegetables except potatoes and almost no fruit and baby hasn't any shoes.
Burton, Alberta

I am a girl thirteen years old... and I haven't got a coat to put on. I have to walk to school four and a half miles every morning and night and I'm awfully cold every day.

Passman, Saskatchewan, Oct. 16, 1933

During the last two weeks I have eaten only toast and drunk a cup of tea every day. Day after day I pass a delicatessen and the food in the window looks so good, and I'm so hungry! The stamp which carries this letter to you will represent the last three cents I have in the world.

Hamilton, Ontario

This is one of Canada's best-known paintings. It is called *The Young Canadian* and is a portrait of Carl Schaeffer, a friend of the artist. The artist, Charles Comfort, was unemployed during the Great Depression. Why do you think the artist chose to paint Carl? What is in the foreground of the painting? What is in the background?

Voices of Canada

Survivors' Stories

Brianne's teacher lent her a book that contained interviews. They were done by Barry Broadfoot. He was an interviewer and historian who had travelled across Canada and talked with people who had survived the Great Depression.

I remember not going to school my fifth grade, about 12 years old, because I didn't have shoes. My sister Helen went, though, because she could use the ones I grew out of... I got around doing chores and that, by making sort of moccasins out of deerskin, rubber from an inner tube and binder twine and staples, but my mother wouldn't let me go to school that way.

Canadian interviewed by Barry Broadfoot

Brianne also found other books with stories that show how Canadians were affected during this time.

I remember Dad had a shoemaker shop... Few people had the money to get their shoes fixed... Dad would leave Mom 25 cents, and that was to feed the family... I remember one day. It was so sad! Dad had to admit that he only made 10 cents for a day's work. He had two rents to pay, house rent was $25 a month, as was the shop rent.

Virginia Sherbo Cosentino

The thing that got to me was my first day at school. I saw kids with holes in their clothes and shoes. Some of them had stuffed cardboard in their shoes to cover the holes. I thought to myself: "... Is this the land of plenty? Is this the place which is supposed to have gold on the streets?"

Annette Morello came to Canada in 1933 at age 7

Thinking It Through

- What five words best describe life during the Great Depression?
- Why might Annette's family have expected Canada to have gold on the streets?

During the Great Depression, Newfoundlanders like the Knee family, shown in this photo, suffered hard times. More than half of the people in Newfoundland had no work. One reason was that no one could afford to buy the cod that fishermen caught. People who had no jobs had no money to spend. Why do you think this photo was taken?

273

Country Life During the Great Depression

Between 1929 and 1939, what happened to the land of the Prairies made people's struggles even harder.

My family calls the Depression years the dirty thirties. I asked why. Everyone had stories about the Dust Bowl, the nickname they gave to the Prairies during that time. Aunt Mary says pictures can't show how dirty it was, and how hot it was in the days before air-conditioning. She says she can still taste and feel the blowing soil.

- There was no rain, year after year. It was so dry that when a rainstorm finally came in 1937, young children cried. They did not know what the rain was. They were so afraid.
- Summer after summer, temperatures were hotter than normal. The 1936 heat wave killed 780 Canadians. The winters were very cold, but there was little snow because there was no moisture.
- Strong, hot winds blew the dry soil like snow in a blizzard. It covered fences and blew into people's houses.
- The weather caused crops to die in the fields. It was useless to plant more crops. Livestock died. Farmers had no crops to sell. Their families had no money.

Voices of Canada

Dust Storm!

There was the blackest, most terrifying cloud I've ever seen on the horizon. It was moving very quickly... The house was sure to be blown away and the nearest neighbor was a mile away... I could never make it... [We] ran for the dugout barn. Already the shadow of the cloud was upon us... dust hung in the air so thick it was clearly visible. Everything—land, air, sky—was a dull gray color.

From Anne Bailey's diary (farmer's wife)

Anne Bailey wrote that after the dust storm, their "feet sank in sand almost to our ankles, and we breathed and tasted sand." What evidence in this photo supports the name "the Dirty Thirties"?

Natural Disaster: Grasshoppers

During the years of drought on the Prairies, crops were often destroyed by swarms of grasshoppers. They could eat through clothes on a clothesline, too. Clouds of these insects were so thick they blocked the sun. Masses of crushed grasshoppers made sidewalks, roads, and railway tracks too slippery to travel on.

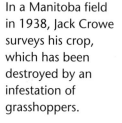

In a Manitoba field in 1938, Jack Crowe surveys his crop, which has been destroyed by an infestation of grasshoppers.

Voices of Canada

More Grasshoppers

Where we lived in the Red River Valley the soil kept some moisture in. So it wasn't as dry as further west. We might have made half a living on the farm during the 1930s, but then the grasshoppers came.

Germaine Alaire, St. Agathe

Do you remember Jimmie Gray from Chapter 9? By 1936 he was writing for a newspaper, which sent him on a car trip to report on the Dust Bowl.

> We were hit by the thickest cloud of grasshoppers... The swarm was upon us so suddenly that our windshield was solidly encrusted with splattered insects in a matter of seconds. We pulled over and stopped... Our car was a ghastly mess. The crashing grasshoppers had given it a sickly green colour. The windshield wipers only created a gooey smear.

The Trans Canada Trail splits into two routes at Moose Jaw, Saskatchewan. The southern route passes through the area known as Palliser's Triangle. This was the area most affected by the drought of the Dust Bowl. Thousands of people moved away from this area in the 1930s. Later, farmers and governments worked together to find better ways to farm this very dry Prairie land.

City Life During the Great Depression

Many people who lost their jobs refused to apply for relief. Give two reasons why they did not.

During the Great Depression, city governments gave poor families relief, or help. They gave out coupons that could be exchanged for rent, fuel, and food. But relief money could not be used to buy streetcar tickets, newspapers, cleaning supplies, or even toothbrushes. No one on relief was allowed to have a telephone, a radio, or a car. Some cities made married men on relief do work like moving rocks from one pile to another, or pulling dandelions on city streets. This was to prove that they were not lazy.

❓ Critical Inquiry TIP

Processing

When you are learning about historical events, it is important to make sure you understand the causes and effects. For example, it might help to draw a web showing the causes of the Great Depression, and another web showing the effects it had on Canadians.

Voices of Canada

Out of Work

Our family had to go on relief when [the railway] laid off 1500 people; father was one of them. I remember the day it happened. We were waiting by the door for dad to return from work. When he came in, he tossed his work gloves up in the air, which signified that he had lost his job. He was unemployed for four years.

Giuseppe Torchia

In the 1930s, Montréal was Canada's largest city. It had many factories and industries. During the Great Depression, these factories either closed down or had to pay their workers much less money. One out of three Francophone male workers in Montréal had no job. Like other families, the Montréal family in this photo could not pay the rent and was forced to leave its apartment.

Not everyone in the cities was poor, though. Some people were able to keep their jobs. Other people occasionally got richer because prices were lower.

Some people who owned factories or stores saw a chance to make more money during these hard times. They forced workers to work longer hours for less pay. They hired children too young to legally work. The workers, who desperately needed money, had no power to fight back.

Many stores went bankrupt during the 1930s. Line-ups wrapped around the block whenever one was advertised, such as this Army and Navy Store in Edmonton in 1931. What does this photo tell you about the availability of jobs? Why did the photographer take this photo?

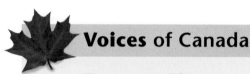

Voices of Canada

Desperate Times

Because I was small, I had to climb into the needles and go between the threads with a little brush... My hands were full of blood. There was no break. It was so hot in the factory. All the windows were closed to keep the humidity so the cotton would stay soft. It could get as hot as [40°C]... Because of the heat, many employees got sick... One of my friends got sick and died.

15-year-old Irène Duhamel, Québec

Unfair Treatment

In the 1930s, people whose families had come from Great Britain owned many of the stores and businesses in Canada. During the Great Depression, these people often only gave jobs to other Canadians of British descent. This meant that Francophones, Aboriginal people, and people of Eastern European ancestry were often denied jobs because of their identity.

My aunt Mary told me that her Eastern European ancestors were treated unfairly when they first came to Canada. Their language, clothing, and customs made them seem different. By the 1920s, their children were being treated a little better. But when the Depression came, Eastern Europeans were again treated poorly. My aunt told me that in the 1930s, she changed her name from Maruca Sobinski to Mary Summers. She said, "Yes, it got me a paycheque, but I felt I lost my identity."

Riding the Rails

In those days, thousands of men... were riding freight trains between Vancouver and Halifax looking for work. When they tried to get off in different cities and towns along the way, the police would say, "OK, fellows, get back on, there's no work here, keep moving." These young men just drifted from one part of Canada to another looking for jobs that did not exist.

Sam Loschiavio

Homeless, Single Men

There was another group of people who suffered greatly during this time. Single men, or men without families, were not given relief in most Canadian cities if they could not find jobs. This meant that the men could not afford houses or apartments. They became homeless.

Homeless men lined up for meals of soup or stew at soup kitchens like this one in Edmonton. Soup kitchens were run by churches, charities, or city governments. Do similar places exist today? Why?

Making *a Difference*

Hannah Taylor and the Ladybug Foundation

Even today, there are still many homeless people in Canada. When Hannah Taylor was five years old, she saw a man eating out of a garbage can. "I was very sad about it," she said. "I asked my mom why he had to do that. My heart was sad. My mom told me that if you do something to change the problem, your heart won't feel so sad."

Hannah started the Ladybug Foundation as a way of raising money to help people who had no place to live. Many Canadian companies donate money to the Ladybug Foundation. The Girl Guides of Canada make ladybug jars in which people can leave their change. Hannah wants people to do more than put coins in jars. She wants people to change "the way we see and help homeless people."

Living Off the Land

Not everyone tried to make a living by working in a city or growing crops during this time. Ike Hill, a Tyendinaga Mohawk Elder, remembers the dirty thirties:

Voices of Canada

Staying Fed

The missus and I managed to keep the kids fed... We used to do the hunting or the trapping so we'd have meat. But folks in the city, they didn't have [anything]. Well, neither did we, but we [were] used to not having anything.

Most Métis and First Nations were used to living off the land. Their ancestors had been doing so for generations. But during the Great Depression, some Prairie farmers were encouraged to move north to the edge of the Shield. There they began hunting, trapping, and fishing—on the same land as First Nations and Métis people. What do you think happens to the animals when too many people are hunting in the same area of land?

More **About...**

Olive Dickason

Olive Dickason's family ended up living off the land in northern Manitoba during the Great Depression. There, her Métis mother taught her how to hunt, fish, and gather food to keep from starving. Dr. Olive Dickason became a university professor and an expert on the history of Canada's First Nations. What did she learn from growing up during the Great Depression?

In the 1930s, the Québec government made its people an offer. They could have free land in the Abitibi area of Québec if they moved away from cities and towns. But the land here was extremely difficult to farm. Describe the people in this picture. Do you think their lives were much different here? What evidence do you have?

How Did People Survive the Great Depression?

Have you ever heard the expression "Necessity is the mother of invention"? It means that when there is great need, people can be very creative and invent new things. During the Depression, people used their creativity to survive. Nothing was thrown out—clothes were mended, and items were re-used or traded among neighbours.

Voices of Canada

Flour-Sack Dresses

You take an empty sack of flour... and give it a good wash... and then you'd turn it upside down and cut two holes for the arms and one at the top for the neck... and put in hems and guess what you had? You had a dress for a nine-year-old girl. I went to school in those dresses, and so did my cousins... Then... another company... put out bags with coloured flowers printed on them... and what did you have? You had a party dress, fit for a queen.

A Saskatchewan woman interviewed by Barry Broadfoot

With no money for fuel or repairs, families hitched horses or oxen to their cars. They nicknamed them Bennett Buggies, after Prime Minister R.B. Bennett. Even if people could afford to have a car, why would it be difficult to operate one on the Prairies during the Great Depression?

Helping Others

Besides thinking of creative ways to use what they already had, people during the Great Depression helped each other get through the hard times. Often what people remember about this period are the stories of Canadians sharing the little bit that they had.

For example, restaurants in those days served sandwiches with the bread crusts cut off. Waitresses collected the crusts in bags and handed them out at the back door. Each evening, men lined up for the crusts.

In 1932, these Bell Canada operators filled Christmas hampers for families in need in Montréal. What do you think is in the baskets? What do people in your community do to help others at Christmas?

Voices of Canada

The Kindness of Strangers

A widow in Williams Lake, British Columbia, told Barry Broadfoot how some First Nations men she did not know found her and her children, hungry and cold.

[They]... looked around the cabin. They see there is no food. Just potatoes and a sack of flour. Next morning two of these guys come across the river riding two horses, leading two others and what do you think they've got? Moose meat on the one horse, all the horse can carry, and dried salmon on the other. They got us through the winter.

Thinking It Through

- What did people do to help survive the Great Depression?
- People who lived through the Great Depression often speak about that time with great pride. Why?

281

Viewpoints

What Did "Fun" Mean During the Great Depression?

You have learned that most people during the 1930s did not have a lot of money. Did this mean that they did not have any fun? What did "fun" mean then? To some children, it was using large pieces of cardboard as sleds in winter and playing with clay-baked marbles in spring. Adults had ways of entertaining themselves, too. Sometimes it just took a bit of creativity.

Mary Travers-Bolduc

One way people amused themselves was with music. Mary Travers-Bolduc was a popular singer and songwriter from Québec. She wrote songs in French about what people were going through. Mary had experienced poverty, hard work, and illness, but she did not give up. She wrote "Ça va venir découragez-vous pas," a song that told people "The time will come, we can't lose hope." Why do you think people needed to hear songs like these during the Great Depression?

And then there were the dances! Ah, what excitement, what anticipation and preparation in readiness for those Friday night frolics. Chilled to the bone from a sleigh ride, or ride in the back of an... old truck, still how exhilarated everyone was upon entering the hall or the schoolhouse. The music, the merriment was infectious!

Ruth Davis and Jenny Kirkpatrick, Mossbank, Saskatchewan

What are the people doing in this photo? How are picnics different today?

One of the happiest things we did when I was a kid in the 1930s was our Saturday night treat of watching people go by. We... could sit on our front step and watch people pass by, go shopping, visit the café, and drive up and down the street.

G. Friedman, Saskatchewan

Child playing on sled in 1934 near Wawota, Saskatchewan

If there weren't enough players to form opposing teams, we had a game for which I cannot recall the English term (all of us spoke French). We called it... "jouer à la vache." Runs were only to first base and back to home plate.

John J. Molgat, Ste. Rose du Lac, Manitoba

We used to play street hockey. Of course we did not have the equipment hockey players have today. We would wrap Eaton's catalogues or thick newspapers around our legs to make very sturdy hockey pads. Old brooms would be our sticks, but the pucks... were formed of frozen papier-mâché, others with candle wax.

Dorothy Nazareth, Winnipeg

Over to You

1. Make a list of the activities mentioned on these two pages. Then make a list of activities *you* do for fun. Compare the lists. What do they have in common? How are they different? Why do you think this is?

2. Interview your family members about what they did for fun when they were younger. How have things changed? How have they stayed the same?

How Did Life in Canada Change After WW II?

This is the time my grandparents—the Watsons and the Lysenkos—call "the good old days." They were my age in the 1950s. How had life in Canada changed since the Great Depression?

In 1939, another war began. It became known as World War II. The war created jobs in the armed forces and in factories. The Great Depression soon ended.

Factories during the war made planes, tanks, and weapons. After the war, factories produced things like cars and refrigerators. There were more jobs, and many new houses were built. By the 1950s, many people had money for a different lifestyle.

Voices of Canada

Our First Car!

Like many people, we moved to the suburbs, a new part of the city on the outskirts. Everyone had a new house... and they all looked almost the same. But we had our own backyard, and we kids got a swing set. Father now had to drive to work rather than taking a streetcar. So we got our first car.

Grandpa Watson

Our First TV!

It was black and white. There was only one channel, and the picture was often fuzzy. But how excited we were! It changed the way we lived. We dashed home from school to see our favourite shows. We ate dinner off metal TV tables in front of the set. My mother even started using the new-fangled frozen food and instant mixes to give her more TV time.

Granny Watson

This photo was taken in 1949. How do you think cars changed people's ways of life?

The Schiefner family watching television in Saskatchewan in 1956

284

More People, More Money

Canada's population grew after World War II. Many immigrants came from Europe because their homes and lives had been destroyed by the war. They wanted peace and new opportunities. Many of these newcomers settled in big cities like Toronto. The baby boom refers to the large increase in children born in Canada shortly after the war—between 1946 and 1964.

More money came into Canada during this time, too. There was high demand for new houses, cars, and other products, which created jobs. The discovery of several minerals and metals in the Shield created jobs, too.

Of course, all these people with their new jobs needed places to live. One of the ways that life in Canada changed after World War II is that many people moved to **suburbs**.

The billboard on the left is announcing that a suburb will soon be built in that spot. The photo on the right shows a suburb outside of Calgary. What are the choices that can be made when choosing land?

Voices of Canada

My First Year at School!

I was born in 1947. I am a "baby boomer." There were so many of us that the school was bursting at its seams. After two months, half of us were moved to a brand-new school at the edge of the prairie. Soon the new school was surrounded by new houses. By the time my younger brother went to school, there were split shifts. Some kids went only in the morning, and the others in the afternoon, until yet another school could be built in town.

Baba Lysenko

New Ways of Life: Fashions, Fads, and Fun

Life in Canada after World War II was very different from life during the Great Depression. Most people did not have to struggle so hard to survive. Even young people had spending money and free time. Clothing was designed just for them. They had their own music, too—rock 'n' roll. They were not children, but they did not have to work for a living yet, as adults did. A new word was introduced to describe these young people—"teenagers."

Do you know any teenagers? Do they dress like the ones in this photograph? Describe some of the differences you see in this photograph between these teens and teenagers today.

Voices of Canada

New Fashions

I remember the poodle skirts, crinolines, and always a little scarf around the neck. And ponytails. And the guys with low-riding jeans, jet boots, combs sticking out of their back pocket, truckers' wallets and leather jackets.

Joanne, Dawson City

Technology Changes Lives

After the war, many new products became available. Several were made of plastic or vinyl, a material that was cheap, easy to shape, and waterproof. Look at the objects in the photos on this page. How do you think each one changed the way people lived?

Voices of Canada

Incredible Inventions

We were the first students to use ballpoint pens instead of inkwells and straight pens. We had the L.P., a twelve-inch, long-playing record, and the seven-inch unbreakable single-play vinyl record. We played these records on portable record-players, the size of a suitcase. We had transistor radios that we thought were miraculously small. Nowadays they seem gigantic. But they allowed us to listen to music separate from our parents, and different than their "old-fashioned" tunes. We were the first generation to be able to do this.

Grandpa Watson

When the TV broke, which happened a lot then, the kids would miss it so much. It was like they forgot how to play... [Also,] there was very little French on TV. Our boys wanted to speak English rather than French because that's what they heard on TV.

Germaine Prénovault, St. Boniface

Thinking *It Through*

■ Change does not always have a positive effect. What are some negative ways that television might affect people?

THEN AND NOW

Technology continues to change. The CD, the computer, and the cellphone are just a few of the inventions of our time. How have they changed our lives? What will they come up with next?

Build Your Skills!

Helping Others in Hard Times

Families who live through an event such as a fire or a flood often face hard times for a little while. They may need help with shelter, food, clothing, supplies, or money. Find an organization in your community, such as the Red Cross, that helps families in emergencies. Use the flow chart on page 271 to plan a way that you can help the organization.

Interpreting Historical Cartoons

This cartoon appeared in a Montréal newspaper in 1929. The father of the family has been hurt at work, but cannot get any help from the government official. What can you tell about the family by the way they are drawn? What can you tell about the government official? How do you think the cartoonist felt about the situation? Why do you think the cartoonist drew this cartoon?

Making a Memory Box

What kinds of things best show how you live today? Choose the five most important parts of your life. Think about family, food, school, entertainment, sports, and pets. Then, choose an item that best represents that part of your life. An item can be a photograph, a toy, a drawing, a poem, or something else you choose. Put all five items in a memory box. Trade your memory box with a partner. Then try to figure out the most important aspects of your partner's life just by looking at the items in the box.

Putting It All Together

I learned a lot about how people lived through the hard times of the Great Depression, and how they had better times after World War II. I decided to put together what I learned in a presentation for my class. First, I recorded the evidence I found, and then I recorded my conclusions.

Evidence	Conclusions
Most Canadians had little money and no work during the Great Depression of the 1930s.	They found really creative ways of taking care of themselves and others.
After World War II, there were more jobs and more money.	My grandparents were lucky to grow up during these good times.
Whether times are good or bad, Canadians find ways to have fun.	I think fun happens when you are with family and friends.
At all times, there are people who do not have enough money to take care of themselves or their families.	We should help others in whatever ways we can.

Review the inquiry questions for this chapter:
- Why was everyone affected by the Great Depression, even people with jobs?
- Consider the ways that life changed for most Canadians after World War II. Decide if all these changes improved their ways of life.

Take Time to Reflect

In this chapter, you learned that there are many ways to help others in your community. Write a poem or paragraph about your experience helping others. How did it make you feel? What were the advantages and disadvantages of working with other people? Add your work to your Canada Collection.

We Are a Country

It was the Winter Olympics in 2002. The players on Canada's hockey teams were excited. They had a secret. There was a loonie under the ice, in the centre of the rink. It was placed there by Trent Evans, the icemaker for the Olympic arena. Evans, an Albertan, put the loonie under the ice because it was a symbol of Canada. He thought it would give the Canadian teams good luck. He painted over the coin, so it would not show through the ice. Only the Canadian players knew it was there.

Canada's women's and men's teams made it to the finals. Both teams had to play hard, but both won gold medals. After each win, the players rushed to congratulate one another. Some had tears of joy in their eyes. One player, Danielle Goyette, was so happy that she fell to her knees and kissed the ice above the loonie.

Fans celebrated throughout Canada. After the Games, the teams presented the loonie to Canada's Hockey Hall of Fame.

Canada: Our Stories Continue

You have learned that the beaver is a symbol of Canada, and that is why it appears on our nickel. Symbols are objects or images that represent an idea or a belief. What symbols of Canada can you find in the story on the opposite page? What symbols do you see in the pictures on these pages?

Some of the symbols you will find represent Canada. But how can one image represent a country so diverse? You have learned that many groups with different backgrounds live here. Yet we all share some experiences and beliefs that join us together. Living in Canada is part of what makes us who we are. It is part of our identity.

? Inquiring Minds

Here are some questions to guide your inquiry for this chapter:

- Why have other countries traditionally thought of Canada as a peacekeeping country?
- Why is it important to have a Canadian identity?

needs to make its own decisions.

decides how it will take part in the world.

has an identity that is shaped by people, events, and values.

A nation

has symbols that people recognize.

has rules for being fair.

has rules about how it will be governed.

Sunjeet's Inquiry

Two girls place their poppies on the wreaths at a Remembrance Day ceremony in Halifax on November 11, 2003.

I always feel proud when I see the Canadian flag at hockey games. I felt the same kind of pride in November, but for a different reason. On November 11, our school has a Remembrance Day service. Several members of the Canadian armed forces were there this year. Some were called peacekeepers. During the service, we were reminded that Canada had been part of two World Wars and the Korean War, which was fought in the 1950s.

Now I understand a bit more about what Canada did in these wars, and how they affected our country.

Remembrance Day is a sad and serious time, yet everyone feels proud to be Canadian. The Canadian flag was on the stage. There was also a framed picture of something called the Charter of Rights and Freedoms. I asked myself:

- Why do people wear poppies on Remembrance Day?
- How did we get our flag?
- What is the Charter of Rights and Freedoms?
- Why does Canada have peacekeepers?

My teacher said that many of these things are symbols of our country. I decided to research these symbols and learn more about them.

Skill Smart

■ Find out why poppies are worn on Remembrance Day. Use three sources to find the answer. Keep track of your sources.

Considering Context

Have your grandparents ever told you that when they were young, they could go to a movie for 25 cents? That sounds cheap, doesn't it? To understand better, you need more information about how much people were paid and how much other things cost at the time. In the 1950s, some people were paid $1.00 an hour for work. Today, some people earn $9.00 an hour, but movie tickets can be $14.00!

We use the word *context* to refer to information that helps us better understand an event. This information can be additional facts, or it can be the story of the events that happened before or afterward. These facts, causes, or circumstances help us to understand the meaning and importance of an event.

Poppies often grow wild in fields in northern Europe. These fields sometimes became cemeteries for soldiers who were killed in World War I. Canadians started wearing poppies to remember the soldiers who were killed in that war. Today we wear poppies to remember Canadians who have sacrificed their lives in wars since 1914.

Practise the Skill

You have already learned that many Canadians died or were wounded in World War I. Use the Internet or library books to learn the context of this information.

1. How many people lived in Canada at the time of the war (1914–1918)?

2. How many Canadian soldiers were killed or wounded during the war?

3. Find a town or city in Western Canada with a population about the same as the number of soldiers who were killed or wounded.

4. How does learning the context help you better understand Canada's losses during World War I?

How Did Canada Change After Confederation?

Canada has changed a lot since Confederation. I know that as I grow up, I get to make more decisions, but I have more responsibilities, too. I wonder if the same thing happened to Canada.

Independent means the ability to make decisions and act for yourself. It also means accepting responsibility for your actions.

On September 2, 1920, people watched as the British flag was raised in front of Memorial Hall in Edmonton. Why do you think many Canadians felt proud to fly the British flag?

Canada became a country in 1867. But in many ways, it was still controlled by Britain. Britain thought our young country was not ready to make all its own decisions. We were allowed to make decisions for things that happened within Canada. However, we were not given the power to declare war, make peace, or make trade arrangements with other countries. Britain made these decisions for us.

Many Canadians did not mind this at first. Britain had a powerful Empire and controlled countries around the world. Some Canadians were proud to be part of the Empire. They flew British flags and sang the British anthem. But others thought Canada should have more powers of its own. They believed Canada should be more **independent.** How did Canada show Britain that it was ready to make its own decisions and accept more responsibility?

Voices of Canada

Canadian Soldiers

As I write, French and English Canadians are fighting and dying side by side. Is their sacrifice to go for nothing or will it cement a foundation for a new Canadian nation, independent in thought, independent in action?

Letter from Talbot Papineau, a Canadian soldier, Europe, 1916

Skill Smart

- Work with a small group to discuss solutions to a problem that exists in your school or community. Consider different viewpoints, possible solutions, and their effects. Discuss what role you should have in making the final decision, and how that decision should be made and why.

Canada Becomes More Independent

When Britain declared war on Germany in 1914, Canada was automatically at war, too. Some Canadians did not want to fight because the war did not involve their country. Others disagreed with the whole idea of war. Some Francophone Canadians did not feel a connection with Britain, and therefore did not want to fight its war. But thousands of Canadians from across the country did join the war as part of the British army in World War I.

Canadians fought bravely in many terrible battles. Our soldiers were very proud when they captured a stronghold at Vimy Ridge in France in 1917. Armies from other countries had tried to do this, but had failed.

Voices of Canada

Identity

When soldiers left Canada for Europe, they did not know that the war would change their identity forever.
I never felt like a Canadian until Vimy Ridge. After that I was a Canadian all the way. We had a feeling that we could not lose (and if all the other allies packed it up we could do the job ourselves).

H.F. Mills, Soldier at Vimy

By the end of the war, Canadian soldiers were fighting in their own army. Canadians had helped to win the war and had earned the respect of other countries. Because of this, and because of the great loss of life that Canada suffered, Canadians were now determined to be recognized as having their own country.

But Britain was not ready to give up control. Canadian leaders argued that Canada had proved it was ready for more independence. Finally, the British Parliament changed its mind. Canada was allowed a place at the peace conference and its own signature on the treaty that ended the war.

Thinking It Through

- Why was Vimy Ridge important to capture?
- What other countries fought battles there?
- How does knowing this information provide you with a context to better understand the important role Canadians played in World War I?

This monument at Vimy is a symbol of the sacrifices Canadians made during World War I. Why is it important for us to remember historic events such as wars?

The Statute of Westminster

In 1931, Britain passed a new law called the Statute of Westminster. This law became a symbol of Canada's independence. It gave Canada the right to make its own laws and decisions when dealing with other countries. The Statute of Westminster meant that Canada now had the choice of whether to go to war when Britain did. When World War II began in 1939, our government decided to help Britain, France, and other European countries defend their freedom.

Canada Becomes a Peacekeeping Country

Once the war was over, Canada knew that it was important to stop new wars from breaking out. Canada worked with other countries to form the United Nations, or UN. The UN is an organization set up to keep peace around the world. But in 1956, it looked as though another world war might begin. Meetings at the UN were unable to bring peace.

At that time, Lester Pearson was in charge of how Canada worked with other countries. He suggested that the UN put together a group of soldiers from countries like Canada that were not at war. These soldiers would go to troubled areas to prevent fighting, without taking sides. This was the world's first *peacekeeping* force. Peacekeeping means working to end conflicts without taking sides.

It was hard work to get warring countries to agree to this plan. The peacekeepers succeeded and the fighting stopped. For his work, Lester Pearson won the Nobel Peace Prize in 1957. Each year, it is given as a symbol to a person or group who has done the most for world peace.

The countries of the world send people to the UN headquarters in New York. There, they work to solve problems peacefully. Why are there so many flags? Why is listening and talking to others a better way to solve conflicts than war?

An eagle feather hangs from the United Nations peacekeeping beret of a Mi'kmaq veteran at a Remembrance Day ceremony in Halifax on November 11, 2002. What do you think the eagle feather symbolizes?

Peacekeepers all wear blue UN helmets or berets. These blue berets are symbols of their role as peacekeepers. Why do peacekeepers need helmets? Why do they need tanks and guns?

Making *a Difference*

Mark Isfeld: A Canadian Peacekeeper

The UN has sent peacekeepers to many parts of the world. More than 125 000 Canadians have served as peacekeepers. More than 100 have been killed on their missions.

Mark Isfeld was a Canadian peacekeeper who did a dangerous job. In 1994, he was clearing land mines in Croatia. Land mines are buried in the ground in times of war. They explode when people step on them. Mark always made time for the local children. He knew what land mines could do. The children did not. He felt he needed to protect them most of all.

Mark Isfeld

Once, when Mark was home on a break, he showed his mother a picture of an abandoned house. In the picture was a doll that a child had lost. Mark's mother, Carol, decided to knit some dolls for Mark to give to children on his return to Croatia. "The dolls are a hit, Mom," Mark wrote in a letter home. "Don't stop making them." He gave out almost 100 dolls. His friends called them "Izzy dolls."

Mark was killed when his vehicle ran over a land mine. To keep his memory alive, Carol kept knitting Izzy dolls. Other mothers across Canada started making dolls for Canadian peacekeepers to give out around the world. They continue to give them out today.

Some Izzy dolls wear the blue peacekeeper's beret.

Thinking *It Through*

- Why do you think peacekeepers are prepared to risk their lives to help others?
- In your view, what makes Canadians good peacekeepers?

How Did Canada Get Its Own Flag?

So far, I've learned that symbols can tell a lot about a nation. The nickel shows how important the fur trade was to Canada. The poppy helps us remember Canadians who fought in Europe for our freedom. Izzy dolls stand for Canadian peacekeepers. Now I'm researching different flags flown in Canada. What does the maple leaf flag tell about us?

Some countries' symbols have existed for a long time, but Canada's maple leaf flag is very young. For almost a hundred years after Confederation, Canada flew the British flag, sometimes called the Union Jack.

How do you think some Canadians of non-British descent felt about using the Union Jack as Canada's flag?

Until 1965, we also used a flag called the Red Ensign. It showed Canada's shield, but it had a Union Jack in the corner.

A flag often represents something important about the people. What do each of the symbols on the shield mean?

298

Canada's New Symbol

In 1964, Lester Pearson was Prime Minister of Canada. Canada was changing. He thought Canada needed a new symbol of its identity because the Red Ensign was too British to stand for all Canadians. He announced that Canada needed a new flag. He did not realize that choosing a new flag would start a great debate.

The flag debate got everybody talking about who Canadians were, and how we could all be represented by one flag. People debated at home, in stores, and on the street. Everyone had strong feelings about which symbols best represented Canada. The leader of the Opposition, John Diefenbaker, wanted a flag that included the British Union Jack.

Why did people feel so strongly? Canada had grown in many ways throughout the years. Canadians felt a new pride in their country. They wanted to be sure they had the right flag. Canadians were disagreeing, but together they were also creating the symbol of their country.

My grandparents remember their families being upset when the Red Ensign was taken down. To them, it was a symbol of their identity.

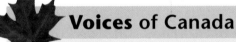

Voices of Canada

Flag

The flag is the symbol of the nation's unity, for it... represents all the citizens of Canada without distinction of race, language, belief, or opinion.

Maurice Bourget, Speaker of the Senate, February 15, 1965

My family told me that Québec has always proudly flown its fleur–de-lys flag.

Thinking *It Through*

- When Lester Pearson represented Canada at the UN, he realized that many people did not understand that Canada was independent of Britain. This was because Canada used the British flag. When our first peacekeeping forces went to other nations, they were often mistaken for British soldiers because their uniforms had the Union Jack on them.

- How does this context help you understand why Pearson was so determined to give Canada its own unique flag?

What symbols do you see? Research this flag. Give reasons for its importance to Québécois.

The Great Debate

My baba said her family wanted a flag with a symbol that was not British or French. They felt this would help people who had come to Canada from other countries feel that they belonged.

My great-great-grandfather fought in World War I under the Red Ensign. So at first, my family wanted to keep it.

Every Canadian had an opinion about what should go on the flag. Many designs were suggested. The maple leaf was an early favourite. Other people suggested the beaver, or a sheaf of wheat, the Rockies, or a codfish. Some made bumper stickers showing their favourite image.

People marched on Parliament Hill in Ottawa. Some protested in favour of one design, while others protested in favour of another. Many Canadians of British heritage protested against any change at all. They still loved the Red Ensign. Some Francophones, especially in Québec, preferred flags with the fleur-de-lys because it represented their heritage and language.

The final decision on the flag had to be made in Parliament. A special committee took over. They argued for months. They met 41 times and looked at more than 2000 designs. In the end, the committee chose three finalists. When the final vote was taken, the winner was the flag we have today.

These are all symbols that can represent Canada. Who might have wanted each one as the symbol for the new flag? What do you think are good criteria for choosing a flag?

I wonder why the maple leaf was chosen as a symbol of Canada. Maple trees sure don't grow where I live! But I do feel proud when I see our flag raised.

The maple leaf flag is the only flag of Canada my family has ever known. People all over the world recognize our flag.

Canada's new flag was raised for the first time over the Parliament Buildings in Ottawa on February 15, 1965. It took just a short while for Canadians to get used to it. Soon the flag was everywhere—on backpacks of Canadians travelling abroad, on Olympic uniforms, and flying from poles in front of people's houses.

Today it is hard to imagine Canada without the maple leaf flag. It is a symbol of our identity. A group of Canadian students were asked what the flag meant to them. They said "peace," "pride," and "freedom."

More About. . .

The Flag

Here is some of what Sunjeet learned from his research on the flag:

- The red maple has been a Canadian symbol for a long time. First Nations such as the Haudenosaunee harvested the sap every spring. The first Europeans learned how to use syrup, and it became part of their way of life, too.
- The maple leaf tells people that Canada is a land of natural beauty.
- Red and white are traditional colours of England and France. Our flag recognizes the role of both peoples in our history.
- The red bars on each side represent oceans on the west and east.

These hikers are in the Rocky Mountains. Why do you think they have Canadian flags on their backpacks? Why would Canadian hikers display Canada's flag when they travel in other countries?

Thinking *It Through*

- Do you think there are people from other countries who would not show the flag of their country when they travel? Why?

How Will Canada Be Governed?

Are there rules about how rules are made and how the government works?

Just like a classroom, a country has a set of rules about how it will be governed. The rules are called the *constitution*. A constitution outlines the main beliefs of a country and the roles of the different parts of the government. It is the highest law in the land. It shapes, and is shaped by, a country's identity.

At the time of Confederation, Canada's Constitution was put in place by the British North America Act, or BNA Act. It was passed in Britain in 1867, when Canada was created. If Canada wanted to change its Constitution, it had to ask the government in Britain. The Statute of Westminster had given Canada more independence, but Britain still controlled our Constitution. This was because Canadians could not decide on the rules for changing, or amending, the Constitution. In 1980, Prime Minister Pierre Trudeau announced it was time for Canada to control its Constitution.

Skill Smart

■ To change the Constitution, all or most of the provincial and territorial governments in Canada have to agree. Look closely at the cartoon on this page. Think about the symbols that the cartoonist has used. Discuss what the pot symbolizes. Count the number of beavers. What do you think they symbolize? Do the beavers agree about what should go in the pot? What is the cartoonist's point of view about changing the Constitution?

Canada Gains Control of Its Constitution

The prime minister and premiers met several times to discuss how changes might be made. One night, after hours of talking, nine provinces and the government of Canada came to an agreement. They wrote a new Constitution, including rules for making changes.

When the new Constitution was written in 1981, the premier of Québec did not agree with it. He believed it did not do enough to permit the government of Québec to protect its language and culture. As a result, Québec did not sign the new Constitution. Since 1981, there have been many discussions to try to find a way to include Québec in the Constitution. It remains a challenge for the future.

On April 17, 1982, the new Constitution was officially made the law of Canada with the passing of the Canada Act by Britain. This was one more step toward becoming a truly independent country.

The new Constitution was signed in Ottawa by Prime Minister Trudeau and Queen Elizabeth II. At last, we had a "made-in-Canada" Constitution. Who else do you think is in the photo?

Aboriginal Peoples and the Constitution

Do you remember that Canada's Aboriginal people were not included in talks about Confederation? In 1980 it looked like they would be excluded again. The first draft of the new constitution did not mention any rights for Aboriginal people.

Aboriginal leaders arranged for a train called the "Constitutional Express" to travel from Vancouver to Ottawa. There, they demonstrated on Parliament Hill, reinforcing that Aboriginal rights should be included in the Constitution. The treaties that had been signed in the past had established these rights, but Aboriginal people wanted them written down in the Constitution.

Aboriginal voices were heard: Section 35 was added. It reads: "The existing Aboriginal and treaty rights of the Aboriginal peoples of Canada are hereby recognized and affirmed."

Larry Pierre was from British Columbia's Okanagan Valley. He was one of 100 people who walked out of the First Nations Constitutional Conference on May 1, 1980, demanding First Nations participation in the Constitutional talks.

At the Remembrance Day service, why was the Charter of Rights and Freedoms on the stage? What is it? Why is it important to Canada?

Voices
of Canada

Protection for All

In a country like Canada—vast and diverse, with eleven governments, two official languages and a variety of ethnic origins—the only way to provide equal protection to everyone is to [honour Canadians'] basic rights and freedoms in the Constitution.

Jean Chrétien, Minister of Justice, 1980–1982

Most of the rights and freedoms... in the Charter are not *totally* new and different. Indeed, Canadians have tended to take most of them for granted over the years. The difference is that now they will be guaranteed by our Constitution...

Pierre Elliott Trudeau, Prime Minister, 1968–1979 and 1980–1984

The Charter of Rights and Freedoms

What would you think if any of the following situations happened?

- The student with the highest marks in Alberta is not allowed to accept a prize because of her race.
- Some people are not allowed to sit anywhere in a movie theatre. They have to sit in the last few rows because of their ethnic background.
- Some people are not allowed to go to medical school because of their religion.
- Two workers do the same job, but are paid different amounts because one is a woman.
- Québec has an English-language school system for its Anglophone minority. But other provinces do not have French-language public schools for their Francophone minorities.

You are probably thinking, "Not fair!" At one time, though, these situations did happen in Canada. Canadians have always had many freedoms and rights that other countries do not have. For a long time, however, these rights were not written down in a Constitution. That meant they could be interpreted differently, or even ignored. Also, they did not apply to provincial laws.

When Canada gained control of its constitution in 1982, the Charter of Rights and Freedoms was added. Because the Charter is part of the Constitution, it is very difficult to change any of the laws that protect us.

The Charter of Rights

- gives us the freedom to believe what we like, and to speak and write about our opinions.
- gives citizens the right to choose their government through elections.
- gives people the right not to be arrested without being given a reason and gives them the right to a fair trial.
- gives citizens the right not to be subjected to cruel and unusual punishment.

The Charter

The Charter gives rights to all Canadians. It also gives "collective" rights to official-language groups and peoples in Canada. Francophone minorities throughout Canada and the Anglophone minority in Québec have the right to be educated in their first language.

These Mounties are guarding the Charter of Rights and Freedoms. It was on display to celebrate the twentieth anniversary of the signing of the new Constitution. The Charter reflects the values of Canadians. We believe people should be treated equally, whatever their ethnic background, religion, or gender. We want our society to accept differences among peoples. The Charter also reminds us of the rights and the shared history of Canada's founding peoples: the Aboriginal nations, the Francophones, and the Anglophones.

As travellers make their way along the Trail, they will be greeted at each province or territory by a Trans Canada Trail Gateway. The first one was opened on the Québec–New Brunswick border on June 19, 1997. The Trans Canada Trail is a team effort between the people, governments, and companies of Canada's ten provinces and three territories. The Gateways symbolize the efforts of Canadians working together.

and Freedoms...

- forbids discrimination for reasons of "race, national or ethnic origin, colour, religion, sex, age, or mental or physical disability."
- guarantees that Canada is a bilingual country, and that English and French are equally important.
- guarantees that Aboriginal peoples have special rights to the land, because they were here first and have rights according to treaties.
- states that we must respect the multicultural heritage of Canada.

Thinking *It Through*

- Why do you think the Charter protects French and English as Canada's official languages? Why is it important that the Charter protects treaty rights and other Aboriginal rights?
- What responsibilities do you think come with the rights set out in the Charter?

What Should Canada's Role Be in the World?

For nearly forty years, Canada was one of the world's leading peacekeeping nations. Canadian soldiers helped to stop conflicts between countries from becoming worse.

But the world started changing. New conflicts were often not between two countries—they were civil wars. People in the same country were fighting each other. It was difficult to enforce and maintain peace.

By 2006, fifty years after Prime Minister Pearson suggested the idea of peacekeeping, Canada was involved in very few "peacekeeping" missions. Now, Canadian soldiers are often involved in **combat** in dangerous places such as Afghanistan. But many people don't agree that this is the role Canada should play. Should we only be peacekeepers or should we also fight wars in other countries?

A soldier from Trois-Rivières, Québec, talks with children at a checkpoint in Kabul, Afghanistan, in May 2004.

words matter!

Combat means fighting against an enemy.

We might call [Afghanistan] peace support… Our grandfathers would call it war.

Jack Granatstein, military historian

Peacekeeping is no longer a simple exercise… It's kind of scary. The Canadian military is more than capable of carrying out a new…role… But should we be playing that role? I think we should be asking our soldiers…if they are building a nation, if they are freeing people.

Sandra Perron, Ile Bizard, Québec—one of the first Canadian women soldiers to face combat duty

Not everyone believes that Canada should be sending troops to fight in other countries. Are there other ways that Canada can help make the world more safe and peaceful?

My parents say that there is too much poverty at home in Canada. They believe our money should be used to improve living conditions here. But of course, when disasters like earthquakes and tsunamis destroy other countries, they always give money for relief aid.

My parents think that Canada should give more money to countries that need food, medical supplies, and help to educate their children. People who are well fed, healthy, and educated are less likely to start wars.

A worker from Doctors Without Borders (Médecins Sans Frontières) helps refugees in Chad, Africa.

My aunt is involved in an organization called Médecins Sans Frontières, or Doctors Without Borders. MSF helps people in other countries when there is an emergency caused by a natural disaster or by war. It doesn't matter whose side the people are on, or what they believe. MSF helps everyone.

Over to You

1. Why might some people support Canadian troops going to fight wars in other countries?
2. What role do you think Canada should have in the world? Why?

Is Canada Still Changing?

The Creation of Nunavut

1970s ● Inuit begin talking to Canadian officials about governing themselves.

1982 ● People of the Northwest Territories vote to divide.

1992 ● People of the Northwest Territories vote on where boundaries should be.

1999 ● Nunavut is born.

How long did it take for Nunavut to be created after the people voted to divide? Why do you think it took so long for decisions to be made?

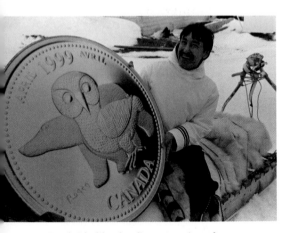

Paul Okalik, the first premier of Nunavut, holds a model of a special coin. What symbols of Nunavut do you see in this picture?

Since 1982, Canada has been a fully independent country. Yet this does not mean we will never change. A good example is what took place on April 1, 1999. Fireworks lit up the skies over Iqaluit in the eastern Arctic. People there were celebrating the birth of a new territory in Canada—Nunavut.

The Creation of Nunavut

Before 1999, the Northwest Territories was a huge area—five times the size of Alberta. Most of the people living in the eastern part were Inuit. Their culture and language are different from those of the Dene and other groups, but the government in Yellowknife made decisions for all peoples in the territory. The Inuit felt that the government was too far away to understand what they needed. They wanted the right to make decisions for themselves. This is called self-government.

The Inuit talked with Canada's government for many years. At first they found it difficult to get the government's attention, but they kept trying, patiently and peacefully. Eventually, the government agreed to let the people of the Northwest Territories vote on their future. They voted to divide, and in 1999, Canada recognized the new territory of Nunavut. It was the first territory created by and for Aboriginal communities. Nunavut opened the way for other Aboriginal communities who want to self-govern.

Skill Smart

■ Measure and record the distance between Iqaluit and Yellowknife, and between Iqaluit and Ottawa. Why do you think the people of Nunavut felt that the governments in Yellowknife and Ottawa did not understand them?

An Interview with
Louis Angalik: Inuit Elder

What did the creation of Nunavut mean to you?

I was really happy because the Inuit could now use the Inuit traditions in governing ourselves. It is also a good thing for the people of Canada and the world. They will see more of Inuit culture now.

Have your hopes for Nunavut come true?

Yes, some have. We are Canadians, but with a different language and a different culture. When Nunavut was created, we started showing up more on television and on the Internet. People are more interested in us. We have the chance to show the world who we are.

How do you feel when you see the new Nunavut flag?

I like the flag. There was a contest to choose it, and I sent in my own design. Mine wasn't chosen, but I like the one that was.

What symbols did you use in your design for the flag?

It had an inuksuk. I also had a bear looking backwards. It's important to look behind every now and again, to see what you have been through. Then you turn and look forward again.

How do you feel about being Canadian?

I feel very comfortable and welcome. I feel attached to Canada.

What are your hopes for the future of Nunavut?

Now our communities are very young. There are many different dialects. We are learning to live together. We are also starting to write down our stories and histories. I used to fear that our stories and culture were being lost, but I don't have these fears anymore. Now we can maintain our language and culture.

More About. . .

Nunavut

- Nunavut has its own flag. The blue and gold symbolize the riches of the land, sea, and sky. The inuksuk symbolizes the heritage of the Inuit. The red represents Canada. The North Star stands for the leadership of Elders in the community.
- The people of Nunavut decide how to run their own schools, courts, and other services.
- "Nunavut" means "Our Land" in Inuktitut.

Thinking *It Through*

■ What do you already know about Inuit traditions, stories, ways of life, and concerns? Why was it important to the Inuit to have their own government?

Build Your Skills!

Explore Context

Do some research on Canadian hockey teams in the Winter Olympics. Find out how many times the men's team has won the gold medal, and how many times the women's team has won gold. Make a chart or graph that shows the years in which each team won gold. Now analyze your chart or graph and tell how many times both teams have won gold in the same year. How does this information give you a context to better understand why Canadians were so happy after the 2002 Winter Olympics?

Think About Identity

Develop a list of ten words that describe what you think it means to be Canadian. Find a symbol for each word. Then use all ten symbols to create a poster about Canadian identity. Explain to your class why you chose each of the ten words and symbols.

Practise Your Research Skills

Research a place in the world where Canadians are or were involved in peacekeeping. Create a PowerPoint® presentation to show your findings.

- Include a map.
- Report briefly on the problems in that area.
- Explain what kinds of work Canadian peacekeepers do there.

Putting It All Together

I went looking for information about our country's symbols. I found that the best way to keep all of the information organized was to make a chart.

Canadian Symbol	What I Think It Symbolizes
Poppies	All the Canadian soldiers who have fought in wars since 1914
The Statute of Westminster	Canada becoming more independent from Britain after World War I
Blue beret	Canada's peacekeepers
Maple leaf flag	How Canadians work together to make decisions
Constitution and Charter of Rights and Freedoms	The rights we have in Canada
Nunavut	How our country is still changing

Review what you've learned in this chapter:
- Why have other countries traditionally thought of Canada as a peacekeeping country?
- Why is it important to have a Canadian identity?

Take Time to Reflect

Design a flag for your family. Try to use symbols and colours that mean something to all the family members. Write a paragraph explaining why you chose those symbols and colours. Add the flag and explanation to your Canada Collection.

12 | Caring for Canada

Think of a natural area that is special to you. What if there was a threat to your special place? What could you do? You might take positive steps as David Grassby did recently.

David Grassby was 12 years old when he read an article about environmental threats to Oakbank Pond near his home in Thornhill, Ontario. David decided to help protect the pond and its wildlife.

David talked to classmates and community members. He discovered that writing letters and informing the media are powerful tools to get action. He wrote many letters to the Town Council, the CBC, and newspapers. He appeared on several TV shows, including *The Nature of Things* hosted by David Suzuki.

In each of his letters and interviews, David explained the problems facing the pond and suggested some solutions. For example, people were feeding the ducks. This attracted too many ducks for the pond to support. David recommended that the town install signs asking people not to feed the ducks.

The media were able to convince people to make changes. David Grassby learned that it is important to be patient and to keep trying. He learned that one person can make a difference.

Today, Oakbank Pond is a nature preserve, home to many birds such as ducks, Canada geese, blackbirds, and herons. It is a peaceful place that the community enjoys.

Please Do Not Feed The Waterfowl

Although people mean well when feeding ducks and geese, it is often in the best interest of the waterfowl and the general public, to allow the birds to find their own natural food.

Canada: Our Stories Continue

What David Grassby did is an example of active citizenship. He noticed a problem in his community and took action to solve it. He did so because he felt responsible for making sure his environment remained healthy. Across Canada, individual citizens, companies, schools, and organizations are choosing to help protect the natural resources of our country.

words **matter!**

To **preserve** means to keep in good condition or protect.

? Inquiring Minds

Here are some questions to guide your inquiry for this chapter:

- What would happen if some of Canada's resources ran out?
- How do parks and protected areas help **preserve** our natural environment?

Our natural resources combine to give Canada a special landscape. The beauty of this landscape inspired Emily Carr. Why do artists paint pictures of the environment they see around them? This painting is titled *Skidegate, Graham Island, British Columbia*.

Katie's Inquiry

My dad works for Parks Canada. This summer, I am going with him when he visits different protected areas in Canada. I looked on the Parks Canada Web site, and there are so many places we could visit—not just parks, but World Heritage Sites and even World Biosphere Reserves. I wonder:

- Why do so many places in Canada need protection?
- How does Parks Canada help to do this?
- Is Parks Canada the only group that is helping our environment?

I am going to take a lot of photos on my trip. I am also going to interview some people. I know my dad cares about the environment, and I wonder if people across Canada have the same feelings.

Canada's World Heritage Sites include national and provincial parks and historic sites. These are chosen by the United Nations because they are important to everyone. The Historic District of Québec (above) and SGaang Gwaii, an island in British Columbia, are two of thirteen sites in our country. There are five World Heritage Sites in Alberta—what are they?

World Biosphere Reserves are areas chosen by the UN because they are special. Their natural resources are conserved or used in a careful way. People usually live in these areas, too. Clayoquot Sound in British Columbia is one of these reserves.

Skill Smart

- Research why we have national and provincial parks in Canada.

Planning an Interview

Interviews are one way we can learn from others. In an interview, one person asks questions and the other person answers them. The questions are usually planned ahead and focus on a specific topic. To plan an interview, follow these steps:

Step 1
Think of a topic about which you would like to learn more. Write a list of questions. Try to make your questions "open" instead of "closed."

Step 2
Find a person who knows a lot about your topic and who would be willing to answer your questions. Arrange a time to interview the person. Be sure you have your list of questions ready.

Step 3
During the interview, listen to what the person has to say. Record the answers to your questions. You can do this by taking notes or by asking the person if you can record their voice.

Step 4
After the interview, think about what you learned. Are there questions you wish you had asked?

More **About. . .**

Closed and Open Questions

Closed questions are questions that can only be answered with *yes* or *no*. One example is "Did you help protect Oakbank Pond?"

Open questions give a person a chance to say more. They often begin with *how* or *why*. An example is "How did you help protect Oakbank Pond?"

Practise the Skill

On page 314, Katie mentions many ways of caring for Canada. Choose the one that interests you most. It could be Parks Canada, World Biosphere Reserves, World Heritage Sites, groups that help the environment, or another topic. Write ten "open" questions. Find an expert on your topic and ask the person if you can do an interview.

What If Some of Canada's Resources Ran Out?

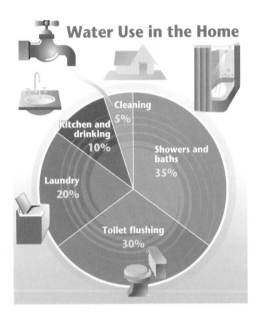

Water Use in the Home

Cleaning 5%
Kitchen and drinking 10%
Showers and baths 35%
Laundry 20%
Toilet flushing 30%

According to this chart, what do Canadians use the most water for? How do you think using water in these ways affects our environment? How could you reduce the amount of water *you* use at home?

Every day, we breathe the air. We use water to flush the toilet, drink, and wash. We eat foods from plants and animals. When we watch TV, play computer games, or turn on a light, we are using electricity. If you think about it, we could not survive without natural resources.

As we go through our daily lives, we often forget the impact we have on the natural resources that make up our environment. We forget that we leave an *environmental footprint*. This footprint is the effect we have on the environment when we use resources, create waste, and cause other changes.

Dirty Footprints

Did you ever wonder where all of our garbage goes? Often it goes to a landfill like the one shown below. It might be hard to believe, but each Canadian throws out about one tonne of garbage each year!

What kind of environmental footprint do you think landfills create? How do they affect the land and animals? How do they affect our quality of life?

Caring About Canada

Since Canada is so huge, it is hard to imagine that any of our natural resources would ever run out. But remember what happened to the bison on the Prairies? They were overhunted and driven out of their habitat by settlers and the building of the railway. Today there are almost no bison left. Can you think of other examples of natural resources running out or being destroyed in an area? What effects would this have?

Cause	Effects
Clearing land for lumber and building houses wipe out resources	→ Fewer natural areas → Destroys animal habitats → More endangered species
Cars and factories create air pollution	→ Polluted air/smog → Health problems for people and animals
Industries dump waste into waterways	→ Polluted water that is not safe to drink → Animals that live in or use waterways die → Water is unsafe for swimming
Companies mine where animals live or migrate	→ Animals cannot find food → Destroys animal habitats

What other causes and effects can you add to this chart? Which of these causes has an effect on your quality of life?

Canadians are faced with a problem. Many of our activities have a negative impact on the environment, and therefore, on us. But we cannot stop building houses, driving, making products, logging, and mining. We depend on these activities for the way we live. They also provide millions of people with jobs. How can we live in our environment and protect it at the same time? Who do you think is responsible for preserving our resources?

317

How Do Parks and Protected Areas Help?

Canada's National Parks, World Heritage Sites, and World Biosphere Reserves

Parks Canada is part of the government. This map will give you an idea of how important they are to all areas of Canada!

Ivvavik National Park

Yuntut National Park

Aulavik National Park

Tuktut Nogait National Park

Kluane National Park

Nahanni National Park

Ukkusiksalik National Pa

Wood Buffalo National Park

Gwaii Haanas National Park

Jasper National Park

Wapusk National Park

Glacier National Park

Elk Island National Park

Prince Albert National Park

Banff National Park

Pacific Rim National Park

Gulf Islands National Park

Mount Revelstoke National Park

Yoho National Park

Kootenay National Park

Waterton Lakes National Park

Riding Mountain National Park

Grasslands National Park

This is Forillon National Park in Québec.

Quttinirpaaq
National Park

Legend

⬛ •	National Park
•	World Heritage Site
○	World Biosphere Reserve

Sirmilik
National Park

Auyuittuq National Park

0   250   500
kilometres

Torngat Mountains
National Park Reserve

Gros Morne
National Park

Terra Nova
National Park

Mingan Archipelago
National Park

Forillon National Park

Cape Breton Highlands
National Park

Saguenay-
St. Lawrence
Marine Park

Prince Edward Island National Park

Pukaskwa
National Park

Kouchibouguac National Park

La Mauricie
National Park

Fundy National Park

Fathom Five
National
Marine Park

Kejimkujik National Park

Bruce Peninsula
National Park

St. Lawrence Islands National Park

Georgian Bay Islands National Park

Point Pelee National Park

Fathom Five National Marine Park in Ontario helps to protect animals and plants of the Great Lakes. Its clear water and more than 20 shipwrecks attract divers.

Kejimkujik National Park is in Nova Scotia. It protects the endangered Blanding's turtle.

Thinking *It Through*

■ Find the national park on the map that is closest to where you live. Why is it important to protect this area?

■ How do you think national parks help Canadians appreciate their country?

■ Why do you think there is at least one national park in every province and territory?

Kluane National Park covers an area of 22 013 square kilometres in the Yukon Territory. It was created to preserve Canada's highest mountains, longest glaciers, and spectacular wildlife.

Interview with Pauline Scott

(Communications Manager, National Parks in Nunavut)

How do parks help preserve natural resources?

Canada's national parks help to protect examples of every natural region found across the country. Within national parks, communities of plants and animals are protected. Life goes on naturally. Some species that are endangered get special protection. Parks can also act as nurseries for species that go missing in areas outside the parks.

Whose responsibility do you think it should be to preserve Canada's national parks?

The Government of Canada thinks it should be a partnership between the people of Canada and the Parks Canada Agency. Aboriginal people help to co-manage some of our national parks. There is a responsibility for visitors to use these parks wisely and for all citizens to care about them.

What do visitors to the parks do that hurts the environment?

There are many fun and exciting activities to do in Canada's national parks. These activities can be done safely and without hurting the environment. It is important to know how to behave in a park. Remember to stay on the trails to avoid damaging fragile plants. Pack out what you pack in. Help keep animals wild by not approaching or feeding them. Keep streams and lakes clean by not polluting them with garbage or human waste.

What can citizens do to help preserve Canada's parks?

The best way is to learn about them and to enjoy them. In this way, we will all care more about our parks. We will want to make sure that we have them in the future for our children and grandchildren. We can also join organizations that support national parks, such as Friends of the Parks groups. We can let our government representatives know that national parks are important to us. Learn all you can and encourage your parents to vacation at national parks and national historic sites.

Provincial Parks

Provinces and territories set aside special areas, too. These areas allow people to enjoy the natural beauty of where they live, but also help to protect the animals and plants. Provincial parks and protected areas do not allow activities that will harm the natural environment. Only activities that leave a small environmental footprint are allowed.

Activities Allowed (but Limited) in Provincial Parks	Activities Not Allowed in Most Provincial Parks
Hiking	Logging
Camping	Mining
Cycling	Hunting
Boating	Trapping
Fishing	

Boating and fishing are allowed, but controlled, in provincial parks. Why do you think this is done?

Parc du Mont-Tremblant is a provincial park in the Laurentian Mountains of Québec. Wolves, bears, raccoons, otters, moose, bald eagles, wolverines, and beavers are just some of the animals protected by the park. What might threaten these animals?

Urban Parks

Imagine that there was no place in your community to play baseball or soccer, or to meet your friends. City governments often create urban parks. These are green spaces within a city where people can walk, cycle, picnic, and enjoy nature. Many of these parks also protect natural resources, such as trees, rivers, and animals.

The Trail length in the Yukon will be 1600 km! It is a real wilderness experience. Here you are more likely to meet a dog team on the Trail than a skier. You can watch salmon and Arctic char in the clear water.

How do urban parks, such as this one in downtown Calgary, improve the quality of life of people living in cities?

How Else Do Canadians Care for Their Environment?

 In school we learn about reducing, reusing, and recycling as ways to care for our environment. As I talked with people on my trip, I learned that there are many other things Canadians are doing.

Making *a Difference*

The SEEDS Foundation

The SEEDS Foundation teaches students to conserve our land. This organization has several programs that encourage students to protect the environment. Students have found hundreds of ways to help conserve natural resources. They turn off lights, collect garbage, build composting sites, educate their parents on how to conserve at home, recycle paper, and several other projects.

The SEEDS Water Challenge encourages students to conserve water so that enough water is available for everyone. It is such a great idea that the government of Canada continues with a national water challenge to help preserve this important resource.

Environment. Energy. Education.
www.seedsfoundation.ca

SEEDS stands for "**S**ociety for **E**nvironment and **E**nergy **D**evelopment **S**tudies." The SEEDS Foundation is a Canadian organization based in Calgary.

The SEEDS Foundation encourages schools to become Green Schools by doing projects that enhance the environment. Imagine if every school in Canada became a Green School. What a difference that would make to our environment!

Skill Smart

- How "green" is your school? How could you encourage others to make it "greener"? Design a persuasive poster that shows different ways of caring for your school environment.

Environmental Groups

You have already learned that Canadians have very diverse backgrounds and experiences. They also have different interests and concerns, including concerns about the environment. Wherever you go in Canada, you will find organizations that are working toward protecting our environment in various ways. Here are just a few of the hundreds of organizations in Canada:

Green Kids

This group focuses on environmental education in elementary and middle schools. They use live theatre to get their message across to kids. Why do you think this is effective?

Pollution Probe

This group works to reduce air and water pollution, and to conserve water and energy.

The David Suzuki Foundation

This foundation works to find ways that we can live in harmony with our natural world. Its members use science and education to share their message.

Zoocheck Canada

This organization works to protect wild animals, especially those kept in zoos and aquariums in Canada. Often, these animals are very poorly treated. Many cannot stay healthy in our climate because Canada is so different from their natural habitat.

Thinking It Through

■ Why do you think there are so many different environmental groups in Canada?

■ If you were going to join a group that works to protect the environment, how would you choose which one to join? What would you want to know before you make your decision?

Some zoos own large areas of land. This allows them to build special animal habitats that are very similar to those found in the wild. How are these zoos, such as the one shown below in Québec, helping to protect natural resources?

Canadian Companies

I know that some factories can create a lot of pollution. I also know that many of these factories—and other companies—are trying hard to take care of the environment. I did a phone interview with one company to find out how it does this.

What does your company do?

We gather [plant] nutrients, which are found in nature, and provide them to farmers. Farmers around the globe use our products to grow crops.

What natural resources is your company involved with?

[One of the nutrients is called potash.] Potash is a salt that was left over from oceans that evaporated millions of years ago. We get potash from the ground.

What does your company do to make sure we will have enough resources in the future?

We put things back the way we found them. For example, when we mine phosphate from the ground, we not only replace any wetlands that may have been [damaged], we also create additional wetlands.

Voices of Canada

Environmental Report Card

Each year we set goals to try and make our company more environmentally friendly. It's kind of like a report card, only it measures how well we are taking care of the air, water and land... Our job is to help feed the 6.6 billion people who are on the planet today, and to manage our resources so that we may feed the 8 billion people who will be on our planet in just 20 years.

Interviewee from PotashCorp, Saskatoon, SK

Other Solutions

Many Canadian companies have come up with ways to protect the environment and use our natural resources at the same time. Several companies recycle, reduce, and reuse, just as you do at home and at school. Logging companies plant new trees to replace the ones they cut down. Hydro companies put young fish into the waterways they use for electricity.

Some companies invent new products that are friendlier to the environment. Have you ever seen a hybrid car? Hybrid vehicles run on both gasoline and battery power. They create less pollution and use less fuel. How does this affect the environmental footprint they create?

Most hybrid cars look the same as non-hybrid cars.

Think about the items you use every day. Most of them were manufactured somewhere. What do you see here at this mill in Grand Forks, British Columbia? What are the workers doing?

? Critical Inquiry **TIP**

Evaluating

When you find information about a company on its Web site, remember to ask yourself:

- What is the purpose of the company's Web site?
- What information might a company *not* put on its Web site?
- Where can I go for more balanced information?

Thinking *It Through*

■ Find out if companies can be recognized for their efforts to minimize negative impact on the environment.

What Other Types of Energy Could We Use?

Have you ever thought about how you get the power that is used to run a computer or TV, or to heat your home? In Alberta, most electricity is produced from burning coal. Most homes are heated using natural gas. Both coal and natural gas are non-renewable energy sources. Once they are used up, no more can be produced. Most cars and trucks use non-renewable energy sources—gasoline and oil.

Some people think we should look for and use renewable energy sources. For example, one Canadian company called Hydrogenics is working on using hydrogen—a gas made from water—to power vehicles. Another company is experimenting with using ocean tides to create electricity. What are some other ways we could replace non-renewable energy sources with renewable ones?

Drake Landing in Okotoks, Alberta, is the first community in Canada to depend almost completely on solar energy. Solar panels on every house will provide 90% of the houses' energy needs.

Six Provinces and the Yukon Use Wind Turbines—Could Produce 20% of Canada's Energy!

Hydroelectricity Creates Over 60% of Canada's Electricity

Ontario has set a goal to shut down coal plants altogether. They are very serious about cleaning up the air, and there simply isn't a better energy choice than wind.

Theresa Howland, Manager of Green Energy Marketing at Vision Quest

Our power plant is burning coal to make electricity and heat in a way that doesn't give off so many emissions.

Genesee Generating Station, Alberta

I saw a commercial today for nuclear energy. It said that nuclear power is cleaner than coal power. But isn't it dangerous, too?

The Seabird Island First Nation housing project has provided us with a unique opportunity to incorporate our traditions but in a modern way... The earth tubes and radiant floor heating and cooling system is far from new technology; our ancestors built their pit homes in-ground where it was cool in the summer and warm in the winter.

Marcie Peters, Seabird Island First Nation Council

Food or Fuel?

Corn is not only a food. It can also be used to make ethanol, a clean-burning renewable fuel. First Nation Ethanol Development in southern Ontario plans to use locally grown corn to make ethanol. The company hopes to start similar businesses across Canada. These businesses will provide jobs for hundreds of First Nations people. They will also help conserve natural gas and create less pollution.

Over to **You**

1. Consider the viewpoints. What is each person trying to accomplish?

Build Your Skills!

Plan an Interview

Choose a topic in this chapter that interests you. Think of someone you could interview to learn more about the topic. Follow these steps:

1. *Think.* Come up with ten questions. They should help you learn as much as possible about your topic.
2. *Pair.* Review the Skill Power on page 315. With a partner, discuss whether each of the questions is "open" or "closed." Change each closed question to an open one whenever possible.
3. *Share.* Explain your changes to another pair of students.

Consider Your Environmental Footprint

Make a board game that shows what you have learned about environmental footprints. You will need
- a game board with a Start, a Finish, and spaces in between
- an object to represent each player
- a way to decide how many spaces each player will move in a turn

In some of the spaces on your game board, write things that Canadians do to help the environment. In other spaces, write things we do that hurt the environment. Players should move forward or backward depending on where their object lands.

Persuade an Audience

Research a park or a World Heritage Site near you. Find out its purpose. Why is it important? What does it protect? What does it teach? What does it provide to the community? Create a brochure encouraging people to visit the site. Remember to use interesting images and persuasive language.

Putting It All Together

My tour of Canada's protected areas was amazing! I learned so much about the environment and about how Canadians are working together to help conserve our resources.

Caring for Canada

Why Should We Care?
• our use of resources leaves an environmental footprint
• need to decide how to use resources but protect them, too

How Do Parks Help?
• protect special areas of Canada and endangered species
• help people enjoy and learn about the environment

How Else Do Canadians Show Their Concern?
• some companies take responsibility for protecting the environment
• many different environmental programs all over Canada

What Other Types of Energy Could We Use?
• renewable energy sources: ocean tides, sun, wind, nuclear
• can use hydrogen and ethanol to run cars

Review the inquiry questions for this chapter:
• What would happen if some of Canada's resources ran out?
• How do parks and protected areas help **preserve** our natural environment?

Take Time to Reflect

CANADA COLLECTION

This year you have learned about the diversity of Canada's resources. Animals, lakes, trees, and land are just a few. Which one means the most to you? Why? Write a paragraph about the resource you care about the most, and the ways in which you can help to protect it. Add your work to your Canada Collection.

Looking Back on Unit 2
Canada, Our Country

Canada as a country

Building Canada

SYMBOLS

UNITY

Government

Our future

Use the words and phrases above to think about how a critical assessment of Canada's history helps lead you to

- understand how historical events shaped the identity of Canada as a country
- appreciate the impact of people's responses to issues and changes over time

Decide what you consider to be the five most important historical events in Canada. What criteria will you use to decide?

You can use a **Cause and Effect** organizer to show your work. Include a component that shows who was involved and one that shows who was affected.

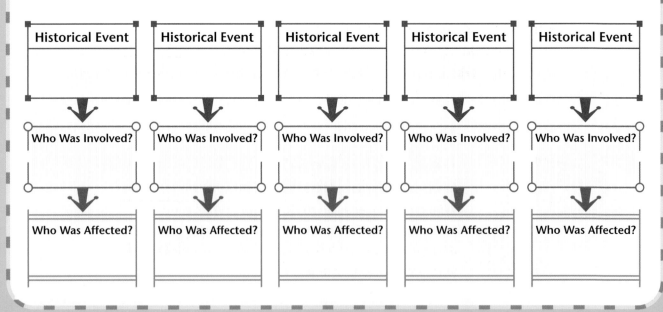

Share What You Have Learned

To share what you have learned in this unit, participate in a "Historic Happenings" presentation. For this, work with a partner or small group to select a historical event, situation, or time period. There are a variety of ways to make your presentation. You might want to create a drama; prepare a slide show or video clips; or make a poster or a diorama.

Whatever type of presentation you decide on, make sure you convey a message that

- provides accurate information about the event, situation, or time period
- explains the impact on the ways of life of people then and now

Here are examples of some topics you might want to create a display around:
- Confederation
- building the railway
- World War I or World War II
- The Famous Five or others who have made a difference
- The Great Depression
- symbols—particularly the new flag
- peacekeeping
- Charter of Rights and Freedoms
- Nunavut
- caring for Canada's natural resources

Tip

- Once all the presentations are complete, work as a class to organize them.

Wrapping Up

Six regions + physical geography + natural resources + diverse people = Canada

Reflecting on the unique features of Canada will help you to
- develop a sense of what gives us quality of life
- develop a sense of citizenship and identity

Develop a Criteria and Evidence chart to show what you have learned about quality of life. Criteria are factors to consider when we judge quality of life. Evidence demonstrates how these factors are visible in a community.

Develop another Criteria and Evidence chart about citizenship and identity. Criteria for deciding what contributes to citizenship and identity are such factors as sense of belonging and active participation. Evidence illustrates the criteria, such as actions, symbols, and ways of life.

Quality of Life

Criteria	Evidence

Citizenship and Identity

Criteria	Evidence

Share What You Have Learned

One way to share what you have learned is to create an information page. You may choose to use a newspaper page; a Web site; a home page; or a "news zine." Whatever you choose, it will be a special edition, reporting on items of citizenship and identity in Canada.

Use selections from your Canada Collection to fill the following categories:

- news articles
- human interest stories
- special interest
- employment
- culture
- entertainment
- viewpoints
- cartoons
- official and other languages

You can create a single information page on your own or with a partner.

Tip

- Try to use a computer program to design your information page.

Canada's Provinces and Territories

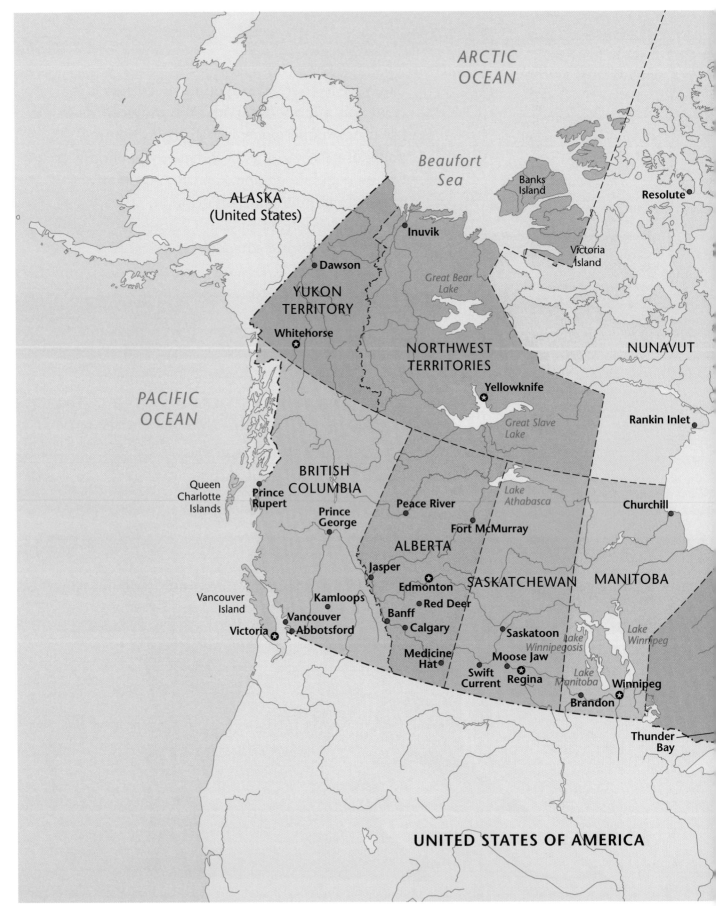

ARCTIC OCEAN

Beaufort Sea

Banks Island

Resolute

ALASKA (United States)

Inuvik

Victoria Island

Dawson

Great Bear Lake

YUKON TERRITORY

NUNAVUT

Whitehorse

NORTHWEST TERRITORIES

Yellowknife

PACIFIC OCEAN

Great Slave Lake

Rankin Inlet

BRITISH COLUMBIA

Lake Athabasca

Churchill

Queen Charlotte Islands

Prince Rupert

Peace River

Prince George

Fort McMurray

ALBERTA

Jasper

SASKATCHEWAN

MANITOBA

Edmonton

Vancouver Island

Kamloops

Red Deer

Banff

Vancouver

Abbotsford

Calgary

Saskatoon

Lake Winnipegosis

Lake Winnipeg

Victoria

Medicine Hat

Moose Jaw

Swift Current

Regina

Lake Manitoba

Winnipeg

Brandon

Thunder Bay

UNITED STATES OF AMERICA

Alert

Legend
- National capital
- Provincial capital
- Cities and towns
- —·—·— International boundary
- ——— Provincial or territorial boundary

ICELAND

GREENLAND

Baffin Bay

Devon Island

Baffin Island

Foxe Basin

Davis Strait

Iqaluit

0 250 500
kilometres

Ungava Bay

Labrador Sea

NEWFOUNDLAND AND LABRADOR

Hudson Bay

James Bay

Labrador City

QUÉBEC

Corner Brook

St. John's

ST. PIERRE AND MIQUELON (France)

Gulf of St. Lawrence

ONTARIO

Lake Nipigon

Chicoutimi-Jonquière

Cape Breton Island
Sydney

NEW BRUNSWICK
P.E.I.
Charlottetown

Lake Superior

Québec City

Moncton
Fredericton

Halifax

Sudbury

North Bay

Montréal

NOVA SCOTIA

Sault Ste. Marie

Sherbrooke

Yarmouth

ATLANTIC OCEAN

Ottawa

Lake Huron

Toronto

Lake Ontario

London

Hamilton

Windsor

Lake Erie

N
W   E
S

First Nations People at Contact with Europeans

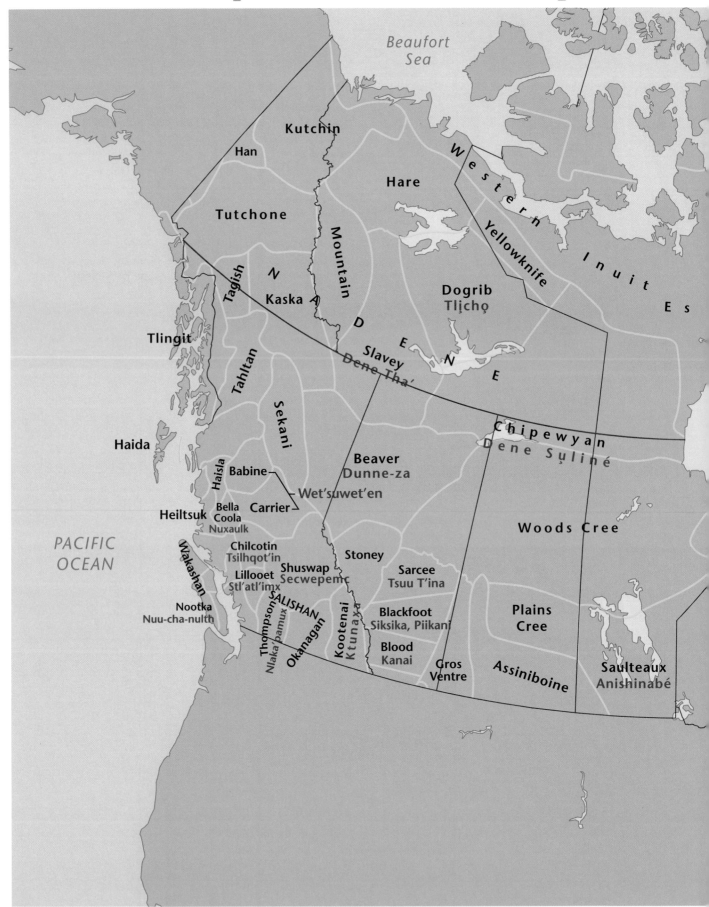

Beaufort
Sea

Kutchin

Han

Hare

Western Inuit Es

Tutchone

Yellowknife

Tagish

N

Mountain

Dogrib
Tlįchǫ

Kaska

A

Tlingit

D

E

Slavey
Dene Tha'

N

Tahltan

E

Sekani

Chipewyan
Dene Sųłiné

Haida

Haisla

Babine

Beaver
Dunne-za

Wet'suwet'en

Bella
Coola
Nuxaulk

Carrier

Woods Cree

Heiltsuk

PACIFIC
OCEAN

Chilcotin
Tsilhqot'in

Stoney

Wakashan

Lillooet
Stl'atl'imx

Shuswap
Secwepemc

Sarcee
Tsuu T'ina

Plains
Cree

Thompson
Nlaka'pamux

SALISHAN

Blackfoot
Siksika, Piikani

Nootka
Nuu-cha-nulth

Okanagan

Kootenai
Ktunaxa

Blood
Kanai

Saulteaux
Anishinabé

Gros
Ventre

Assiniboine

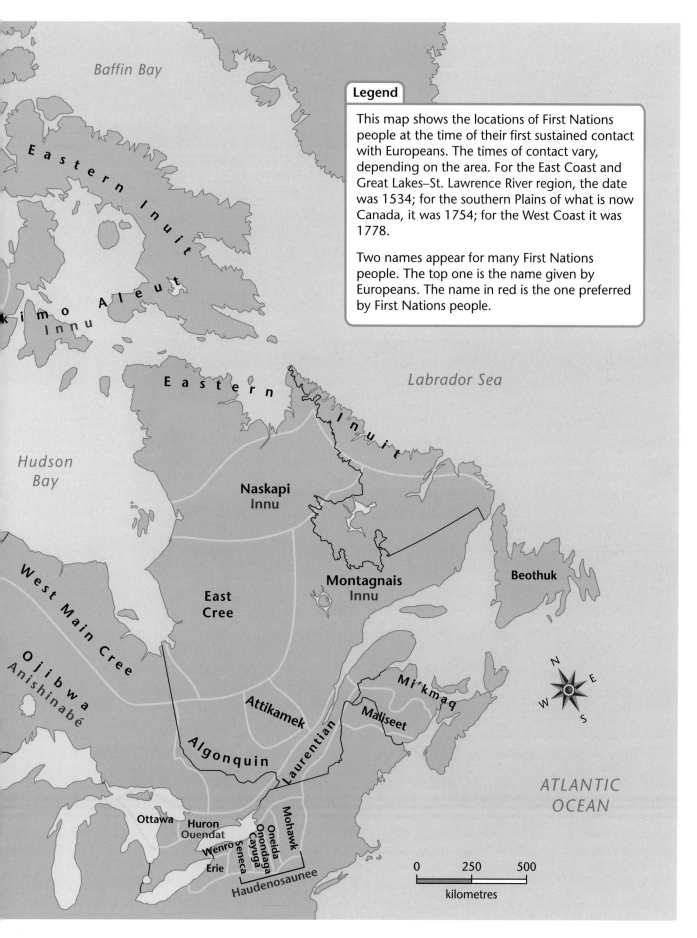

Legend

This map shows the locations of First Nations people at the time of their first sustained contact with Europeans. The times of contact vary, depending on the area. For the East Coast and Great Lakes–St. Lawrence River region, the date was 1534; for the southern Plains of what is now Canada, it was 1754; for the West Coast it was 1778.

Two names appear for many First Nations people. The top one is the name given by Europeans. The name in red is the one preferred by First Nations people.

Baffin Bay

Eastern Inuit

Innu Aleut

kimo

Innu

Labrador Sea

Hudson Bay

Eastern Inuit

Naskapi
Innu

West Main Cree

East Cree

Montagnais
Innu

Beothuk

Ojibwa
Anishinabé

Mi'kmaq

Attikamek

Maliseet

Algonquin

Laurentian

ATLANTIC OCEAN

Ottawa

Huron
Ouendat

Wenro

Erie

Seneca

Mohawk
Oneida
Onondaga
Cayuga

Haudenosaunee

0   250   500

kilometres

Territorial Evolution of North America

1608–1763

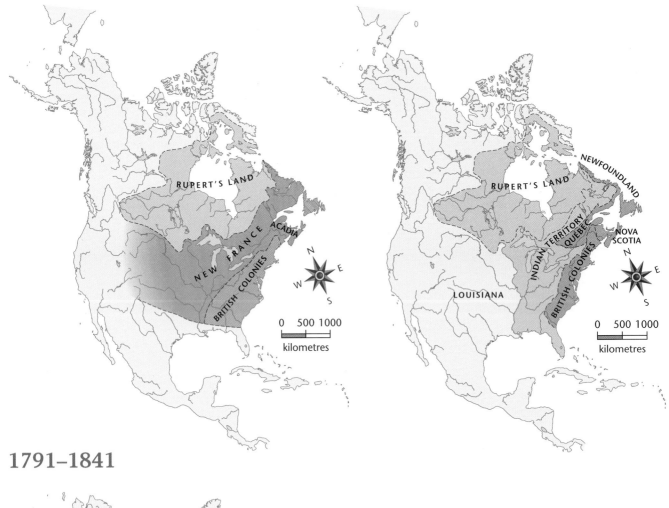

RUPERT'S LAND

NEW FRANCE

ACADIA

BRITISH COLONIES

0 500 1000
kilometres

1763–1791

NEWFOUNDLAND

RUPERT'S LAND

INDIAN TERRITORY

QUEBEC

NOVA SCOTIA

BRITISH COLONIES

LOUISIANA

0 500 1000
kilometres

1791–1841

ALASKA

THE NORTH-WESTERN TERRITORY

NEWFOUNDLAND

RUPERT'S LAND

OREGON TERRITORY

UPPER CANADA

LOWER CANADA

UNITED STATES

MEXICO

0 500 1000
kilometres

Legend

- ▨ British
- ▨ French
- ▨ American
- ▨ British/American
- --- Colonial or territorial border

After 1776, the British Colonies became the United States.

The term "Indian Territory" is historical. Today we use "First Nations."

Territorial Evolution of Canada

1866

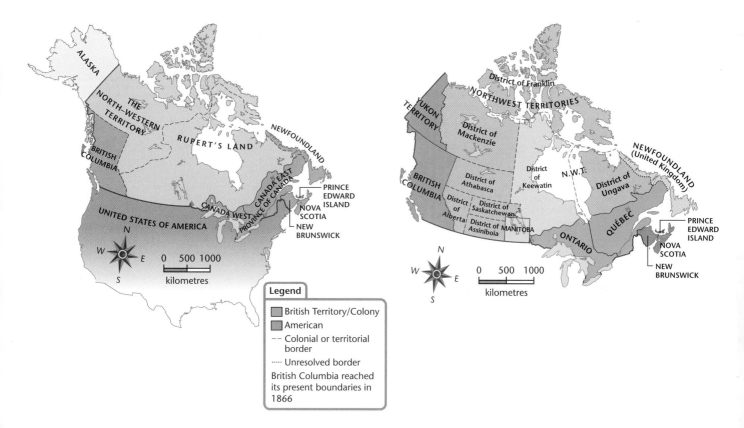

- ALASKA
- THE NORTH-WESTERN TERRITORY
- BRITISH COLUMBIA
- RUPERT'S LAND
- NEWFOUNDLAND
- CANADA EAST PROVINCE OF CANADA
- CANADA WEST
- PRINCE EDWARD ISLAND
- NOVA SCOTIA
- NEW BRUNSWICK
- UNITED STATES OF AMERICA

0 500 1000 kilometres

Legend
- British Territory/Colony
- American
- -- Colonial or territorial border
- ···· Unresolved border
- British Columbia reached its present boundaries in 1866

1898

- District of Franklin
- YUKON TERRITORY
- NORTHWEST TERRITORIES
- District of Mackenzie
- BRITISH COLUMBIA
- District of Athabasca
- District of Keewatin
- N.W.T.
- NEWFOUNDLAND (United Kingdom)
- District of Ungava
- District of Alberta
- District of Saskatchewan
- District of Assiniboia
- MANITOBA
- QUÉBEC
- ONTARIO
- PRINCE EDWARD ISLAND
- NOVA SCOTIA
- NEW BRUNSWICK

0 500 1000 kilometres

1905

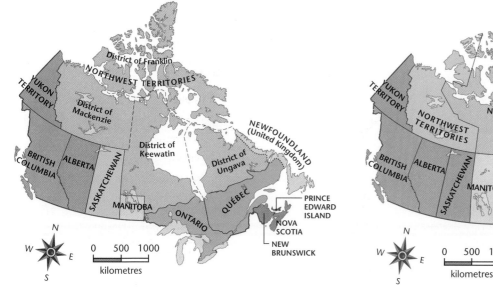

- District of Franklin
- NORTHWEST TERRITORIES
- YUKON TERRITORY
- District of Mackenzie
- BRITISH COLUMBIA
- ALBERTA
- SASKATCHEWAN
- District of Keewatin
- NEWFOUNDLAND (United Kingdom)
- District of Ungava
- MANITOBA
- ONTARIO
- QUÉBEC
- PRINCE EDWARD ISLAND
- NOVA SCOTIA
- NEW BRUNSWICK

0 500 1000 kilometres

2001

- YUKON TERRITORY
- NORTHWEST TERRITORIES
- NUNAVUT
- BRITISH COLUMBIA
- ALBERTA
- SASKATCHEWAN
- MANITOBA
- ONTARIO
- QUÉBEC
- NEWFOUNDLAND AND LABRADOR
- PRINCE EDWARD ISLAND
- NOVA SCOTIA
- NEW BRUNSWICK

0 500 1000 kilometres

Physical Features and Regions of Canada

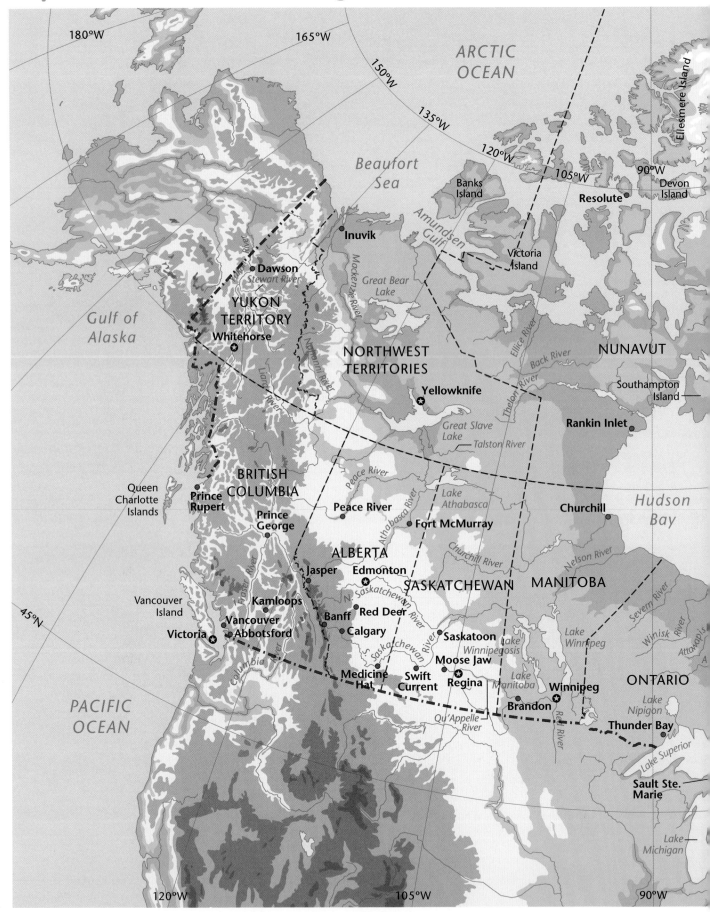

180°W

165°W

150°W

ARCTIC OCEAN

135°W

120°W

105°W

90°W

Ellesmere Island

Beaufort Sea

Banks Island

Resolute

Devon Island

Amundsen Gulf

Inuvik

Victoria Island

Dawson

Stewart River

Mackenzie River

Great Bear Lake

YUKON TERRITORY

Whitehorse

Ellice River

Back River

NUNAVUT

NORTHWEST TERRITORIES

Yellowknife

Thelon River

Southampton Island

Gulf of Alaska

Liard River

Nahanni River

Great Slave Lake

Talston River

Rankin Inlet

Queen Charlotte Islands

BRITISH COLUMBIA

Prince Rupert

Peace River

Athabasca River

Lake Athabasca

Churchill

Hudson Bay

Prince George

Peace River

Fort McMurray

Churchill River

Nelson River

45°N

Vancouver Island

Fraser River

Jasper

Kamloops

ALBERTA

Edmonton

N. Saskatchewan River

SASKATCHEWAN

Red Deer

Severn River

Lake Winnipeg

MANITOBA

Winnisk River

Attawapi

Vancouver

Banff

Saskatoon

Lake Winnipegosis

Victoria

Abbotsford

Calgary

S. Saskatchewan River

Moose Jaw

Lake Manitoba

ONTARIO

Columbia River

PACIFIC OCEAN

Medicine Hat

Swift Current

Regina

Brandon

Winnipeg

Red River

Lake Nipigon

Qu'Appelle River

Thunder Bay

Lake Superior

Sault Ste. Marie

Lake Michigan

120°W

105°W

90°W

340

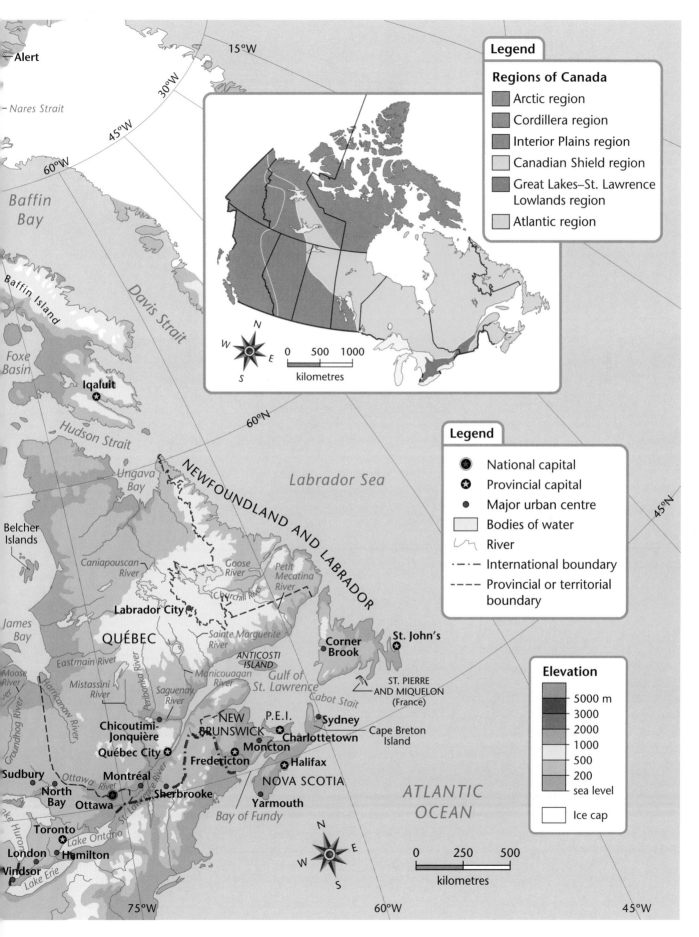

Alert

Nares Strait

15°W

30°W

45°W

60°W

Baffin Bay

Legend

Regions of Canada

Arctic region

Cordillera region

Interior Plains region

Canadian Shield region

Great Lakes–St. Lawrence Lowlands region

Atlantic region

Foxe Basin

Baffin Island

Davis Strait

Iqaluit

N

W — E

S

0 500 1000

kilometres

Hudson Strait

Ungava Bay

Labrador Sea

60°N

NEWFOUNDLAND AND LABRADOR

45°N

James Bay

Belcher Islands

Caniapouscan River

Goose River

Petit Mecatina River

Churchill River

Legend

National capital

Provincial capital

Major urban centre

Bodies of water

River

International boundary

Provincial or territorial boundary

Labrador City

QUÉBEC

Sainte Marguerite River

Eastmain River

ANTICOSTI ISLAND

St. John's

Corner Brook

Moose River

Mistassini River

Peribonka River

Manicouagan River

Saguenay River

Gulf of St. Lawrence

ST. PIERRE AND MIQUELON (France)

Harricanaw River

Chicoutimi-Jonquière

Québec City

P.E.I.

NEW BRUNSWICK

Sydney

Cape Breton Island

Cabot Strait

Charlottetown

Elevation

5000 m

3000

2000

1000

500

200

sea level

Ice cap

Groundhog River

Sudbury

Ottawa River

Montréal

Moncton

Fredericton

Halifax

North Bay

Ottawa

Sherbrooke

St. Lawrence River

NOVA SCOTIA

ATLANTIC OCEAN

Toronto

Lake Ontario

Lake Huron

Yarmouth

Bay of Fundy

London

Hamilton

Windsor

Lake Erie

N

W — E

S

0 250 500

kilometres

75°W

60°W

45°W

The World

ARCTIC OCEAN

GREENLAND
(Denmark)

ALASKA
(United States)

CANADA

ICELAND

IRELAND

UN
KI

NORTH
ATLANTIC
OCEAN

PORTUGAL   SPAI

UNITED STATES
OF AMERICA

MOROCCO

WESTERN
SAHARA

HAWAII
(United States)

CUBA
THE BAHAMAS

MEXICO

DOMINICAN
REPUBLIC

MAURITANIA

M

JAMAICA

BELIZE

HONDURAS

SENEGAL
GAMBIA
GUINEA BISSAU

BURKI

PACIFIC
OCEAN

GUATEMALA
EL SALVADOR

NICARAGUA

GUINEA
SIERRA LEONE

GHAN

COSTA RICA

VENEZUELA

GUYANA
SURINAME
FRENCH GUIANA

LIBERIA

IVORY COAST

TO

PANAMA

COLOMBIA

CAN

EQUATORIAL

Equator

ECUADOR

PERU

BRAZIL

SOUTH
ATLANTIC
OCEAN

BOLIVIA

PARAGUAY

URUGUAY

ARGENTINA

CHILE

Falkland Islands
(United Kingdom)

South Georgia Island
(United Kingdom)

180°W 165°W 150°W 135°W 120°W 105°W 90°W 75°W 60°W 45°W 30°W 15°W

342

ARCTIC OCEAN

90°N
75°N
60°N
45°N
30°N
15°N
0°
15°S
30°S
45°S
60°S
75°S

SWEDEN
FINLAND
POLAND
BELARUS
UKRAINE
RUSSIA
KAZAKHSTAN
MONGOLIA
NORTH KOREA
JAPAN
SOUTH KOREA
GEORGIA
ARMENIA AZERBAIJAN
TURKEY
UZBEKISTAN
KYRGYZSTAN
TURKMENISTAN
TAJIKISTAN
CHINA
ITALY
GREECE
TUNISIA
CYPRUS
LEBANON
ISRAEL
SYRIA
IRAQ
JORDAN
IRAN
AFGHANISTAN
PAKISTAN
TAIWAN
LIBYA
EGYPT
KUWAIT
BAHRAIN
QATAR
SAUDI ARABIA
UNITED ARAB EMIRATES
OMAN
NEPAL
BHUTAN
INDIA
MYANMAR
BANGLADESH
LAOS
VIETNAM
PHILIPPINES
GER
CHAD
ERITREA
YEMEN
THAILAND
CAMBODIA
BRUNEI
FEDERATED STATES OF MICRONESIA
SUDAN
DJIBOUTI
SOMALIA
RIA
CENTRAL AFRICAN REPUBLIC
ETHIOPIA
SRI LANKA
SINGAPORE
MALAYSIA
GABON
UGANDA
KENYA
ZAIRE
RWANDA
BURUNDI
PAPUA NEW GUINEA
SOLOMON ISLANDS
TANZANIA
INDONESIA
TUVALU
ANGOLA
MALAWI
MOZAMBIQUE
INDIAN OCEAN
PACIFIC OCEAN
ZAMBIA
ZIMBABWE
MADAGASCAR
MAURITIUS
RÉUNION
VANUATU
FIJI
NAMIBIA
BOTSWANA
NEW CALEDONIA
SWAZILAND
AUSTRALIA
SOUTH AFRICA
LESOTHO
NEW ZEALAND

0   1000   2000   3000
kilometres

ANTARCTICA

15°E   30°E   45°E   60°E   75°E   90°E   105°E   120°E   135°E   150°E   165°E   180°E

343

Population Distribution of Canada

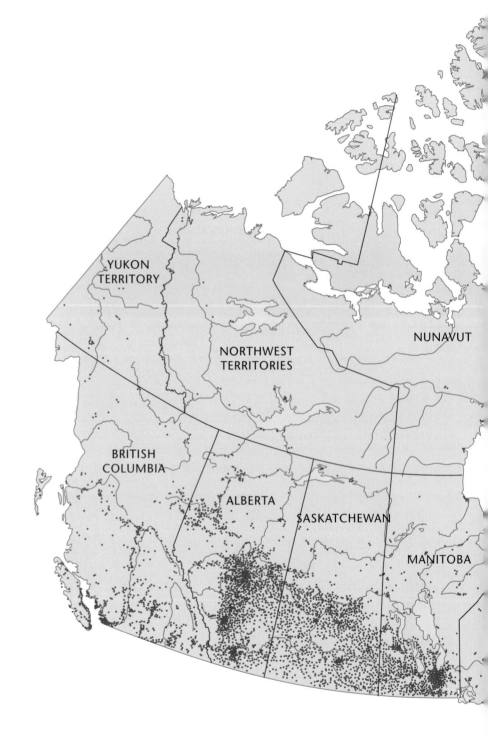

NEWFOUNDLAND AND LABRADOR

QUÉBEC

ONTARIO

PRINCE
EDWARD
ISLAND

NOVA
SCOTIA

NEW
BRUNSWICK

0   500   1000

kilometres

Francophone Population in Canada

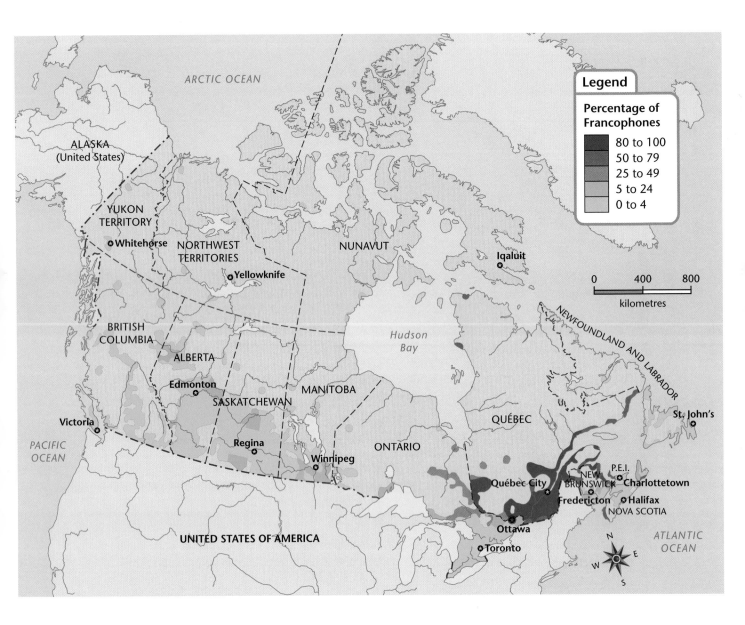

Legend

Percentage of Francophones

- 80 to 100
- 50 to 79
- 25 to 49
- 5 to 24
- 0 to 4

0   400   800
kilometres

ARCTIC OCEAN

ALASKA
(United States)

YUKON
TERRITORY

Whitehorse

NORTHWEST
TERRITORIES

Yellowknife

NUNAVUT

Iqaluit

NEWFOUNDLAND AND LABRADOR

Hudson
Bay

BRITISH
COLUMBIA

ALBERTA

Edmonton

SASKATCHEWAN

MANITOBA

QUÉBEC

St. John's

Victoria

Regina

Winnipeg

ONTARIO

Québec City

P.E.I.
Charlottetown

NEW
BRUNSWICK

Fredericton   Halifax
NOVA SCOTIA

PACIFIC
OCEAN

UNITED STATES OF AMERICA

Ottawa

Toronto

ATLANTIC
OCEAN

N
W   E
S

Climate of Some Canadian Cities

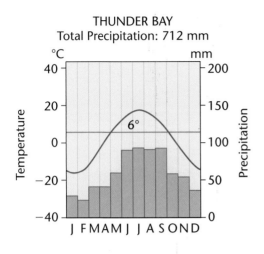

THUNDER BAY
Total Precipitation: 712 mm

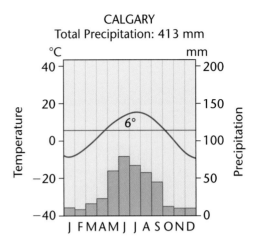

CALGARY
Total Precipitation: 413 mm

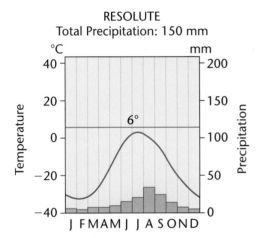

RESOLUTE
Total Precipitation: 150 mm

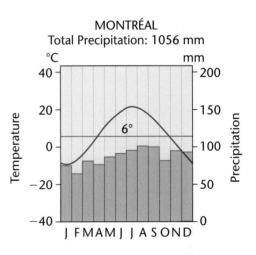

MONTRÉAL
Total Precipitation: 1056 mm

VANCOUVER
Total Precipitation: 1199 mm

HALIFAX
Total Precipitation: 1508 mm

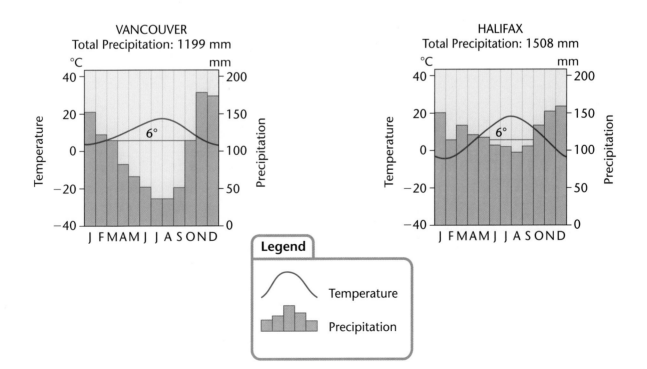

Legend

Temperature

Precipitation

Vegetation in Canada

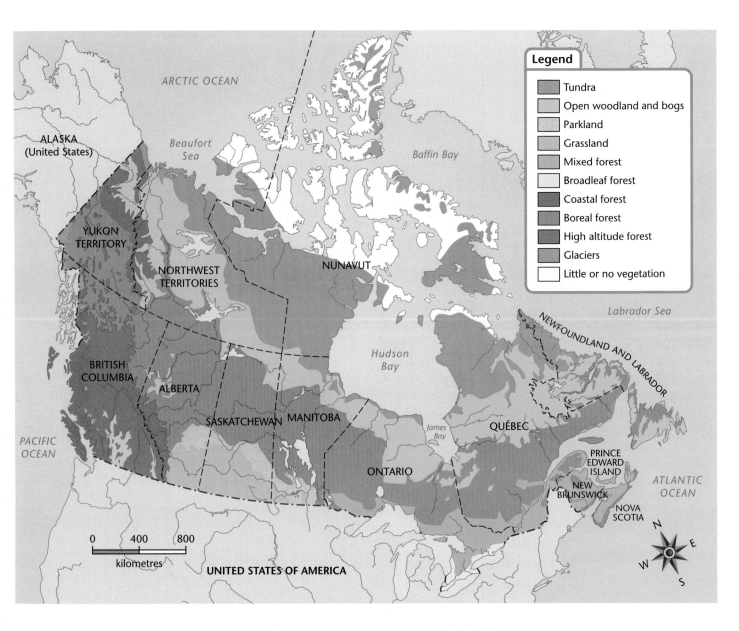

Legend

- Tundra
- Open woodland and bogs
- Parkland
- Grassland
- Mixed forest
- Broadleaf forest
- Coastal forest
- Boreal forest
- High altitude forest
- Glaciers
- Little or no vegetation

ARCTIC OCEAN

ALASKA
(United States)

Beaufort
Sea

Baffin Bay

YUKON
TERRITORY

NORTHWEST
TERRITORIES

NUNAVUT

Labrador Sea

BRITISH
COLUMBIA

Hudson
Bay

NEWFOUNDLAND AND LABRADOR

ALBERTA

SASKATCHEWAN   MANITOBA

James
Bay

QUÉBEC

PACIFIC
OCEAN

ONTARIO

PRINCE
EDWARD
ISLAND

ATLANTIC
OCEAN

NEW
BRUNSWICK

NOVA
SCOTIA

0   400   800

kilometres

UNITED STATES OF AMERICA

Energy Resources in Canada

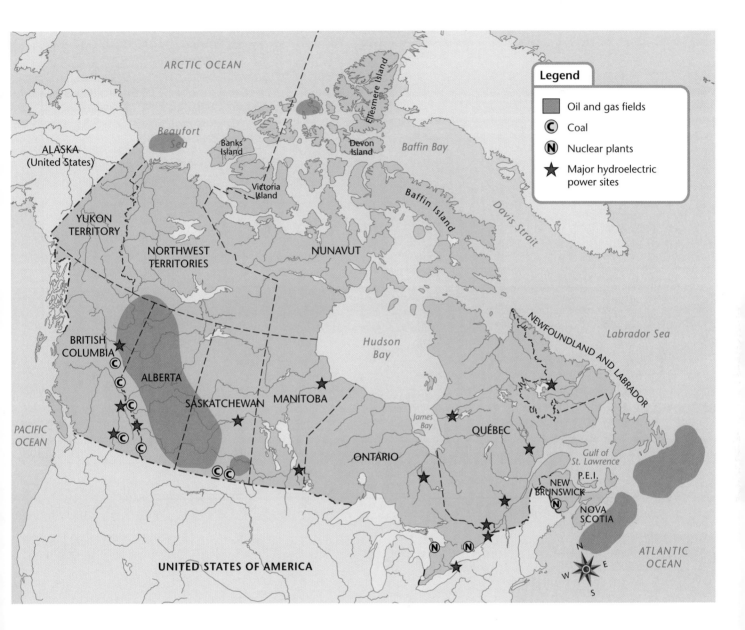

Agricultural Products and Forestry Resources in Canada

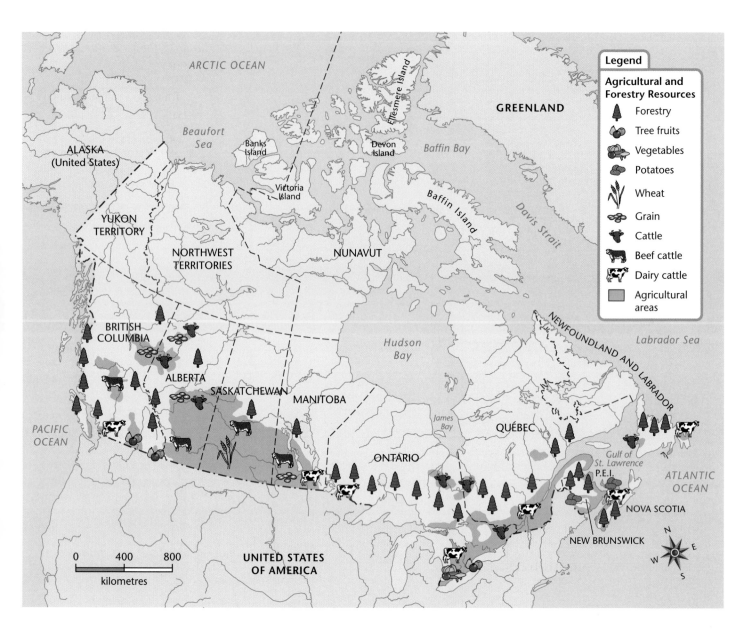

Transportation in Canada

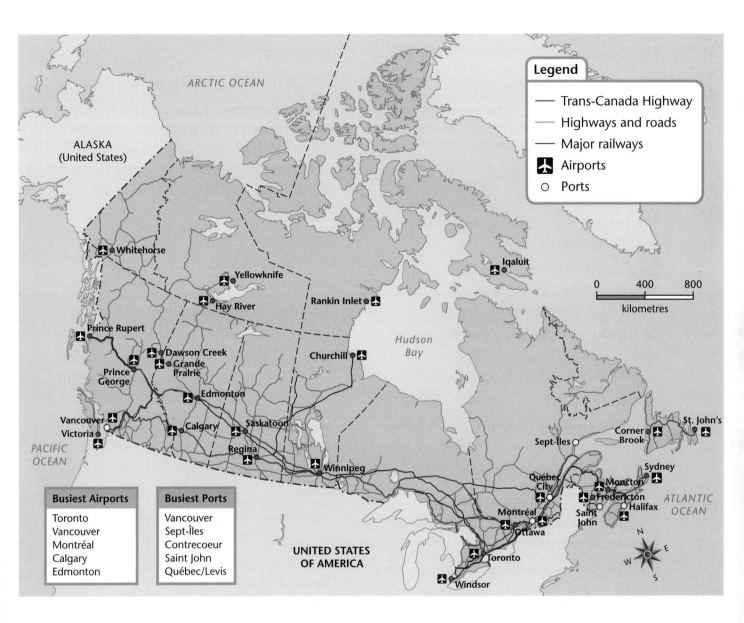

Legend
- Trans-Canada Highway
- Highways and roads
- Major railways
- ✈ Airports
- ○ Ports

ARCTIC OCEAN

ALASKA
(United States)

Whitehorse

Yellowknife

Hay River

Iqaluit

Rankin Inlet

Prince Rupert

Dawson Creek
Grande Prairie

Churchill

Hudson Bay

Prince George

Edmonton

Saskatoon

Vancouver

Victoria

Calgary

Regina

Winnipeg

PACIFIC OCEAN

0   400   800
kilometres

Sept-Îles

St. John's

Corner Brook

Sydney

Québec City

Moncton
Fredericton

ATLANTIC OCEAN

Montréal

Saint John

Halifax

Ottawa

Busiest Airports	Busiest Ports
Toronto	Vancouver
Vancouver	Sept-Îles
Montréal	Contrecoeur
Calgary	Saint John
Edmonton	Québec/Levis

UNITED STATES OF AMERICA

Toronto

Windsor

N
W   E
S

Glossary

absolute location describes exactly where a place is using lines of latitude and longitude

allegiance loyalty to a nation or country

ally someone who cooperates with and helps you in a debate, an argument, or a war

ambassadors people who are chosen to represent or speak for a group

ancestors the people in your family who came before you

aquaculture raising fish in protected areas until they are big enough to harvest for human consumption

archeologist someone who studies the way people once lived by looking at their homes, tools, and clothing

bastion a word that means "stronghold"; protection often is provided by a natural rock formation

bilingual able to understand, speak, and write two languages

bison also called buffalo

bodies of water rivers, lakes, oceans

British North America the term for the British colonies in North America after the United States became independent from Britain

Canadien a Francophone born in New France

cavalry a group of soldiers or police who use horses

Chinook Jargon the name given to a special language that was developed among the different First Nations people of the Cordillera region

climate the kind of weather an area has over a long period of time

colonies settlements that are under the control of another country, such as Britain or France

combat fighting against an enemy

Confederation on July 1, 1867, Nova Scotia, New Brunswick, Québec, and Ontario came together to form the Dominion of Canada, when the British Parliament passed the British North America Act

cordillera a chain of mountains

coureurs des bois a French term meaning "runners of the woods"

Creator a word used by First Nations to refer to Great Spirit

delta a broad, flat area of land formed where a river drains into a large body of water

diverse made up of people from a variety of cultures, backgrounds, and beliefs

droughts long periods without rain or snow

elevation the height of land compared to sea level or the ocean surface

equator the starting point for measuring lines of latitude

factor the HBC employee in charge of the trading post

fertile soil rich with nutrients that plants need for good growth

gales fierce windstorms

Grand Dérangement, le the deportation of more than ten thousand Acadians by the British; also called "the Great Upheaval"

Great Depression, The a time between 1929 and 1939 when thousands of Canadians lost their jobs and could not find new ones; most people had little money

Great Migration, The a time between 1815 and 1850 when 8 million immigrants, mostly from Britain, Scotland, and Ireland, came to the British colonies in Canada

habitants French settlers in New France who cleared and farmed the land

heritage what has been passed down to you from the past

Highlands a mountainous area in Scotland

highway a large road that connects towns and cities

homestead land that is owned by a settler

hurricanes large storms that form in the ocean

identity how we are shaped by the places we live, the languages we speak, the groups we belong to, where we came from, and how we see ourselves

independent the ability to make decisions and act for yourself; accepting responsibility for your actions

industries businesses that produce goods or services

inquiry an investigation to find answers to questions

interpretation what you think something means

Inuktitut the language of the Inuit

Iroquois Confederacy six First Nation peoples make up this alliance; it is one of the world's oldest democratic societies

irrigation water supplied to dry land using pipes, ditches, or streams

landforms the different features of the land, such as mountains, hills, or plains

lines of latitude imaginary lines that run east and west on a map or globe; the equator is the starting point for measuring these lines

lines of longitude imaginary lines that run north and south on a map or globe; the prime meridian is the starting point for measuring these lines

logo a special sign that gives key information

longhouses long houses where several related Ouendat or Haudenosaunee families lived

majority the largest in number of two or more groups

Métis people who had one parent who was First Nations and one who was Canadien; later, Métis also had Scottish and British ancestry

minority the smallest in number of two or more groups

muskeg swamp or bog formed from the buildup of moss, leaves, and other plants

non-renewable resource a resource that can never be replaced once it is used up

official languages ones that have equal status in the government; Canada has two official languages—English and French

organic farming no chemicals on plants or animals are used

paska Ukrainian Easter bread

patriotism showing support or loyalty toward a country

pemmican dried meat pounded to a paste and mixed with melted fat and berries

permafrost soil that stays frozen all year

physical features landforms, such as mountains, hills, and plains; also bodies of water, such as oceans, rivers, and lakes

potash a substance mainly used in fertilizer and rich in potassium; an important nutrient for plants

potlatch a ceremony or feast held by Aboriginal peoples of North America's West Coast

preserve to keep in good condition or protect

prime meridian the starting point for measuring lines of longitude

prospectors people who search for valuable minerals such as gold

region an area of land that has unique features, such as climate, landforms, and natural resources

relative location means a place is somewhere close to a known place

renewable resource a resource that can be replaced if it is used carefully

scale a tool used to compare the distance on a map to the actual distance on Earth's surface

scrip a coupon given to Métis by the Canadian government that could be exchanged for land or money

scurvy a disease that is caused by a lack of vitamin C

seigneurs land owners in New France who rented land to habitants who cleared and farmed it

slaves people owned by another person and made to work for little or no money

suburbs areas of housing on the outlying part of a city or town

suffrage the right to vote; people who fought for women's right to vote were called suffragists or suffragettes

tides daily changes in the level of the ocean

Trans-Canada Highway a highway in Canada that spans from St. John's, Newfoundland, to Victoria, British Columbia

treaty an agreement between countries; also an agreement between the government and First Nations people

tsunami an ocean wave produced by an underwater earthquake

tundra a treeless area in northern Canada where only grasses and small plants grow

uranium an element used to create both nuclear energy and X-rays

urban sprawl when cities spread quickly and more land is used than is needed

voyageur a French word meaning "traveller"; voyageurs travelled by canoe, working for fur-trading companies

waterways rivers and lakes that can be used by people as highways for travel

weather daily conditions: for example, rain, sunshine, or snow

wigwam comes from "wikuom" [wiguom], the Mi'kmaq word for dwelling

wildfires grass or forest fires that are not set on purpose

World War I (1914–1918) fought mainly in Europe and involved many countries, including Canada; also called the Great War

Index

Credits

The publisher would like to thank the following people and institutions for permission to use their © materials. Every reasonable effort has been made to find copyright holders of the material in this text. The publisher would be pleased to know of any errors or omissions.

PHOTO CREDITS

CP:	Canadian Press Photo
LAC:	Library and Archives Canada
bg/i:	background/inset
t/c/b/l/r:	top/centre/bottom/left/right

2 bl Stephen Saks/Lonely Planet Images; **i** Courtesy of Fondation du Sentier transcanadien/Trans Canada Trail Foundation; **3** Patrick Doyle/CP; **4** Thinkstock Images/JupiterImages; **6 l** Image Source/Getty Images; **6 c** Alison Wright/The Image Works; **6 r** David Young-Wolff/Photo Edit; **7 l** PM Images/Taxi/Getty Images; **7 r** Steve Skjold/Alamy; **8 t** Ryan McVay/Taxi/Getty Images; **12, 13 bg** Shutterstock; **14, 15 bg** John E Marriott/Alamy; **i** Tim Clark/CP; **16 tl** WaterFrame/Alamy; **bl** Michael Melford/The Image Bank/Getty Images; **br** Keith Levit Photography/Firstlight; **17 t** Don Johnston/Alamy; **c** Mark Tomalty/Masterfile; **b** Blaine Harrington III/Corbis; **20** Danita Delimont/Alamy **22 b** Richard Buchan/CP; **23 l** Brian Sytnyk/Masterfile; **r** Galen Rowell/CORBIS; **24 l** Mark Wiens/Masterfile; **lc** Bill Brooks/Masterfile; **rc** Peter Griffith/Masterfile; **r** Guy Grenier/Masterfile; **26** James Marshall/CORBIS; **27** Brian Atkinson/Alamy; **28 tl** Keith Levit/Alamy; **bl** Bryan & Cherry Alexander Photography/Alamy; **tr** Albert Normandin/Masterfile; **br** William A. Bake/CORBIS; **29 tl** Bryan & Cherry Alexander Photography/Firstlight; **cl** Kevin R. Morris/CORBIS; **bl** Andrew Vaughan/CP; **tr** Eric Dufresne/Alamy; **cr** Craig Aurness/CORBIS; **br** Paul A. Souders/CORBIS; **30** Brian Summers/Firstlight; **31** Troy and Mary Parlee/Alamy; **34, 35 bg** Scott Leslie/Firstlight; **36 c, b** Dale Wilson/Masterfile; **37** Philip Scalia/Alamy; **38 b** ImageState/Alamy; **39 t** Nova Scotia Tourism, Culture and Heritage; **c** Mike Dembeck/CP; **b** Michael Melford/The Image Bank/Getty Images; **br** George Blonsky/Alamy; **40 t** CORBIS SYGMA; **b** Pierre Perrin/CORBIS SYGMA; **42** Courtesy of Daniel N. Paul; **43** Courtesy of Daniel N. Paul; **44 r** Courtesy of Lalia Harvie Kerr; **45 t** History Collection, Nova Scotia Museum; **bl** LAC C-038862; **br** Taken from James Patrick Howley, *The Beothucks, or Red Indians, the Aboriginal Inhabitants of Newfoundland*, (Cambridge: University Press, 1915. Courtesy of Dr. Hans Rollman **46 bl** LAC PA-110814; **br** Robert Estall photo agency/Alamy; **47 t** Nova Scotia Archives and Records Management 1979.147.154/N-6097; **bl** McCord Museum of Canadian History Museum of Canadian History; **br** McCord Museum of Canadian History; **48** Michael S. Yamashita/CORBIS; **49** History Collection, Nova Scotia Museum; **50 t** James Leynse/CORBIS; **b** Courtesy of photographer Troy Johnstone; **51** Jim Merrithew *Images of New Brunswick/Images du Nouveau-Brunswick*; **52 b** LAC C-115424; **53 l** LAC PA-170244; **r** Courtesy Dr. Stephen Kimber; **54 b** PANB Albert Hickman Photographs: P13-122; **55 t** Canada Science and Technology Museum/Musée des Sciences et de la technologie du Canada; **b** Nova Scotia Archives and Records Management NSARM #20040026; **56** Andrew Vaughan/CP; **57** Daniel Templeton/Alamy; **58 l** Courtesy of Dr. Moira Brown; **r** Florida Fish and Wildlife Conservation Commission/NOAA; **59 b** Greg Agnew/CP; **60** public domain; **61** Alan Dawson Photography/Alamy; **64, 65 bg**

Canadian Heritage Gallery #20682/LAC C-023633; **i** Canadian Heritage Gallery #10129/LAC C-013396; **66 b** Bob Turner/Alamy; **67 t** Alt-6/Alamy; **b** Barry Gray/CP **68 b** Jeremy Woodhouse/Masterfile; **69 tl** Kevin Dodge/Masterfile; **tc** Bill Brooks/Alamy; **tr** Authors Image/Alamy; **b** Jeff Speed/Firstlight; **70 b** McCord Museum of Canadian History; **72 l** Courtesy of the Canadian Canoe Museum; **r** Courtesy of Canadian Museum of Civilization; **73 t** Megapress/Alamy; **bl** Photos.com Images/JupiterUnlimited Images; **br** Kennan Ward/CORBIS; **74 b** *The Three Sisters*, Courtesy of Iroquois Indian Museum, Howes Cave N.Y.; **76 b** Canadian Heritage Gallery #20057/Metropolitan Toronto Reference Library, T31616; **77 tr** Lee Snider/Photo Images/CORBIS; **lc** LAC C-016952; **br** Megapress/Alamy; **78** JupiterMedia/Alamy; **79** Canadian Heritage Gallery #10072/Ste. Marie Among the Hurons; **80 b** Canadian Heritage Gallery #20673/LAC C-002834; **82 b** Canadian Heritage Gallery #10204/LAC C-002481; **83 t** Arco Images/Alamy; **b** Courtesy of David Kanowakeron Hill Morrison; **84** LAC POS-000941; **85 b** McCord Museum of Canadian History; **86** LAC PA-136924; **87 t** Megapress/Alamy; **br** Chris Schwarz/CP; **bl** Glenbow Archives NA-1030-36; **88 t** André Nantel, Digital Apoptosis; **b** William A. Bake/CORBIS; **89** Jacques Boissinot/CP; **90 l** Toronto Archives; **r** Jeremy Woodhouse/Masterfile; **91** Richard Buchan/CP; **92** Gonzalo Azumendi/AGE Fotostock/Maxx Images; **95** Robert Taylor/Edmonton Sun/CP; **96 c** Jim West/Alamy; **b** Paul A. Souders/CORBIS; **97 t** Andre Jenny/Alamy; **b** photocanada.com/B. Lowry; **98 t** Arco Images/Alamy; **b** Greg Locke/Firstlight; **99 t** Danita Delimont/Alamy; **tc** Garry Black/Masterfile; **bc** Janet Foster/Masterfile; **br** Jim West/Alamy; **100 b** Viktor Pivovarov/CP; **102** Bryan & Cherry Alexander Photography/Alamy; **103** Daryl Benson/Masterfile; **104 t** Hudson's Bay Company, used with permission; **b** LAC C-005746; **105** McCord Museum of Canadian History; **r** Comstock Images/Alamy; **107 t** LAC C-002771; **109** Tony Avelar/CP; **110** GA NA-3421-14; **111 l** McCord Museum of Canadian History; **r** Courtesy of Adam Raffee; **112** Joe Bryksa/CP; **113 b** LAC POS-000424; **114** LAC C-006896; **115 tl** Ken Davies/Masterfile; **bl** Danita Delimont/Alamy; **c** Barry Tessman/National Geographic/Getty Images; **br** Bob Anderson/Masterfile; **117** Jimmy Sam, Cree Photographer, Chisasibi, Québec; **118** Don Johnston/Alamy; **119 bl** Courtesy of Esma Erdic, Emma-O Productions; **tr** Doug Hamilton/Firstlight; **120** Artist Bonnie Devine. Courtesy Centre for Contemporary Canadian Art; **124 t** By Bruce McDonald. From the book *Where the River Brought Them* by Pat McDonald; **124 bg** Reproduced with the permission of the Champlain Society www.champlainsociety.ca; **125** Shaun Cunningham/Alamy; **126 cl** Brian Sytnyk/Masterfile; **br** Daryl Benson/Masterfile; **127 t** Wally Bauman/Alamy; **c** Robert Postma/Firstlight; **b** Dave Pattinson/Alamy; **128** Glenbow Archives NA-1646-8; **129 (2)** Brian Atkinson/Alamy; **(3)** Charles Gupton/CORBIS; **(4)** Sandland Photography/Alamy; **130 b** Dick Hemingway Photographer; **131 l** Glenbow Archives NA-670-38; **r** Glenbow Archives NA-3596-76; **132 l** Government of the NWT, Scanned by Industry Tourism and Investment; **r** W. Eryk Jaegermann/AGE Fotostock/Maxx Images; **133 tr** Robert Dall/CP; **bl** Glenbow Archives NA-2672-14; **134 t** Glenbow Archives NA-4209-2; **b** Ed Gifford/Masterfile; **135 b** public domain; **136 t** Saskatchewan Archives Board; **b** Glenbow Archives NA-1709-35; **137 bl** Canadian Heritage Gallery #10042, LAC C-26182; **tr** WorldFoto/Alamy; **139** Glenbow Archives NA-47-13; **140** Glenbow Archives NA-659-29; **141** Don Denton/CP; **142 b** Glenbow Archives NA-949-15; **143** Glenbow Archives NA-1063-1; **144 c** Gary Herbert Photographer; **145 tl** Glenbow Archives PA-3703-3; **br** Layne Kennedy/CORBIS; **146** LAC NAC-a010150; **147 r** Bill Brooks/Alamy; **148 bl** John

Courtesy of David Grassby, **b** The Bridgeman Art Library/Getty Images; **314 c** Roy Rainford/Robert Harding World Imagery/Getty Images; **b** Blaine Harrington III/CORBIS; **316** Jeff Mermelstein/Stone/Getty Images; **317 t** Pat O'Hara/CORBIS; **(2)** Dennis MacDonald/Alamy; **(3)** Mike Derer/CP; **(4)** Paul Niklen/National Geographic/Getty Images; **318 c** Robert McGouey/Alamy; **b** Yves Marcoux/Firstlight; **319 t** Kevin Spreekmeester/Firstlight; **b** Stephen Saks Photography/Alamy; **320 bg** Ron Watts/Firstlight; **i** Courtesy of Pauline Scott; **321 t** alt-6/Firstlight; **b** Pictures Canada/Firstlight; **323** sébastien Baussais/Alamy; **325 l** © britishcolumbiaphotos.com/Alamy; **r** D. Hurst/Alamy; **326** Courtesy of Drake Landing Solar Community Project; **327 l** Courtesy of Seabird Island; **r** Picture Arts/Firstlight

LITERARY CREDITS

4 *Speech on the Occasion of a State Dinner Hosted by Her Excellency Tarja Halonen, President of the Republic of Finland,* Helsinki, Monday, October 6, 2003. Reproduced courtesy of the Privy Council Office and with permission of the Minister of Public Works and Government Services Canada, 2007; **31** Reprinted with permission from Pier 21, www.pier21.ca; **43** Todd Labrador, Waterdancer Mi'kmaq Arts; **49** Reprinted with permission of Patricia Doyle-Bedwell (2004) and CBC.ca; **50** The Department of Canadian Heritage. Reproduced with permission of the Minister of Public Works and Government Services Canada, 2006; **53** "Africville: Urban Removal in Canada," Pamela Brown; **53** Joe Sealy, Blue Jade Productions; **56** "Anger From the Deeps," John Demont, *Maclean's,* January 24, 2001; **56** "One Last Whistle," *Maclean's,* August 6, 2001; **57** Courtesy of the Canadian Broadcasting Corporation; **57** Buddy Wasisname and the Other Fellas written by Wayne Chaulk, www.buddywasisname.com; **73** "The Medicine Plants," Suzanne Brant; **78** Reprinted with permission from *Canada: A People's History* and CBC.ca; **80** Courtesy of the Canadian Broadcasting Corporation; **83** David Kanowakeron Hill Morrison UE; **84** *The Freedom Seekers: Blacks in Early Canada,* Daniel G. Hill, Agincourt: Book Society of Canada, 1981; **84** *Niagara's Freedom Trail: A Guide to African-Canadian History on the Niagara Peninsula* by Owen A. Thomas, The Corporation; (1996); **89** Courtesy of the Canadian Broadcasting Corporation; **89** Courtesy of the Canadian Broadcasting Corporation; **94** Dare to Dream 2005, www.daretodream2005.com; **102** © Innu Education Authority and Innu Nation; **102** "From the Hands of the Master," *Canadian Geographic,* May–June 1994, v. 114, no. 3, p. 64(7); **109** Our Voices; **110** *Voices from Hudson Bay: Cree Stories from York Factory,* Flora Beardy, et al. McGill-Queen's University Press (1996) p. 75; **112** "Métis Canoe Expedition 2", The Métis Nation of Ontario; **121** *Canadian National Parks Atlas,* Industry Canada (1996); **128** Canadian Education Association; **132** Government of Déline; **132** *Nitsitapiisinni: The Story of the Blackfoot People,* Pat Provost, Toronto: Key Porter, 2001, p. 5; **133** Adapted from "Valley of Legend," Dave Yanko, Virtual Saskatchewan; **133** Edmond Lavasseur; **134** Beaumont History Book Committee, 1985; **135** Mark McCallum **136** Billy Joe Laboucan; **141** © 2006 HER MAJESTY THE QUEEN IN RIGHT OF CANADA as represented by the Royal Canadian Mounted Police (RCMP). Reproduced with permission of the RCMP; **143** Billy Joe Laboucan; **144** *Pioneer Settlers: Ukrainians in the Dauphin area, 1896–1926,* Michael Ewanchuk (1988); **145** "Childhood Recollections," Tanya Postnikoff; **145** Mennonite Historical Society of Alberta; **145** Manitoba Historical Society; **146** *Saskatchewan History Magazine;* **147** Organic Agriculture Protection Fund; **156** Spirit Bear Youth Coalition; **165** Reprinted with permission of Dorothy Kennedy, Bouchard and Kennedy Research Consultants; **165** Reprinted with permission from Haida Gwaii Museum; **166** YET SUN HEYWA "We are going somewhere" University of Victoria's Maltwood Museum and Art Gallery; **166** Aboriginal Peoples: Building for the Future, Kevin Reed. Oxford University Press. (1999); **167** British

Columbia Archives, Sound Heritage, vol. 7, No.1 Pages 54–55; **170** Sound Heritage Series 26, vol. 8, no. 3; **171** Courtesy of Canadian Pacific Railway; **172** Aya's Story; **177** Richard Black; **177** Reprinted with permission of Friends of Clayoquot Sound; **178** Reprinted with permission of Kelowna Daily Courier; **178** "The State of Canada's Forests 2003–2004," Canadian Forest Service, Natural Resources Canada; **182** © Robert Service; **185** David Pitt-Brooke; **187** Darcy Dobell; **198** © Inuktitut Magazine, published by Inuit Tapiriit Kanatami, www.itk.ca; **199** Nunavut '99; **199** Sheila Watt-Cloutier; **200** © Inuktitut Magazine, published by Inuit Tapiriit Kanatami, www.itk.ca; **202** Reprinted with permission of Nunatsiaq News; **210** "Inuit See Signs in Arctic Thaw," by Doug Struck, Washington Post Foreign Service, March 22, 2006; **210** Reproduced with permission of the Minister of Public Works and Government Services Canada, 2007 and Courtesy of Natural Resources Canada, Geological Survey of Canada; **210** "Signs of Thaw in a Desert of Snow: Scientists Begin to Heed Inuit Warnings of Climate Change in Arctic," DeNeen L. Brown, Washington Post Foreign Service, May 28, 2002; **211** © Inuktitut Magazine, published by Inuit Tapiriit Kanatami, www.itk.ca; **213** Nunia Qanatstaq; **213** © Inuktitut Magazine, published by Inuit Tapiriit Kanatami, www.itk.ca; **230** Jordan Brown; **235** *The Unjust Society,* Harold Cardinal, Douglas McIntyre (1999); **246** *The Boy From Winnipeg,* James H. Gray, Macmillian of Canada (1970); **250** *Canada: A People's History,* vol. 2, Don Gillmor, McClelland & Stewart; **251** *The Boy From Winnipeg,* James H. Gray, Macmillian of Canada (1970); **252** *Great War and Canadian Society: An Oral History,* Daphne Read, Toronto: New Hogtown Press, 1978; **254** The Years of Agony, 1910–1920, John Craig, Toronto: Natural Science of Canada (1977); **259** The Western Producer; **261** The West Beyond the West: A History of British Columbia, Jean Barman, Toronto: University of Toronto Press, 1991. p 306; **264** Skyscrapers *Hide the Heavens: A History of Indian-White Relations in Canada,* J. R. Miller, Toronto: University of Toronto Press, (2000) p. 319; **264** A Woman in a Man's World, Thérèse Casgrain Toronto: McClelland and Stewart, (1972.) p. 17, 19; **268** © Barry Broadfoot; **272** Bennett papers. Public Archives Canada.; **272** *Towards Tomorrow: Canada in a Changing World: History,* Desmond Morton, Harcourt Brace Jovanovich (1988); **273** © Barry Broadfoot; **273** Reprinted with permission of the University of Manitoba Press; **274** *Canada: A People's History,* vol. 2, Don Gillmor, McClelland & Stewart; **275** Germain Alaire; **275** *The Winter Years: The Depression on the Prairies,* James Gray, Coteau Books (2004); **276** Reprinted with permission of the University of Manitoba Press; **278** Reprinted with permission of the University of Manitoba Press; **278** Courtesy of the Ladybug Foundation Inc.; **279** I'll Sing 'Til the Day I Die, Beth Brant, McGilligan Books (1995); **280** © Barry Broadfoot; **281** © Barry Broadfoot; **282** Text copyright © 2001 by Eileen Comstock, Reprinted with permission of Fitzhenry & Whiteside Publishers, 195 Allstate Parkway, Markham, ON L2R 4T8, Canada; **283** Text copyright © 2001 by Eileen Comstock, Reprinted with permission of Fitzhenry & Whiteside Publishers, 195 Allstate Parkway, Markham, ON L2R 4T8, Canada; **286** *Remembering the 50's: Growing Up in Western Canada,* Lorraine Blashill. Orca Books (1997) p98; **287** Germaine Alaire; **295** *Canada: Our Century, Our Story,* Fielding, J., Evans, Rosemary. Nelson (2001); **299** The National Flag of Canada. Dept of Canadian Heritage; **304** The Charter of Rights and Freedoms: A Guide for Canadians, Department of Justice, 1982. Reproduced with permission of the Minister of Public Works and Government Services Canada, 2006; **306** Sandra Perron; **309** Curriculum and School Services Division and Department of Education/Nunavut; **320** Pauline Scott; **324** PotashCorp; **327** © TransAlta Wind; 327 Used with permission of the New Brunswick Environmental Network; **336–337** Adapted by Bob Beal from a map by Ives Goddard in Vol. 17, *Handbook of North American Indians* (1996), Smithsonian Institute